CW00403300

"Credibly documents what appea[...]
response to Christ among Muslir[...]

"From an analysis of recent p[...]
house churches, one can now und[...]
have bowed their knee to the Lor[...]

– Greg Livingstone, founder of Frontiers mission agency and author of *You've Got Libya*

"When I want to understand what is happening behind the opaque walls surrounding modern-day Iran, I always turn to Mark Bradley. Mark's lucid writing and extraordinary research provide the reader with an unforgettable experience of seeing what God is doing and how He is at work giving birth to His kingdom today inside the Islamic Republic of Iran. I highly recommend to any follower of Jesus Christ, Mark's latest book: *Too Many to Jail*."

– David Garrison, author, *A Wind in the House of Islam*

"We have worked with Elam for many years. We feel privileged to have personal connection with some of those whose stories Mark tells, and count them our friends. It is a privilege to endorse this book."

– Stuart and Jill Briscoe

"Without exception history proves that persecution always provides fertile soil for the growth of His church through the Gospel. Read and see this truth delineated in the story of Iran."

– Pastor Johnny Hunt, former President, Southern Baptist Convention

"A precise, honest and informative account of the ordeals of a growing (Muslim-background) Christian population inside Iran. This affirming message of perseverance, hope and faith will excite and challenge the reader... a must read."

– Dr Mike Ansari, Director of Operations, Mohabat TV

"This is a compelling, inspirational and hopeful book. Once I started reading I could not put it down. Mark Bradley skilfully and accurately leads us through the story of the church in Iran today. This book is an act of great service to those who want to know what has happened and is happening with the church in Iran. Through reading *Too Many to Jail* my admiration and appreciation for the church in Iran – and Iranians – has grown, along with an understanding of the circumstances in which such remarkable growth is taking place. If you are tempted to believe that God does anything the same way twice, read this book and let this Iranian story teach you. If you are tempted to believe there is anything more beautiful on the planet than the church of Jesus Christ, read this book and let God speak to you through the Iranian church in the middle of its weakness, empowering and glory."

– Viv Thomas, Hon Teaching Pastor St. Paul's Hammersmith and associate International Director OM International

"As the son of Iranian martyr, Haik Hovsepian Mehr, I can relate to many instances in this book. I admire Mark Bradley, who has so carefully researched and presented the facts about the persecuted believers in Iran. He gives a 360 degree view of the fastest growing church in the world, in the face of political and governmental oppression. *Too Many to Jail* is not merely an informative read that helps us stand with Iranians in prayer, but it inspires us by their stories to grow in our walk with the Lord."

– Joseph Hovsepian , Founder/Director of Hovsepian Ministries

"Be aware! When you read Mark Bradley's *Too Many to Jail*, you will encounter Eugene Peterson's interpretation of Jesus' saying 'the invisible moving the visible'! In his most recent book Mark has carefully examined three effective elements in the huge and widespread house church movement in Iran. There is no wall that could stop the Holy Spirit. There is no wall in Iran that could stop satellite TV signals! The Holy Spirit is using satellite TV as a bridge to the fastest growing house churches in the world. By reading this book you will see that this bridge makes Jesus' encounter a growing possibility; Christian growth a responsibility; and the expansion of God's Kingdom a reality. So Petersen's translation rings true: 'the invisible', the presence and power of the Holy Spirit, is indeed 'moving the visible', with lives being changed as people encounter Jesus and the church growing in houses of Iran."

– Rev. Mansour Khajehpour, Executive Director of SAT-7 PARS

"Too Many to Jail is an insightful and reflective book about a new emerging church with echoes as old as the house churches of the Acts of the Apostles and as wide as the global church.

"Too Many to Jail is a story of 'lovely pain': a story of unfailing and costly love not only about Iranian converts and house churches, but also about the manifestation of Christ in Iranian society and cultures. On the one hand it describes pain, struggles and challenges; on the other it tells of hope, growth and courage.

"Too Many to Jail is not only about Iranian converts and house churches; it is about church planting. Thank you for giving me the privilege to read it."

– Sara Afshari

"I often remind Western Christians that Jesus is running around loose in many parts of the Middle East and especially in the Islamic Republic of Iran! The Spirit of God is on the move in Iran and Jesus is fulfilling His promise that He is going to build His Church! Mark Bradley's new book, *Too Many to Jail,* is the most thorough and well-documented book on what God is doing in Iran in drawing people to Himself. In the midst of much suffering and persecution, the house church movement in Iran is spreading like wildfire! If you want to know how God is at work in Iran read this book and be inspired by God's beautiful sovereignty."

– Rev. Dr Sasan Tavassoli, preacher and author

Published by Monarch Books
an imprint of
Lion Hudson plc
Wilkinson House, Jordan Hill Road,
Oxford OX2 8DR, England
Email: monarch@lionhudson.com
www.lionhudson.com/monarch

ISBN 978 0 85721 596 3
e-ISBN 978 0 85721 597 0

First edition 2014

Acknowledgments

Scripture quotations marked ESV are from The Holy Bible, English Standard Version® (ESV®) copyright © 2001 by Crossway, a publishing ministry of Good News Publishers. All rights reserved. Scripture quotations marked RSV are from The Revised Standard Version of the Bible copyright © 1346, 1952 and 1971 by the Division of Christian Education of the National Council of Churches in the USA. Used by permission. All Rights Reserved. Scripture quotations marked TNIV are taken from the Holy Bible, Today's New International Version. Copyright © 2004 by International Bible Society. Used by permission of Hodder & Stoughton Publishers. A member of the Hachette Livre UK Group. All rights reserved. "TNIV" is a registered trademark of International Bible Society.
pp. 80, 83, 84, 85, 92. Extracts taken from *Then They Came for Me* by Maziar Bahari. Copyright © Maziar Bahair, 2013. Extract reproduced with permission of Oneworld Publications, London. pp. 174, 175, 190, 191, 194, 195: Extracts taken from "Christians in Parliament: All Party Parliamentary Group Report on the Persecution of Christians in Iran" copyright © 2012, Christians in Parliament. Used by permission. p. 197: Extract taken from "The Cost of Faith: Persecution of Christian Protestants and Converts in Iran" copyright © 2013, International Campaign for Human Rights in Iran. Used by permission. p. 89: Extract taken from "Violent Aftermath: The 2009 Election and Suppression of Dissent in Iran" copyright © Iran Human Rights Documentation Center. Used by permission. pp. 87, 188, 189, 202: Extracts taken from *Captive in Iran* by Maryam Rostampour & Marziyeh Amirizadeh. Copyright © 2003. Used by permission of Tyndale House Publishers, Inc. All rights reserved.

A catalogue record for this book is available from the British Library

Printed and bound in the UK, September 2015, LH26

TOO MANY TO JAIL

The Story of Iran's New Christians

Mark Bradley

With a foreword by Sam Yeghnazar

MONARCH
BOOKS

Oxford, UK & Grand Rapids, Michigan, USA

Published by Monarch Books
an imprint of
Lion Hudson plc
Wilkinson House, Jordan Hill Road,
Oxford OX2 8DR, England
Email: monarch@lionhudson.com
www.lionhudson.com/monarch

ISBN 978 0 85721 596 3
e-ISBN 978 0 85721 597 0

First edition 2014

Acknowledgments

Scripture quotations marked ESV are from The Holy Bible, English Standard Version® (ESV®) copyright © 2001 by Crossway, a publishing ministry of Good News Publishers. All rights reserved. Scripture quotations marked RSV are from The Revised Standard Version of the Bible copyright © 1346, 1952 and 1971 by the Division of Christian Education of the National Council of Churches in the USA. Used by permission. All Rights Reserved. Scripture quotations marked TNIV are taken from the Holy Bible, Today's New International Version. Copyright © 2004 by International Bible Society. Used by permission of Hodder & Stoughton Publishers. A member of the Hachette Livre UK Group. All rights reserved. "TNIV" is a registered trademark of International Bible Society.
pp. 80, 83, 84, 85, 92. Extracts taken from *Then They Came for Me* by Maziar Bahari. Copyright © Maziar Bahair, 2013. Extract reproduced with permission of Oneworld Publications, London. pp. 174, 175, 190, 191, 194, 195: Extracts taken from "Christians in Parliament: All Party Parliamentary Group Report on the Persecution of Christians in Iran" copyright © 2012, Christians in Parliament. Used by permission. p. 197: Extract taken from "The Cost of Faith: Persecution of Christian Protestants and Converts in Iran" copyright © 2013, International Campaign for Human Rights in Iran. Used by permission. p. 89: Extract taken from "Violent Aftermath: The 2009 Election and Suppression of Dissent in Iran" copyright © Iran Human Rights Documentation Center. Used by permission. pp. 87, 188, 189, 202: Extracts taken from *Captive in Iran* by Maryam Rostampour & Marziyeh Amirizadeh. Copyright © 2003. Used by permission of Tyndale House Publishers, Inc. All rights reserved.

A catalogue record for this book is available from the British Library

Printed and bound in the UK, October 2014, LH26

This book is dedicated to all the
known and unknown Christians who
have suffered for their faith
in recent years

CONTENTS

Graphs

ACKNOWLEDGMENTS

I would like to thank all those who have helped make this book possible, especially all those who are standing with Iran's new Christians as they seek to shine for Jesus Christ, despite the ongoing persecution there. They cannot be named for security reasons.

Special thanks go to Sam Yeghnazar for his support and the contribution of the foreword.

And many thanks also to Chrissy Taylor for writing Appendix 2, which gives a detailed account of the persecution Iran's new Christians are enduring. Chrissy also worked on all the graphs, provided much of the research for Chapter 8, and gave valuable input on the rest of the book.

Due to the ongoing hostility of Iran's government to Christianity many names in this book have been changed.

FOREWORD

At heart I am a house-church Christian.

I became a believer sixty years ago in Iran, in my own home. From 1956 until 1960 my father held a house-church meeting in Tehran – *every night.*

In these house-church meetings there was worship, intercession, and Bible teaching, and we left wanting to win others to Jesus Christ.

Of course in many ways our meetings were very different to those happening all over Iran today. But I still see connections between them, especially when I see the spiritual zeal of today's house-church Christians. Their enthusiasm reminds me of the enthusiasm we all felt as we worshipped God in our home all those years ago. I count it an extraordinary privilege that God has allowed me to be so involved with this story of Iran's new Christians. What a blessing to be able to rejoice with them and to weep with them. I wish I could take you with me to the Iran region and let you meet them. You would laugh a lot, and perhaps cry a lot too, and I promise you, you would return to your own situation with your faith in Jesus Christ refreshed.

You would discover that Iranians are incredibly open to the Gospel. They have always had a special love for Jesus, and now, after thirty-five years of experience of the Islamic Republic, they are ready – more than ever before – to hear about Jesus.

You would also see for yourself that the Scripture "whoever calls on the name of Lord will be saved" (Acts 2:21) is true: for the Iranians who turn to Jesus experience Him in wonderful ways. You would have to spend several weeks with me if you wanted to hear all the true stories about Jesus rescuing Iranians from miserable situations. I can tell you about suicidal people kept from taking their own lives, drunks becoming sober, drug addicts delivered, shattered marriages being restored, abused women forgiving their tormentors. Our Jesus is in Iran, serving the broken-hearted.

Iran's new Christians have paid a high price for their faith. Hundreds have been arrested. Sixty are in prison as I write. But still the house churches have continued to grow. There is no turning back, even for those who have suffered. Jesus has proved Himself to them; they are not willing to deny Him. Because they have experienced His love so much they love Him, even from behind dark prison bars.

When I was in my twenties, while working with established churches, I travelled over all Iran with a small team of volunteers giving out Scriptures. We visited hundreds of towns and villages. And we prayed that God would establish churches in these seemingly small and obscure places of which most people had never heard.

Building churches in all these towns and villages did not seem practical then. When later the Islamic government unleashed its hostility against Christianity, it was completely impossible. To enable the Gospel to spread, we needed house churches.

And I knew house churches would work, because of my own experience as a young Christian in my father's house church. But it is not just the format that has impact in people's lives. Behind my father's house church lay the power of prayer. My father spent many days seeking God and had an overwhelming experience with the Holy Spirit in the mid-1950s.

Much spiritual water was to flow from my father seeking God. He started what was almost certainly one of Iran's first house churches. Some of Iran's later Christian leaders can trace their spiritual foundations back to that prayer meeting. The superintendent of the Assemblies of God churches in

Iran, Haik Hovsepian Mehr, and his younger brother Edward both became Christians in my father's house. In January 1994 I was conducting a baptismal service when news came that my dear friend Haik had been murdered. In his role as superintendent he had been campaigning for the release of Mehdi Dibaj, a Muslim convert sentenced to death for apostasy from Islam. Mehdi Dibaj also used to attend my father's house church.[1]

Another Christian leader who attended those initial meetings was Tateos Michaelian. He went on to become the Moderator of the Presbyterian churches of Iran. He was the translator of over sixty Christian books into Persian. Just like Haik and Mehdi, he too became a martyr. Before his death he had graciously accepted my invitation to be a member of the translation team for the New Millennium Version of the Bible. After his martyrdom we call this translation endeavour "The Michaelian Project".

My faith was formed in my father's house church, and when I talk to people involved in today's Iranian house churches, I see they are learning what I had learned in my father's meetings: intensity, vibrancy, zeal for the Gospel. My heart rejoices, and somehow I see a connection between my father's intense prayer life and the house church he started, and today's house-church movement. In our meetings back in the 1950s there was a lot of intercession for all of Iran. Those prayers have continued, all over the world. Now in recent years we are starting to see the answer to those prayers.

I – and other leaders of my generation – rejoice. We are also aware that we have a great responsibility. We are thankful that Iran's new Christians do not have an arrogant, unteachable spirit, but that they look to us older Christians for help and support and encouragement: to be their spiritual fathers and mothers.

---

1   See Appendix 3 for his final testament.

I believe the story of Iran's new Christians is an important story for the wider church. The story shows that God has special times. Thirty years ago Iranians were not so open to Jesus Christ; now they are. We must know what hour it is and act accordingly.

The story also shows that formal church structures in countries like Iran are limited. House churches have a vital role to play in the growth of the church – not just in Iran, but elsewhere too. It also shows how crucial the role of the wider church is, and how older Christians have a duty to join with new churches to help and support them. This book emphasizes that this is not just a story about Iran's new Christians; it is a story about Iran's new Christians – in partnership with the church at large.

Finally, the story shows that we are all engaged in a serious business. There is a price to pay. Being a true Christian in Iran is not for the faint-hearted. The knock on the door from the police can come at any hour of the day or night. But even when there has been suffering, as this story already shows, it is the church that triumphs, not its enemies. Because of the church in Iran having been persecuted for the last thirty-five years, it is fitting that this book is dedicated to all those who have suffered. But the end of the story does not take us to a lonely prison cell, but to thousands and thousands of homes across Iran where God is worshipped in the Spirit through Jesus Christ.

I repeat. This is an important story, and I commend Mark Bradley for telling it to the wider church. I trust that, as you read, you will be encouraged.

Sam Yeghnazar
Founder and Director of Elam ministries

INTRODUCTION

In early 2011 the wife of a Christian prisoner was called to report to the offices of the MOIS (Ministry of Intelligence and Security[2]) in Tehran. This is the Ministry that had orchestrated the arrests of at least 114 Christians in fourteen cities across Iran since the end of 2010. By the end of 2012 the agency would have arrested over 300 Christians.

During the interrogation the wife of the Christian prisoner was asked if she knew why her husband was in prison. She replied, "Because of his Christian faith."

She was surprised by her interrogator's response.

"Of course not. Your husband isn't in prison because of his religious faith. If we arrested people for religious reasons, there would be no room in the prisons."

MOIS has a vast budget and many staff. No expense has been spared to monitor the activities of Christians. Phones are bugged, suspects are trailed, and when Christians are arrested their laptops and mobiles are confiscated so contact lists can be analysed. This is almost certainly the organization that knows more accurately than any other exactly how many house-church Christians there are in Iran.

And here's the answer: too many to jail. For when the interrogator said "religious reasons" he was making reference to the fact that according to Islamic law, a person born into the Muslim faith cannot convert to another faith. This is the

2   Known as Ettela'at in Iran. Vezarat-e Ettela'at Jomhuri-ye Eslami-ye Iran, literally Islamic Republic of Iran's Ministry of Intelligence, is the primary intelligence agency of the Islamic Republic of Iran. It is also known as VEVAK (Vezarat-e Ettela'at va Amniyat-e Keshvar) or VAJA, as well as MOIS. I shall use "MOIS" in this book.

"religious reason" the state employs to imprison Christians.[3]

So, there are too many Christians to jail in Iran, one of the most closed countries in the world. Given the hostility of the Islamic Republic to active Christians for the last thirty-five years resulting in the murder of at least six evangelical pastors, the closure of churches, the banning of the Bible and Christian literature, and the arrests of hundreds, one might have expected the Iranian church to have withered away.

The opposite has happened. Instead, the church has been growing vigorously. New branches have appeared in towns and villages of which most church leaders have barely even heard.

In my earlier book, *Iran: Open Hearts in a Closed Land*, I looked at what made Iran such a closed country and why the Iranian people were so open to the Christian Gospel. That book, at just over 100 pages long, was published in 2007. I expanded this subject in more detail a year later in *Iran and Christianity: Historical Identity and Present Relevance*.

A lot has happened since then: Mahmoud Ahmadinejad's presidency; the bitterly disputed 2009 elections; Iran's ongoing showdown with the West over its nuclear programme; a very marked increase in the government's persecution against Christians; and overwhelming evidence that there has been dynamic growth in the new house-church movement, the home of Iran's new Christians.

3   While Iran is an Islamic Republic and the judiciary is dominated by the clergy, nevertheless the Sharia interpretation of how to punish apostates from Islam (death for men; life imprisonment for women) has not been cemented into the country's legal system. It was a part of a draft proposal for a new legal code in 2008, but this failed to win the approval of parliament. This reflects a reasonably consistent theme in the Islamic Republic: when something Islamic threatens the Republic – the wholesale execution of Christians and others would create an international storm, if not a casus belli – pragmatism and the Republic wins. The rejection of the implementation of Sharia law regarding apostates is, however, not just about pragmatism; it also reflects that within the Iranian body politic there is this other non-Islamic identity that tends to be more tolerant. This is discussed in Chapter 5. For more information about Iran's constitution and apostasy see: http://scholarlycommons.law.northwestern.edu/cgi/viewcontent.cgi?article=1156&context=njihr Accessed 2 July 2014.

This is a big story – a dramatic story. It is full of tears of joy – and tears of grief. As I write, at least sixty known house-church Christians are in prison. They and their families are suffering. Hundreds more have been forced into exile. One day they have normal lives, the next their world is squeezed into a suitcase and they are heading for a strange land. They too are suffering.

Yet out of this suffering Iran's new house churches have experienced unprecedented growth. Indeed, in the modern era there have never been so many Christians in Iran. And – as you will see as you read on – their numbers are almost certainly set to rise.

The purpose of this book is to tell this story. Chapter 1 establishes that all the talk about the church growing in Iran is not Christian hype. It is reality. It is where all the available evidence leads. The following three chapters examine how the average Iranians' relationship with their national religion became first bruised by the Islamic Republic, and then, under Ahmadinejad, infected. Many became disillusioned with Islam. But why were so many wanting to find out about Jesus Christ? This question is addressed in Chapter 5.

Iranians are open and are joining house churches. This is reported in the Christian press. But what exactly is meant by a "house church"? This question is discussed in Chapter 6 in which I look at the different stories of five house churches (there are many others). Drawing on what we learn from these five accounts, Chapter 7 asks what it is that connects these house churches together and how it is that they have been playing such a crucial part in Christianity's growth in Iran.

The story ends, in Chapter 8, by looking at the strange equation of suffering and growth that appears in so much church history, including the last ten years of Christianity in Iran.

While I very much hope that this book will help you understand the growth of the church in Iran, I also hope it will inspire you afresh to give yourself to intercede for Iranian Christians – both for those who are suffering in prison, and for those who seek to be salt in their ancient land.

This book is dedicated to them.

CHAPTER 1

HOSTILE GOVERNMENT: FASTEST-GROWING CHURCH IN THE WORLD

Mahmoud Ahmadinejad: "I will stop Christianity in Iran."[4]

Along with many other Muslims, the former president of Iran, Mahmoud Ahmadinejad, has two problems with Christianity. One is that he sees the faith as being inferior – it came before Islam, God's final revelation. This is the theological issue. The more pungent problem is that he sees Christianity as being deeply corrupt.

A brief glance at the "Christian"[5] nations of the world soon provides ample evidence of this corruption for many Muslims. Most obvious is the brazen promotion of sexual lust. Nudity is emblazoned on advertisement hoardings, paraded on stages, and broadcast onto millions of TV screens. In terms of mental images the difference between Islam and Christianity is not theological, but physical. Muslim women cover up; Christian women bare all.

Now the "Christian" West has given the final proof to all decent Muslims that its depraved, dissolute, and degenerate societies will soon be pounded by Allah's wrath: some Western governments have legalized homosexual "marriage".

4   https://www.worldwatchmonitor.org/2006/01-January/newsarticle_4166.html
5   Many Iranians, especially those who have not travelled abroad, consider the West (America, Europe, and Australia) to be Christian. The actual number of churchgoers in these countries is irrelevant to this perception.

21

The Islamic revolution (1979, also known as the Iranian Revolution) mixed together Shia Islam's backing for the oppressed with a left-wing loathing for Western imperialism and stirred this into Iranian nationalism. This powerful political concoction brought millions to the streets. Ahmadinejad and his supporters still see the world in this way – and hence find Christianity guilty of gross corruption. For it is the creed of the imperialist: the Spanish in South America; the Russians in the Caucasus; the French in North Africa; worst of all the British – and most recently the Americans – all over the world, and at present[6] on three of Iran's borders: in Iraq, the Gulf, and Afghanistan.

Built into the DNA of the Iranian Revolution is a hatred for the Western imperialism that turned vast swathes of the Islamic world into Christian-controlled colonies.[7] The whole point of the Islamic revolution was to expel all the influence of these "arrogant" powers, together with their corrupt religion from Iran – and the whole of the Middle East.

The most noxious example of imperialism in the Middle East for Muslims like Mahmoud Ahmadinejad is Israel. And Christianity is very much a guilty partner in what they consider as an invasion of Palestinian land. While the father of political Zionism is considered to be Theodore Hezl (1860–1904), a Jew, in fact the idea in modern times for the Jewish people to have Palestine as their homeland originated with Christians. Puritans wrote about it during the Reformation period, and then Zionism became popular in the nineteenth century when the Plymouth Brethren leader, John Nelson Darby (1800–82), the man behind dispensational theology,[8] made Zionism a

---

6   As of February 2014.

7   To appreciate the humiliation felt by Muslims over Western imperialism see Bernard Lewis, *What Went Wrong?*

8   Darby taught that history should be divided into several dispensations – that is, different periods of God's dealing with Man from creation to the final judgment. This paradigm has had significant influence on American Christianity through its promotion in the Scofield Bible.

precondition for the return of Christ. While Darby's teaching has been questioned by many Christian leaders,[9] nevertheless it is still very popular, especially in the southern states of the USA. Well-known Christian preachers have been ardent advocates. In alliance with the Israeli lobby their voice has influence in Washington. It is not surprising, then, that Iranians of Ahmadinejad's ilk easily think of Christianity and Zionism as almost being one and the same.[10]

Linked to imperialism, and providing further proof of Christianity's corruption, are the well-documented atrocities committed by the Western powers. First on the list is the Crusades, especially Richard I of England's sack of Jerusalem, followed by the murder of all the city's Muslim residents. There was also the genocide of the American Indians by the "Christian" settlers; the genocide of the aborigines by the "Christian" settlers in Australia; the slave trade – the Christian British selling of Africans to the Christian Americans. And each time Ahmadinejad courted curses by questioning the scale of the Holocaust he reminded the world that the barbaric burning of the Jews happened in a Christian country. The Nazis were voted into office by a country where 94 per cent of the population were registered as Christians.[11]

Sexual lust, imperialism, Zionism, atrocities – these are the associations that come with the word "Christianity" when mentioned by President Ahmadinejad and his supporters. For a strong Iranian leader to give any quarter for inferior Christianity to spread would not only be insulting the Islamic faith, God's final revelation on earth, but, much more dangerously, it would

9   Examples include John Stott, Colin Chapman, and, most recently, Stephen Sizer.
10   Christians are often accused of being Zionist. In July 2013, for example, 28-year-old Ebrahim Firouzi was arrested and charged with "promoting Christian Zionism" by "attempting to launch a Christian website, contact with suspicious foreigners and running online church services". See www.worldwatchmonitor.org/2013/07/2623421/ Accessed 11 June 2014.
11   http://jdstone.org/cr/files/hitlerworkingthechristiancrowd.html states "According to the *Encyclopedia Britannica*, in the 1930s Protestants constituted 49 percent of the German Christians; Catholics about 45 percent." Accessed 11 June 2014.

open the door to decadence, licentiousness, and the habitual imperialism of the "Christian" powers, recently on display in Afghanistan and Iraq.

Given this association it is then not surprising to find that when Ahmadinejad became president in 2005 he proclaimed: "I will stop Christianity in Iran." As a president who enjoyed the full support of the Supreme Leader, the Revolutionary Guards, and the judiciary, Ahmadinejad had access to all the levers of power by which to crush Christianity in Iran. The law was firmly on his side. Christians from Muslim backgrounds were said to be guilty of "apostasy", a crime in religious courts, which, at the discretion of the judge, could carry the death sentence for men and life imprisonment for women. Given the nature of the international church, Christians could easily be framed as a threat to national security. During Ahmadinejad's presidency hundreds of Christians were arrested and there was indeed an unprecedented attempt to "stop Christianity".[12]

But Christianity has not been stopped.

The complete opposite has happened.

Christianity has been present in Iran since at least the second century. The faith thrived there until the arrival of Islam in the seventh century. Despite restrictions, the church remained a vibrant presence until the savage attacks of Tamerlane in the fourteenth century. Then Christianity became associated with two minority ethnic groups: the Assyrians who trace their roots back to the early Nestorian church, and the Armenians who were brought to Iran in the seventeenth century[13] (see Appendix 1 for an account of Christianity pre-1979).

After the Arab invasions it was unheard of for thousands of Iranian Muslims to become Christian. However, in our generation, at a time when Iran is ruled by a government

12   See Chapter 8.
13   The Assyrians and Armenians who generally belong to the Eastern Orthodox family of Christians are still a presence in Iran. However since 1979 there has been a dramatic decline in their numbers (see Chapter 8). Whenever the Islamic Republic refers to Christians, it means these ethnic minorities specifically.

implacably opposed to Christianity, this is exactly what has happened – and continues to happen.

Mahmoud Ahmadinejad vowed to "stop Christianity".

Here is irony.

During those very years when Ahmadinejad was president the church grew more rapidly among Muslims than at any other time in Iran's recent history.

Church growth – it's where the evidence leads

In 2007 a conservative estimate[14] for the number of Persian-speaking Iranian Christians from a Muslim background in Iran was put at between 50,000 and 100,000.[15] Seemingly a small figure in a country of (then) 66,000,000 inhabitants, 100,000 Muslim converts in Iran was, relative to the past, a historic number. Twenty years earlier there were around just 500 Christians from a Muslim background. Something significant had been going on.[16]

Now in 2014 the most cautious estimate is definitely 100,000,[17] and the conservative estimate is 370,000.[18] Another view[19] argues that due to satellite TV and the internet there are now thousands of isolated unconnected believers, and this source believes the more likely figure is 700,000.

14 There were then a number of preachers who enthusiastically talked of there being over a million Christians in Iran in 2007. The figure probably had more to do with their enthusiasm than with accurate research.

15 The numbers of ethnic Assyrian and Armenian Christians have been decreasing since the 1979 Revolution.

16 This is fully explored in the author's *Iran: Open Hearts in a Closed Land*.

17 The author was verbally given this figure by a house-church leader with an extensive network inside Iran; and the same figure was quoted by a senior leader from a satellite TV agency.

18 The mission agency Open Doors states this: "An estimated 200 Muslim Background Believers (MBBs) were living in Iran 40 years ago, according to Open Doors. Now, the number of MBBs is estimated to be 370,000." www.christianpost. com/news/open-doors-growth-of-christianity-in-iran-explosive-71946/ Accessed 6 February 2014.

19 This is the view of a senior leader in an agency with a long history of serving the church in Iran.

If the 370,000 figure is correct this then means that Christianity among Iranians from a Muslim background has grown by 200 per cent in the last seven years; about 28 per cent per year. This means that Iran has the fastest-growing church in the world.[20] This conclusion is backed by one of the most respected sources for statistics on church growth in the Christian world, Operation World. This agency records Iran's church growth among evangelicals as being 19.6 per cent.[21]

There is no exact picture, but there are three areas of evidence that when put together confirm there has been serious church growth in Iran in recent years. It is not borne of hype and Christians getting over-excited. The available evidence might only be able to paint an impressionistic picture, but the impression left is very clear. In this closed Muslim land there has been church growth.

The three areas that can be looked at are:

1. the response of Iranians inside Iran to ministry (Scriptures, books, TV, internet);

2. reports from those involved in church planting;

3. the high numbers of arrests.

Response to ministry to Iran

Scriptures and books

The ever-increasing demand for Bibles and New Testaments is double-edged evidence. First of all the demand shows that Iranians in general want to read the Christian Scriptures. But there is more. As a rule whole Bibles are not given to non-

---

20   Landinfo, a human rights group that produces reports for the Norwegian Immigration Department, emphasizes it is impossible to say what the true number of converts to Christianity is. However, these researchers make this significant statement: "In the opinion of Landinfo, and source material on which this report is based indicated a tendency towards growth in the volume of house churches during recent years." See "Iran: Christians and Converts", Landinfo, July 2011, p. 10. See http://www. landinfo.no/asset/1772/1/1772_1.pdf Accessed 22 May 2014.

21   http://www.operationworld.org/hidden/evangelical-growth Accessed 13 May 2014.

Christians, but only to believers with some sort of standing in a house church. The agency Elam Ministries, one of the most active in bringing Scriptures to Iran, has printed 1.2 million copies of their new translation of the New Testament in the last ten years. Many of these will have been used in evangelism. However, they have also printed over 40,000 whole Bibles since 2007.[22] These are for believers. The graph below, based on figures from another agency with close involvement in the region, tells the same story: an increase in demand both for New Testaments – and whole Bibles.

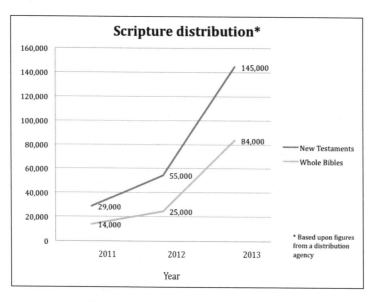

Scripture distribution*

Despite the thousands of New Testaments and Bibles these agencies are dealing with, their leaders say they cannot keep up with demand. Elam Ministries is keen to print another 1 million New Testaments and provide hundreds of thousands of whole Bibles. Yet another agency would like to have at least half a

22   From the 1990s Elam Ministries has been providing the Iran region with what is known as the 1895 Persian Version. In September 2014 the New Millennium Version of the whole Bible was published. This is a modern and accurate translation, comparable to the New International Version or English Standard Version in English.

million Bibles and New Testaments a year to meet the demand.[23]

Reports from inside the region reveal three constants about the response of Iranians to the Christian Scriptures. One is that more are always wanted. The second is that 99 per cent of people receive them warmly (there are many beautiful stories of Iranians who seek a message from God who are then being given some Scriptures). The third is the hostility of government authorities. One group of smugglers were told: "You can bring in alcohol, you can bring in drugs; but never bring in these (New Testaments)." There is even a report that the authorities burnt confiscated Scriptures.[24]

The response to books also shows there is great interest in Christianity in Iran. Agencies such as Elam Ministries report there is a constant demand for more Christian books in Persian in Iran. All books have to be sent in to the country as it is illegal to print Christian literature in Iran. When they arrive, they essentially disappear – such is the demand.

Satellite TV and internet

Christian satellite TV has been beaming into Iran since 2001. The broadcasters are certain that people are not only watching their programmes, but also responding. This was proved in 2006 when one of the channels, "Mohabat" (Love), asked a professional marketing company to carry out research within Iran to get a feel for how many people were watching their programmes. They were encouraged by the results. After interviewing 1,500 individuals in three different cities the researchers report that 200 of those interviewed (13 per cent) watched Mohabat programmes, and 40 (3 per cent) said they had wanted to experience Christ after watching the broadcasts.[25]

Seven years on and Mohabat's annual report of 2013 shows

23   As revealed in conversation with a leader from that agency.
24   http://www.beliefnet.com/columnists/watchwomanonthewall/2011/08/iran-launches-bible-burning-campaign.html Accessed 11 July 2014.
25   The author was given private access to this report.

the interest in Christianity is increasing. There has been a 160 per cent increase in their viewing figures; a 23 per cent increase in the number of people becoming Christians through their programmes; and a 300 per cent increase in the number of people being connected to house churches. Response to their internet ministry tells the same story (see graph).

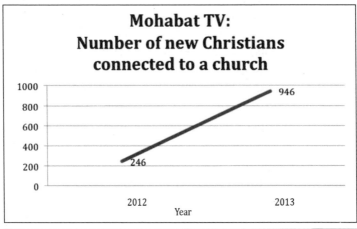

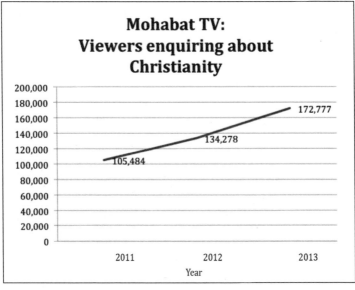

Research from the Christian broadcaster Sat 7 Pars reaches the same conclusion. A 2011 survey carried out inside Iran showed that 1.7 million people over the age of fifteen watched Sat 7 Pars programmes, and a further 5 million were aware of the channel.[26] And, as the graph shows, there has been a dramatic increase in the number of viewers contacting them – over 240 per cent.[27]

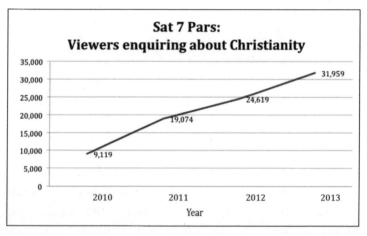

Sat 7 Pars:
Viewers enquiring about Christianity

Another major Christian broadcaster is Dr Hormoz Shariat whose channel Network 7 provides round-the-clock programming, seven days a week. Dr Shariat has no doubt that his programmes attract millions of viewers. And it is clear viewers want to find out more. Dr Shariat's agency Iran Alive Ministries reports 10,000 visitors per month in its evangelistic web chat rooms. There have also been plenty of conversions: since 2002 his agency has recorded over 27,000 documented decisions of Iranians turning to Christ.[28] However, Dr Shariat

26 http://www.sat7uk.org/about/countries/iran Accessed 27 March 2014.

27 Figures contained in an email from Sat 7 Pars staff received 31 March 2014.

28 In a private letter to the author Dr Shariat wrote: "One hard stat is the number of people who have contacted us for the last twelve years that we have been on the air. Over 150,000 people have contacted us and we have the names of over 27,000 people who have either prayed with us to receive Christ or have indicated that they have done so through watching TV programs."

is certain that many more Iranian Muslims are becoming Christians – but believes they are keeping quiet about their new faith because of the security situation. This is very likely. Dr Shariat suggests that for each recorded decision, there are another nine unrecorded ones.[29] This would then mean that his ministry alone has seen well over 200,000 come to faith in the last thirteen years. Given that up to 50,000,000 Iranians have access to satellite TV[30] it is of course impossible to give an exact figure regarding how many have come to faith in Christ through Christian programming.

One of the most comprehensive sources for evidence about the interest in Christianity in Iran is the internet ministry "Farsinet". Launched on 21 March 1996 this was one of the first Christian websites for Persian speakers. From the very start the agency has used an independent web service[31] to track responses to its site and the story painted by the statistics is easy to understand – it shows there has been a year-by-year increase. In the first ten years (1996–2006) the number of page requests shot up from under 200,000 to 13 million. Remarkably, the statistics so far for 2014 show that the requests now number 20 million.

29   The former head of programming at Sat 7 Pars makes the same point regarding viewers who believe, but are shy about their faith. In a private email to the author it was stated: "There are many people (we witness some of their testimonies every day on our channel) for whom public concern and honor and shame play a big role: for example a young teacher in a village called us telling us that he observed that there are many people there watching our channel and some accepted Christ, but they do not want to admit it or speak about their new faith." (Email received 12 May 2014.)
30   Sara Afshari, "An examination of the Growth of Christianity and the Contribution of Farsi Christian Media in Contemporary Iran", August 2013. Unpublished MA thesis for Edinburgh University. In this essay Ms Afshari, the former head of programming at Sat 7 Pars, states that in 2011 64 per cent of Iranians had access to satellite TV. Ms Afshari based this figure on the findings of a police report reported on the website www.entekhab.ir and another agency, Shargh News.
31   http://extremetracking.com/open;sum?login=farsinet Accessed 31 March 2014.

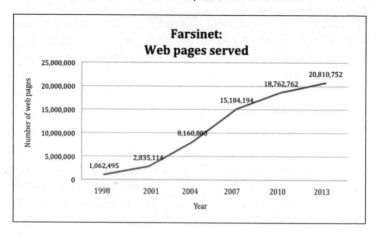

What the church planters say

A leader involved in house churches was asked how many Christians there were in his fellowships. I was expecting to hear the answer of around several hundred. This was not the case: it was a lot more than I had anticipated.[32] And the growth is happening quickly. About six months later the same leader was asked the same question, and by this time the number had grown a lot more.

This "a lot more" was also the answer given by two other church planters. It was also clear from their answers that the churches are not limited to just a few cities. One church planter talked of working in many towns. The reports regarding the number of house church Christians in Iran are not that helpful. But the answer to the central question, "Is house-church Christianity growing in Iran?" is important. Eyewitness evidence declares that yes, there is *significant* growth.

---

32   For security reasons the exact figure cannot be given.

The arrests

Ironically, perhaps, the most important evidence regarding the spread of Christianity in Iran comes from the security forces that harass the church. It is known that the MOIS has a full-time team dedicated to monitoring the activities of Christians.[33] This team taps phones, monitors people's travelling, and infiltrates Christian groups. When – as has regularly happened in recent years – Christians are arrested, the security forces interrogate them for hours in order to get more information about the house churches. They also trawl through thousands of emails and files from the computers they have confiscated from Christians. There is no doubt that it is this team that has the most accurate information about the size of Iran's new Christians. And, as we have seen, their view is that there are too many Christians to jail.

This is also the impression that sometimes appears on websites and in news outlets linked to the security forces. In evidence given to a UK tribunal in May 2008, Iran expert Dr Anna Enayat[34] referred to an official of the Ministry of Education, Hasan Mohmamadi, who in 2004 had complained to a group of high school students that "unfortunately, on average, every day 50 Iranian girls and boys convert secretly to Christian denominations in our country". Dr Enayat also made reference to the Deputy Director of Religious Propaganda and Applied Training of the Qom Seminaries. He said in 2005 that "Christianity had become extremely active in academic circles. He referred to Christian missionaries establishing house churches in Tehran, and proselytising. He was concerned by the way in which the young were being attracted to Christianity,

33   An Iranian with knowledge about Iran's security forces gave this information to the author.
34   Dr Enayat is fluent in Persian and was previously a lecturer in Economic Sociology at Tehran University (1971–79). Dr Enayat has been a Senior Associate Member of St Antony's College since 1983. She is a prolific writer on Iran, and for many years was on the editorial board of I.B. Tauris, a publisher of academic titles.

and said that statistics gave rise to grave concern. He said the religion appealed to youth, because it set no limits."[35]

The fact that the numbers of Iran's new Christians had become a national issue for the Islamic Republic was confirmed in October 2010 by the Supreme Leader. In a speech in Iran's religious capital, Qom, which was broadcast across the nation, Ayatollah Khamenei warned against the "network of house churches" that threaten the Islamic faith and deceive young Muslims.[36] We can deduce from this that the reference to the house-church networks gave them, albeit negatively, official recognition; the use of the word "threat" meant that their numbers were a serious concern.

Shortly after this speech there was a coordinated attempt by the government to crush the house-church movement. Ironically it is this attack that has provided the most solid evidence that Christianity is spreading in Iran. From 2010 through to the summer of 2011 there were over 300 documented cases of Christians facing arbitrary arrest in over forty-eight towns and villages across Iran.[37] It is likely there are many other cases that have not been reported.

These figures prove two characteristics about the house-church movement. First, we are most certainly talking about a movement of thousands. The Christians arrested were active in their faith; they were the pastors and teachers responsible for others. During one of the arrests a scene with echoes of Gethsemane were re-enacted. In a city in the south the security forces entered the house of a Christian pastor who had two or three from his fellowship there. The police wanted to arrest all the Christians but the pastor said, "I am the leader; I am the one

35   https://tribunalsdecisions.service.gov.uk/utiac/37748

36   Sara Afshari, "An Examination of the Growth of Christianity", quoted from www.aftabir.com, p. 11.

37   *Christians in Parliament All Party Parliamentary Group Report on the Persecution of Christians in Iran*

you need to talk to. You have no need to arrest my friends."[38] It is almost certain that some of the Christians arrested represented many others. Some would say, ten; others, a hundred. If the leader arrested was responsible for ten other Christians, then the figure for the arrests represents 3,000 believers; if a hundred, then the figures point to a total of 30,000. It is also important to note that some of the house churches remained successfully below the radar and managed to escape the attention of the authorities.

The second characteristic of the house-church movement that these arrests highlight is that it is a movement that is widespread across the country. Thirty years ago Christianity was almost entirely an urban affair. There were Protestant congregations in most of the largest cities – Tehran, Mashad, Isfahan, Shiraz, Tabriz, Ahvaz, Kerman – but there were hardly any evangelical Christians who were of a Muslim background who lived in Iran's thousands of smaller towns and villages. Now – due primarily to satellite TV and the internet – there are. And the proof were these arrests of Christians in unfamiliar places like Dezful, a small town north of Ahvaz; or Arak, another small town 135 kilometres south-west of Qom; or Bandar-E-Mahshahr, another small town just over 100 kilometres east of Abadan – and many more. In an interview regarding this, Revd Edward Hovsepian Mehr, one of Iran's most senior church leaders, made exactly this point in connection to persecution:

> As the result of persecution, worship in the church is no longer contained or limited to a handful of churches in the mega cities; it has now moved, according to the statements by the state officials, to remote areas and villages.[39]

These figures from TV and internet agencies, the demand for Scriptures, complaints about the numbers of Christians from

---

38 An eyewitness from the fellowship told this story to the author.
39 Sara Afshari, "An Examination of the Growth of Christianity", p. 30.

officials, the numerous reports from those engaged in ministry to Iran, and the number and extent of the arrests of activists all combine to affirm that the estimates from Operation World regarding the size and growth rate of the church in Iran are probably reliable.

The church is probably 370,000-strong and is growing at a rate of 19.6 per cent a year. If this growth rate continues this means that by 2020 there will be (at least) 1,000,000 Christians who are of a Muslim background in Iran.[40]

This is not wishful thinking. This is not Christian hype. This is where the available evidence leads. There are too many Christians in Iran to jail.

As Jesus said, "The wind [Spirit] blows where it wills" (John 3:8, RSV); in other words without divine intervention nobody can become a Christian, and certainly nobody can plant a church. However, in Iran's case it is also possible to see how recent events have helped that wind blow more freely over Iranian hearts.

To better understand the story of Iran's new Christians, it is helpful to first see how recent history has impacted many Iranians' receptivity to Jesus Christ.

---

40   Suggested growth rate might look like this: 2013: 360,000; 2014: 430,560; 2015: 514,949; 2016: 615,879; 2017: 736,591; 2018: 880,962; 2019: 1,053,630; 2020: 1,260,141.

CHAPTER 2

IRANIANS AND THEIR NATIONAL RELIGION: A WOUNDED RELATIONSHIP

The story of Iran's new Christians begins with the religion of their birth: Shia Islam. All of Iran's new Christians were born into Shia Muslim families – some devout, some less so – but Shia Islam was their national religion. Even if they were not ardent believers, nearly all had an emotional attachment to the religion of their land, even if it was borne purely of patriotism.

By becoming Christian they renounced Islam. This was not a small step; it was an immense turnaround in their lives that required both determination and courage. They faced the wrath of their families and employers, which could leave them ostracized and without work. They also risked facing the hostility of a government whose *raison d'être* was to uphold Shia Islam. And of much more importance was the spiritual risk. All their lives they had heard that only the followers of Islam go to heaven. Now they were burning that bridge. They were risking their souls being flung into the eternal flames.[41]

This has happened not for a small number of Iranians, but for several hundred thousand new Christians: they have renounced Islam.

Certainly there is a divine element in their story. The Holy Spirit has convinced them to turn from the religion of their birth and put their hands into the wounded hands of Jesus.

41 The author has talked to hundreds of Iranians who have become Christians, and a number of times he has heard how the fear of going to hell looms large when a Muslim considers turning to Christ.

Seemingly the divine has used recent history to make it much easier for Iranians to turn to Christ than it had been in the past.

This recent history concerns a deep disillusionment of Islam that has developed in Iran. For many Iranians – and certainly those who have become Christians – their relationship with their national religion was first wounded, and then infected.

This is the background to the story of Iran's new Christians.

We will first look at the impact of Ayatollah Khomeini, his successors, when Iranians' relationship with their religion became wounded, and then at the man who tried to claim Khomeini's mantle, the former president, Mahmoud Ahmadinejad, for it was on his watch that Iran's relationship with its religion first became infected.

Ayatollah Khomeini[42]

In 1979, with steely determination and a cunning that ran rings around his opponents, Ayatollah Khomeini swept away Iran's ancient royal throne and installed his "Government of God".

The human face of this divine administration was the "Supreme Jurist", soon to become known as the "Supreme Leader", the religious leader considered to be best able to interpret Islamic laws. In 1979 that was Ayatollah Khomeini. So, with the support of 99 per cent of the voters, the state and the Shia religion were cemented into one entity. Now everything that happened under the new government happened in the name of Islam.

And that is the reason why there was a dislocation between Iranians and their national religion: under Ayatollah Khomeini things happened that made people feel uneasy about Islam.

42   The story of how the rule of Ayatollah Khomeini and his successors caused disillusionment towards Iran's national religion is told in more detail in the author's *Iran: Open Hearts in a Closed Land*, pp. 46–72; and also in his *Iran and Christianity*, chapters 4–7. Much of the following section is based on that material.

Political blood

When Ayatollah Khomeini appointed his first prime minister, Mehdi Bazargan, he said: "I hereby pronounce Bazargan as the Ruler and since I have appointed him he must be obeyed." So Iranians began to taste political authoritarianism under the "Government of God". No dissent was tolerated. Enemies deemed to be a threat were dealt with violently.

First the royalists were rounded up and executed. Next it was the turn of the Islamic socialists, the Mojahadin, who had played a very active and violent part in the overthrow of the Shah. They also enjoyed about 20 per cent support across the country and expected their leader, Masoud Rajavi, to have a place in the new political order. Instead the Mojahadin were hounded down as hypocrites – as "Monafaghin". By the end of 1981 Amnesty International estimated that about 2,500 of their members had been executed and thousands more, mainly teenagers, imprisoned.[43]

Once this threat had been dealt with, the Islamic regime turned its attention to the Tudeh Party – the communists – who had abetted the new government in its war against the Mojahadin because they were keen to be the sole voice of the left in Iranian politics. This was naïve. There was to be no left or right in Khomeini's world and when the Tudeh party dared to criticize his decision to continue the war with Iraq the sword of the Supreme Leader turned on them. Most of the Tudeh leaders managed to flee the country but about 5,000 of their followers were executed.

43   The Mojahadin is a cult-like militant group that mingled Marxism with Islam. It was very active in bringing about the overthrow of the monarchy, and so expected a seat at the table of the new government. However Ayatollah Khomeini always loathed the group and excluded them. This then initiated a violent civil war. There are some Western politicians who naively think this group could establish a democratic Iran. They are deluded. This group is probably more authoritarian than the Khomeinists. To understand how deceptive and cult-like the Mojahadin are see Masoud Banisadr's *Masoud*. The author, the cousin of the former president, was a senior figure in the Mojahadin

Before Khomeini died in June 1989 he unleashed one final murderous assault on his opponents. His victims were the thousands of Mojahadin teenagers who had been arrested in 1981, some for just possessing a piece of the socialist group's literature. In 1988, based in Iraq as an ally of Saddam Hussein, the Mojahadin leader Masoud Rajavi fantasized that his amateur army could invade Iran. On 26 July 1988 Rajavi sent his soldiers in to Iran telling them they would hardly need to fight because all the people would rise up, along with all their comrades in prison who would pour out of their jails and carry the invaders like fish in a river towards Tehran.[44] But the amateur army was annihilated, and a few weeks later, under the orders of Ayatollah Khomeini,[45] three judges toured the prisons and oversaw the execution of 2,000–4,000 Mojahadin inmates.[46]

By the early 1990s there was bitter disillusionment amongst Iranians over this brutal political violence. It is not surprising that when people heard about these executions, or worse actually knew the victims, there was a feeling of uneasiness about the religion in whose name the victims were killed.

44   See Shirin Ebadi, *Iran Awakening*, Rider, 2007, p. 8.
45   Ayatollah Khomeini's decree was published by Ayatollah Montazeri in July 1988. Ayatollah Khomeini wrote: "It is decreed that those who are in prison throughout the country and remain steadfast in their support for the Monafeqin [Mojahedin], are waging war on God and are condemned to execution. The task of implementing the decree in Tehran is entrusted to Hojjatol-Islam Nayyeri, the religious judge, Mr Eshraqi, the Tehran prosecutor, and a representative of the Intelligence Ministry [MOIS]." See http://www.iranrights.org/english/document-106.php Accessed 18 December 2013.
46   Some believe the background to this purge was the invasion; others believe that Ayatollah Khomeini had long been planning such a purge to ensure opposition activists could not threaten the regime. See http://www.pbs.org/wgbh/pages/frontline/tehranbureau/2009/08/the-bloody-red-summer-of-1988.html Accessed 18 December 2013.
In April 2010 the aythor met an Iranian Christian from a Muslim background whose brother had mistakenly been executed during this purge. His brother had had no contact with the Mojahadin. Another victim was the nephew of Shirin Ebadi, the 2003 winner of the Nobel Peace Prize, for her work as a human rights lawyer in Iran. Her nephew was arrested in the early 1980s, just for owning some Mojahadin literature. In 1988 he was executed.

War blood

Eighteen months after Ayatollah Khomeini set up his "Government of God" Iran was at war[47] with Iraq. By the summer of 1988, when at last the Iran–Iraq conflict ended, 300,000 Iranians had died, another 500,000 wounded.[48] They are not forgotten. They appear in huge painted murals that look down on Tehran's traffic jams and in the well-kept memorials in the country's cemeteries. Mahmoud Ahmadinejad, when mayor of Tehran, even turned some of the city's public parks into graveyards. He and fellow veterans from the Iran–Iraq conflict are determined that the post-war generation do not betray what these martyrs died for.

But this is where the constant reference to the war hits a problem: what did those Iranians die for? The government's answers do not add up. They cannot have died to defend their homeland because everyone knows the Iraqi forces had retreated back to their own borders by the summer of 1981, with Saddam Hussein suing for peace. However, the carnage of war continued until 1988 because Ayatollah Khomeini had ordered the liberation of Jerusalem – via Baghdad. So now Iranians were dying to stamp out Baathism in Baghdad and Zionism in Palestine. Thousands did die, including children as young as thirteen, who were used in human wave attacks. Despite a massive offensive in 1987 when at least 65,000 Iranian troops were killed, the armies of the Islamic Republic did not even manage to capture Basra, the city nearest the southern border with Iran. When the war ended in 1988 Iran had not

47 It should be noted that before the invasion Ayatollah Khomeini had been sending in agents to destabilize the Baath regime. There was even a nearly successful assassination attempt on Saddam Hussein's deputy, Tariq Aziz, on 1 April 1980. Some historians, such as Efraim Karsh, argue persuasively that the main aim of the Iraqi invasion was to serve as a warning for Iran to pull back its agents and cease its constant calls for the overthrowing of Saddam Hussein. While Iraq started the war, what is without doubt is that Ayatollah Khomeini then perpetuated it. Saddam Hussein sued for peace nine times.

48 http://www.globalsecurity.org/military/world/war/iran-iraq.htm Accessed 8 January 2013.

even gained a millimetre of Iraqi soil.

The reality of this was obvious to every Iranian. Nothing had been achieved. The deaths had been in vain; the war has continued to scorch Iran's relationship with her religion. Ayatollah Khomeini claimed the battle with Iraq was for Islam. The soldiers were God's warriors fighting God's war. But if it was God's war, why didn't God win? Why did Saddam Hussein survive? The answer for many is that it was not God's war. It was Ayatollah Khomeini's war. At best he was thought of as having been mistaken or deluded to have sent young men to their deaths to liberate Jerusalem via Baghdad; at worst he was manipulative. Either way, the war proved to most Iranians that Ayatollah Khomeini was not in touch with God, and this again made them feel uneasy about the religion he claimed to be representing.

Social and cultural claustrophobia

In Iran the walled garden is not just a place of beauty, it is a recognized place of privacy. And for over thirty years the Iranian government has climbed over those walls, trying to control what its citizens read and watch and consume, and of course how they worship God. The impact of this has not been as bloody as that of the political authoritarianism, but still this constant threat of interference in their private lives has caused intense irritation. Likewise the strict dress codes and segregation of the sexes in public continues to be frustrating, as seen in regularly updated YouTube clips and along with pictures of the "morality police" harassing sharply dressed women.[49]

The root cause of this cultural authoritarianism is no secret. It is Shia Islam as interpreted by Ayatollah Khomeini. This is well illustrated by a seemingly innocent interview on the national radio broadcast in the early 1980s. A woman was asked who her female role model was. She replied it was a Japanese soap opera star. Ayatollah Khomeini was either listening (he was said to be

49   For example https://www.youtube.com/watch?v=uACNXxkmXok Accessed 5 June 2014.

a devotee to the radio) or someone mentioned this interview to him. He was furious. What the interviewee should have said is that her role model was Fatimeh, the Prophet Mohammad's daughter. In this particular case Ayatollah Khomeini's fury reached over the walls of quite a few people's gardens. The director of the radio station in Tehran was sentenced to five years' imprisonment; three of the staff to four years, and all involved were to get fifty lashes. Later he pardoned them, but Khomeini had made his point for all to understand: there was to be no cultural freedom in his Iran.[50]

As an ever-present irritant administered in the name of religion, this lack of cultural freedom has contributed to the dislocation of the relationship between Iranians and their religion.

Economic storms[51]

As soon as Ayatollah Khomeini's "Government of God" began its rule in 1979, cold winds shook Iran's economy. The once strong Iranian rial began falling against the US dollar as US sanctions arrived and foreign investors, who were unwilling to risk their fortunes with a government that had declared that all business within Iran had to be Islamic, withdrew. Meanwhile, banks and major industries were industrialized in line with Ayatollah Khomeini's antipathy towards imperialism and international capitalism. Soon the government and its friends controlled about 70 per cent of the economy. Competition was unlikely to flourish. The government also gave special treatment to their main political backers at street level, the *bazaaris* (merchants). This again dampened competition. As the champion of the poor, Ayatollah Khomeini also needed to be seen to be providing for the *mostazafin*, the deprived.

50   See Sarvenaz Bahar, *Guardians of Thought: Limits on Freedom of Expression in Iran*, Middle East Watch (now Human Rights Middle East Watch), 1993, p. 66.
51   For a detailed analysis of the economic hardship faced by Iranians from 1979 until the Ahmadinejad presidency, see the author's *Iran and Christianity*, Chapter 6.

Generous subsidies for life's necessities, such as gas, electricity, and petrol, were made. Soon they accounted for 25 per cent of Iran's GDP. The net result of these policies was, unsurprisingly, inflation, which was felt by every Iranian.

Then, in 1980, came the war, turning the cold winds of Ayatollah Khomeini's economy into a freezing blizzard. Oil revenues slumped as Saddam's planes smashed the oil producing areas, and foreign exchange reserves nearly dried up as the bills for providing for the military billowed. To save money the government cut non-essential imports, so by the mid-eighties paper was scarce, and some Iranians were even having to make their own soap. Inflation soared – so much so that many breadwinners now had to take on two jobs just to survive. One salary or pension in the family simply did not put enough food on the table.

While Iranians endured economic pain during Ayatollah Khomeini's rule, the official line from Tehran was that the suffering made sense. The enemies of Iran, determined to overthrow the Islamic Republic, were waging a ruthless war against Iranians. Economic stress was a part of the price; other Iranians were giving their lives. And the author of the revolution, Ayatollah Khomeini, was known to be a man with a spartan lifestyle. As he had famously said, his revolution was not about dealing with the price of watermelons. His agenda was grander.

It is important to note that there is in fact little evidence to suggest that anger about the economy transmuted into anger against Islam in the 1980s; this came later. For now, the seeds were being sown.

In the 1990s the new Supreme Leader, Ayatollah Khamenei, and the then president, Akbar Rafsanjani, set about reviving Iran's war-torn economy by initiating a programme of privatization. They enjoyed some success. During this decade the economy grew at about 8 per cent a year and profits from manufacturing rose by 12 per cent. Living standards slowly began to rise.

The sting in the tail of this programme was that the privatization was generally kept within the ruling elite, so about 80 per cent of the Tehran Stock Market was owned either by the state or by the *bonyads*, the huge Islamic charities that are operated like personal fiefdoms by senior clergy. Insider trading was common, and some families were becoming fabulously wealthy, particularly the architects of the privatization. Ayatollah Khamenei's business empire is estimated to be worth $95 billion; in 2003 Akbar Rafsanjani's family was estimated by Forbes to be worth over $1 billion.[52] And there were about seven other senior clergy whose personal wealth was considered to be more than $200 million.[53]

For Iranians grappling with making ends meet there was always this pointed question in their minds: Why were they less well off than their counterparts in Europe or America when Iran owned nearly 16 per cent and 9 per cent of the world's gas and oil reserves?

A kinder answer assumed economic incompetence. The more cynical one pointed to all the money swimming around their new rulers and assumed corruption.

And that impression inevitably increased the disillusionment some were already feeling about the religion in which their wealthy leaders professed to be experts.

Disenchantment

By the mid-1990s the political violence, the blood of the war, the invasion of people's privacy, and the odour of economic incompetence and corruption meant there was serious disenchantment with Ayatollah Khomeini's "Government of God" and its heirs.

---

52   As mentioned on http://www.pbs.org/wgbh/pages/frontline/
tehranbureau/2010/04/the-middle-road-of-hashemi-rafsanjani.html Accessed 10 July 2014.
53   For more detail on the wealth of Iran's clergy see, "Millionaire Mullahs" by Paul Klebnikov, http://www.forbes.com/forbes/2003/0721/056.html

This was proven in 1997 when Mohammad Khatami ran as a presidential candidate for the Reformists, an influential group of politicians and intellectuals who believed that the main actors within the political establishment had to become more accountable to the rule of law in order for the Islamic Republic to succeed. As recognized by his opponents, this was a tacit admission that leaving ultimate political authority with an Islamic expert had failed.

The electorate agreed with this assessment: Mohammad Khatami won over 70 per cent of the popular vote. The disenchantment was official.

The failure of Mohammad Khatami's presidency

Mohammad Khatami's government and a new Reformist press, which sprang to life as newspaper rules were eased, challenged the entrenched powers of the revolutionary elite, especially in the judiciary, who had got used to acting with impunity. There was talk of a "Tehran Spring", a new chapter in the revolution's history when the country's institutions would become more accountable to both the electorate and the rule of law.

For a few months the Conservatives lost ground to the Reformists. There was hope that the Islamic Republic was going to sail on calmer seas. And one result of this would have been a dampening of the anger and disillusionment that had been building up against Iran's religion in whose name people had endured so much suffering.

However when the Supreme Leader, Ali Khamanei, acting as head of the army and the Revolutionary Guards, called on "officials" to silence the "pen-holders" who were "writing against Islam", the Conservatives soon found the confidence to fight back. Reformist newspapers were closed down, editors imprisoned, and when in 1999 students across the country staged large demonstrations in protest at the newspaper closures, they were silenced by violence.[54]

President Khatami did not support the students. In fact the Reformist leader, who had previously brought in press freedom, now denounced the students who were protesting for that very press freedom. The reason is simple. When thousands of students were still protesting in the streets in the summer of 1999, twenty-four Revolutionary Guards sent President Khatami an open letter published in the government's newspaper *Keyhan*. They warned him that their "patience was exhausted". In other words, the political war between the Conservatives and Reformists would turn violent, and the Conservatives had all the fire power.

So on 16 July the President publicly criticized the students, and, the following day, over 1,000 were arrested. Everyone now knew that the Reformists could not stand up to the hardliners. They were men with ideas that had wide support across the country. But they were not willing to see rivers of blood and answer violence with violence. For Iran's relationship with her national religion, the defeat of the Reformists meant the bruising of the relationship was not just going to worsen – it would become infected. This happened in its fullness under the Presidency of Mahmoud Ahmadinejad, to whom we now turn.

54   www.hrw.org/reports/1999/iran/Iran99o-02.htm

CHAPTER 3

MAHMOUD AHMADINEJAD: THE WOUND WIDENS

Iran's new Christians tend to be young. Many are under thirty, born after the Islamic Revolution. They were only babies or young children when Ayatollah Khomeini's wars saturated the battlefields in Iraq and the prisons in Iran with Iranian blood. They grew up with only second-hand reports of what the Islamic Republic had meant in practice in its first decade or so. This alone meant that some were already starting to question Iran's religion.

And then in 2005 Mahmoud Ahmadinejad stepped onto Iran's political stage. He was a "Principalist", the man determined to take Iran back to the true teachings of Ayatollah Khomeini. All of Iran's new Christians have a direct experience of Mahmoud Ahmadinejad. Second only to Ayatollah Khomeini, he has done more than any other Iranian leader to strain Iran's relationship with its national religion and thus has made it easier for Iran's new Christians to renounce Islam.

Over 17 million Iranians (61 per cent of the 42 million eligible to vote), including some Christians, voted for Ahmadinejad to become president of Iran in the 2005 elections.[55]

His victory was a direct result of the Reformists' failure to stand up to the bullying of the hardliners. Why vote for the Reformist candidates, Mehdi Karroubi and Mostafa Moeen when the Reformists had failed so dramatically to curb the excesses of the police and judiciary? And why vote for the

---

55   Kasra Naji, *Ahmadinejad: The Secret History of Iran's Radical Leader*, p. 86.

former president Hashemi Rafsanjani, an architect of the Islamic Republic, worth over a billion dollars, whose name was synonymous with corruption, when you can vote for a man with no establishment baggage, such as Mahmoud Ahmadinejad.

Ahmadinejad was an outsider and a Mr Everyman. His looks, speech, and style complete with occasional cheeky cockiness told the working-class Iranians that he was one of them. For middle-class voters deeply disillusioned by the failure of the Reformers, Ahmadinejad's story was also attractive. The son of a village blacksmith who had studied hard, got into university, and made a success of his life, he was the example all middle-class parents wanted their children to follow. Neither had political power gone into Ahmadinejad's pockets. During the election campaign Ahmadinejad, then the mayor of Tehran, invited TV cameras into his house. They filmed a sparse living room with some cushions and a cheap carpet. There was no furniture. Like millions of other Iranians the Ahmadinejads sat on the floor in his home.[56]

His election campaign was also appealing. Ahmadinejad promised to beat down inflation, root out corruption, cut out all luxury from government and put Iran's oil money on people's supper plates. Ahmadinejad then massively strengthened his role as the ordinary man's hero by spending much of the election campaign in the provinces, pressing the flesh of the rural poor. In contrast the likes of Rafsanjani hardly bothered to leave Tehran. The hostility to the West and to secularism was very hard line, but it was normal rhetoric. It did not lose Ahmadinejad votes. The economy and corruption were the electorate's main concern, not ideology.[57]

By 2013 those 17 million voters were deeply disappointed. Over eight years, Ahmadinejad had aggressively demanded all

56   Ibid. p. 70.
57   "The defeat of Rafsanjani and the reformists also showed that political and social freedoms were not high on the minds of the masses. Battling poverty and unemployment clearly was." Ibid. p. 90.

Iranians to be 1979 Islamic revolutionaries once again; there were severe embarrassments on the international stage as well as the frightening prospect of a military attack. And the economy deteriorated very severely. All this disappointment was in the name of Islam. The wound between the Iranian people and her religion was becoming an open sore.

"We must all be revolutionary, again"

Ahmadinejad's script was simple. The Iranian Revolution was pure, radical, and full of goodness. However, its goodness had first been diluted by corrupt pragmatists (Rafsanjani), and then nearly destroyed by the silky sophisticated Reformists (Khatami) who were out to betray Islamic Iran to the democratic values of the West. In response, ordinary Iranians had risen up in their millions and swept aside Pragmatists and Reformists and elected one of their own, a "Principalist", who unashamedly stood by the values of the 1979 revolution. In this script one of Ahmadinejad's duties was clear: by all means possible he had to re-assert revolutionary values.

Ahmadinejad had already started doing this as the mayor of Tehran (2003–2005). He had imposed gender segregation in local government offices (one elevator for men, another for women); had closed down American-like fast food outlets where young couples dated; and most controversially of all, when the deserts of Iraq gave up the corpses of the dead, Ahmadinejad ordered these martyrs be buried, not in Tehran's vast main cemetery, but in public spaces, especially the leafy parks in the wealthier suburbs in the north of the city. The rich who pined for the West needed to be reminded of the great sacrifices made for the independence of Iran. But the young also needed reminding, so some corpses were earmarked for burial within the grounds of the University of Tehran.[58]

58   Michael Axworthy, *Revolutionary Iran*, p. 374. The reaction of the students was not positive – they rioted.

As president, Ahmadinejad now waged this cultural war across the whole of the country. Its extent was thorough, the impact bruising. As a revolutionary student leader in April 1980 Ahmadinejad had eagerly responded to Ayatollah Khomeini's call to root out liberal influence from Iran's universities. At that time he actively got involved in closing down the Iran University of Science and Technology where he had been an undergraduate.[59] According to his simple script, under the treacherous Reformists enemies of Islam had no doubt infiltrated the universities again. Now another purge was needed. Ahmadinejad started with the country's most prestigious institute of higher learning, the University of Tehran. In November 2005, amidst much protest, a hard-line cleric with no secular academic qualifications was installed as chancellor. Ayatollah Zanjani got to work quickly and in the next year he had forced forty lecturers into retirement. In the same spirit many other university lecturers across the country lost their jobs. The estimates of total job losses range from 200 to 1,000.[60]

Art was treated with the same suspicion. Writers, musicians, and film-makers all felt a cold wind blowing from the president's office. As usual new books had to be passed by the censors of the Ministry of Culture and Islamic Guidance. For some genres this had become a formality, but now nearly all titles were examined and changes made. According to the Ahmadinejad script it was obvious that under Khatami corrupt texts would have been approved, so now the censors were asked to review titles that had already been published. Many were removed, including Tolstoy's *Anna Karenina* "which normalised relationships between unmarried couples..."[61]

---

59   Naji, p. 239. While Ahmadinejad was a very active student leader for the revolution there is no evidence that he took any part in the attack on the US Embassy (4 November 1979 – 20 January 1981). See Axworthy, p. 371 for a discussion on this.

60   Naji, p. 238 has 200. Amir Taheri, in *The Persian Night: Iran Under The Khomeinist Revolution* (Tradeselect, 2009) estimates over 1,000 lost their jobs between 2006 and 2008.

61   Naji, p. 245.

On 19 December 2005 President Ahmadinejad banned all "Western and vulgar" music from state TV. This was completely in line with the script. Ayatollah Khomeini had declared that music "dulls the mind because it involves pleasure and ecstasy... it destroys our youth who become poisoned by it."[62] However under the Pragmatists and Reformers standards had slipped and Iranians could hear musicians like The Eagles or Eric Clapton on state TV.[63] Under Ahmadinejad they were to be silenced. Classical music also suffered as the government rarely gave out licences for public concerts. And cinema, Iran's most revered art form after poetry, also suffered. Films, even by such geniuses as Dariush Mehrjui, director of *The Cow* and *Leila*, ran into problems;[64] two of Iran's most famous directors, Mohsen Makhmalbaf and Abbas Kiarostami continued their careers in exile so they could make the sort of films they wanted. Their friend, Jafar Panahi, however, did not leave. For the alleged crime of creating propaganda against the state he has been banned from making films for twenty years and is currently under house arrest.

All of this segregation, censorship, and banning was happening – again – in the name of Iran's religion, with an Ahmadinejad twist. With the battle dead arriving in Tehran's leafy parks for burial, so his religion proclaimed: Pleasure is forbidden, life must not be enjoyed. Iranians must welcome war and death.

The impact of this cultural authoritarianism was to further widen the wound between Iran and its national religion. Later it would be infected with the poison of political authoritarianism, which was brutally poured into the wound in the aftermath of the 2009 presidential elections.

---

62   http://www.history.com/this-day-in-history/ahmadinejad-bans-all-western-music-in-iranian-state-television-and-radio-broadcasts Accessed 18 July 2013.
63   See http://news.bbc.co.uk/1/hi/world/middle_east/4543720.stm Accessed 18 July 2013.
64   Naji, p. 246.

We will look at that in the next chapter, but first it is important to see how the wound got much worse – first because of Ahmadinejad's antagonistic style of diplomacy, and then because of his dismal record on the economy.

Ahmadinejad on the international stage

Crucial to Ahmadinejad's narrative was an Iran threatened by hostile powers. And in this script only Ahmadinejad could save the nation from the aggressive plots being hatched in London and Washington. The "Pragmatists" and certainly the Reformists could not be trusted. They were ready to talk to the West. Worse, the Reformist leader Mohammad Khatami as president from 1997 to 2005 had campaigned successfully on the international stage for "a dialogue of civilizations".[65]

This was anathema to hardliners. For Ahmadinejad Islam was God's final revelation and so Islamic civilization was the best. There is nothing to "dialogue" about. More pertinently Khatami's stance was treacherous naivety. With the West (the UK and the US) there is no dialogue. These "arrogant powers" only lecture the weak[66] and threaten countries that do not kowtow to their will. So while Khatami smiled for dialogue, disgracefully saying Iran would give up its right to nuclear technology, in 2002 President Bush accused Iran of being a part of an "axis of evil" (along with Iraq and North Korea), and his officials waged proxy, cyber, and economic wars against Iran. For Ahmadinejad and his allies, nearly all veterans of the first

65   Mohammad Khatami chose this title to counter the very influential book by the late Samuel Huntington entitled *The Clash Of Civilizations*. The Harvard professor argued that future conflicts would be based on cultural and religious identities, not ideologies.

66   Ahmadinejad was dismissive of talking to the West because they would not negotiate in good faith: "If this issue is resolved they will bring up human rights; if human rights is resolved, they will bring up animal rights." Quoted in Ray Takeyh, *Guardians of the Revolution*, Chapter 11, p. 248.

Gulf War,[67] Khatami's naivety was a sickening betrayal of Iran's revolution that had shaken off the country's imperial masters.

It is no surprise that once in power Ahmadinejad was determined to bury dialogue. His mission was to reassert Iran as the defiant regional power in the Islamic Middle East, ready to take on any "imperialist" power. The whole point of his foreign policy was confrontation with the West.

If they didn't know already, Khatami's appointees in the Foreign Office soon knew Ahmadinejad was in charge: just two months after taking office in August 2005, he sacked more than forty ambassadors and senior diplomats.[68] A Khatami appointee could not be trusted to speak for Iran in foreign parts; it was loyal hardliners who were needed.

The rest of the world soon realized a cold wind was blowing in from Tehran. Apart from a few countries like Venezuela, Bolivia, and Syria, the response to Ahmadinejad's foreign policy from the world community was usually intense anger. At other times, his foreign policy was greeted with bemusement. After his first speech to the UN General Assembly in September 2005, President Ahmadinejad told reporters there had been a halo of light around his head when he spoke and that no delegate had blinked throughout the 28-minute speech. The president's conclusion? Mahdi, the hidden Imam, was with him.[69]

67   The majority view among these veterans regarding the Iran–Iraq war is that Saddam Hussein's invasion had the approval of the West hoping to crush the new regime in Tehran. Throughout the war the US supported Iraq with supplies and satellite information and finally in 1988 the US cruiser USS Vincennes shot down an Iran Air civilian flight. These veterans therefore felt they had no reason to trust the US.
68   See http://www.theguardian.com/world/2005/nov/03/iran.brianwhitaker Accessed 10 September 2013.
69   Ahmadinejad let everyone know he was fervent believer in the imminent return of Mahdi, the Twelfth Imam who went into hiding in the ninth century, and according to Shia theology is due to return with Jesus Christ at the end of the world. Ahmadinejad told the Supreme Leader at his inauguration that he expected his presidency to be temporary as he would be handing over to Mahdi; he claimed Mahdi helped him with decisions and there were reports that the return of Mahdi was once on the cabinet's agenda which brought the urgent suggestion that many new hotels needed to be built to deal with the flood of pilgrims the return would cause. And, in a speech in the south-eastern province of Kerman, the president told his audience that

There was also largely bemusement, though the content bordered on the offensive, when later the president sent long rambling letters to Chancellor Merkel, suggesting Aryan Germany and Iran form an alliance against the victors of World War II who were oppressing other states; and another letter to President Bush, inviting him to become a Muslim to deal with all the contradictions and evil in the world. There was a lot of laughter too when President Ahmadinejad addressed students at Columbia University in 2007 and said there were no homosexuals in Iran.[70]

However, on the international stage the usual response to Ahmadinejad was intense anger – especially when he spoke on the topic of Israel.[71] In October 2005, just months after becoming president, Ahmadinejad spoke at a conference entitled "World Without Zionism". There was nothing original in his speech for Iranians, but the tone was harsh, the stance hardline. Israel was a Western bridgehead for the invasion of the Muslim world and thus was the front line between Islam and the world. There could be no compromise. If any Muslim nation recognized Israel it would be in effect signing "the document of capitulation" for the entire Islamic world. The president was confident the "shameful blot" of Israel would soon be removed from the Middle East.[72] The only options Ahmadinejad was putting on the table were the elimination of Israel as a state – or war. For most diplomats grappling with the Palestine–Israel conflict the speech created a diplomatic nightmare.

It was to get worse. Shortly after this speech Ahmadinejad told Muslim leaders in Saudi Arabia that the Jewish homeland

the US was employing special teams to try and hunt down Mahdi to stop him setting up a government. Ahmadinejad also did much to improve the site of the Jamkaran Mosque on the outskirts of Qom where Mahdi was once seen. See Naji, Chapter 3.

70   See http://edition.cnn.com/2007/US/09/24/us.iran Accessed 12 September 2013.

71   This section dealing with Ahmadinejad and Israel is based on Naji's excellent chapter "Ahmadinejad vs the World".

72   Naji, p. 146.

should move to Europe. As Europe had oppressed the Jews, why should the Palestinians pay the price? This idea on the streets of the Middle East was old, but for a president to suggest the relocation of Israel become official policy for Muslim nations was new – and of course absurd. The Saudis, allies of the USA, were embarrassed – and very angry.

Enjoying his role as radical maverick and baiter of the West, Ahmadinejad had even more to say at this particular conference. It was deeply offensive. Regarding the six million Jews murdered by the Nazis, he said, "We do not believe this claim". In a speech a few weeks later in Zahedan, Iran, Ahmadinejad went even further: "They [the Europeans] have created a myth in the name of Holocaust", and a transcript of his words give the reason for the myth: "the Zionists are being supported because of this [the Holocaust's] excuse."[73]

The Iranian president had crossed a line. In the uproar of protest from the rest of the world a few voices could be heard supporting the Iranian president. These were the Holocaust deniers, aligned to neo-Nazism and other rabidly anti-Semitic groups. They were treated as criminals in some countries and as oddballs to be ignored in most.

One of them, Michael Hoffman, an American white supremacist and anti-Semite, praised Ahmadinejad for "giving us all an opportunity to smile at the expense of the mandarins of Judeomania". And he had a suggestion for the Iranian president: "Open your nation to the revisionists, bring us to your nation… to conduct teach-ins, seminars, symposia…"[74]

Woefully unaware of how repugnant Holocaust denial was for most, this is exactly what President Ahmadinejad did. His government organized a two-day "International Conference to Review the Global Vision of the Holocaust" in Tehran in December 2006. During the opening speech Iran's

73   See http://www.adl.org/israel-international/iran/c/ihow/iranian-president-2005. html#.U85TV47VwRk Accessed 12 September 2013.
74   Naji, pp. 163–64.

Foreign Minister Dr Manouchehr Mottaki declared that if the Holocaust were thrown into doubt, then the nature and identity of Israel would be thrown into doubt, tying the whole event to Ahmadinejad's confrontational approach. Since most of the guests were fanatical right-wing extremists, such as David Duke, a former leader of the Ku Klux Klan, or George Thiel, an apologist for Hitler, it was a foregone conclusion that the Holocaust would be "thrown into doubt" – inside the conference hall.[75]

Outside of this conference, the rest of the world noted that Iran under Ahmadinejad had sunk to a new low. There was intense anger, which was displayed whenever Ahmadinejad went to New York to address the UN General Assembly. Many delegates (mainly from the USA and Europe) refused to listen to him, walking out in 2007 when Ahmadinejad attacked America's "War on Terror"; in 2008 when he talked about "Zionist murderers"; in 2009 when he attacked America's role in Afghanistan and Iraq and its "murderous" Israeli regime; in 2010 when, perhaps most shockingly, he accused the US government of engineering the 9/11 attacks to justify the "War on Terror"; and in 2011 when he again referred to the "mystery" of the 9/11 attacks and questioned the Holocaust.

President Ahmadinejad had succeeded in letting the world know Iran was ready to defy the Western way of seeing things – but it was an empty success. It seems that nobody in Ahmadinejad's team had thought through what would actually happen in the real world as a result of siding with neo-Nazis and treating the baseless conspiracy theories of the Middle East as facts. The results were, not surprisingly, very dangerous for Iran.

When President Ahmadinejad began his presidency in 2005 there was already intense concern in Israel and the West about Iran's nuclear programme. Hawks in Tel Aviv and

75   For a vivid description of the conference and detailed background on the participants see Naji, pp. 164–74.

Washington were threatening a military response; diplomats were urging caution. Now onto the stage walks Ahmadinejad, a friend of neo-Nazis, talking about wiping Israel off the map and insisting Iran has a right to nuclear technology.

All this sealed the case in favour of the hawks. So from 2006 until 2009, when Barack Obama became the US president, a military attack on Iran became a dangerous possibility. It was constantly talked about in the media, with Tel Aviv and Washington always insisting a military response was an option. Indeed, as early as December 2006 many in the USA assumed an attack on Iran was President Bush's official policy, so much so that Democrats petitioned President Bush with the words, "We oppose your proposal to attack Iran."[76]

The threat of military action was more than verbal. In 2007 Israel bombed Iran's ally Syria, destroying an unfinished nuclear reactor, and in June 2008 Israel carried out a training exercise named "Glorious Spartan 08" in preparation for an attack on Iran. This was followed in July by 15,000 military personnel from the USA and its allies participating in the exercise "Operation Brimstone", which was also seen as a warning to Iran.

With the arrival of Barack Obama in the White House the tone toward America's enemies was softer. The famous "We will extend a hand if you are willing to unclench your fist" in his inauguration speech was widely interpreted as an olive branch to Tehran. However the new administration still refused to rule out military action against Iran and contingency planning continued.

Israel, under Benjamin Netanyahu, was absolutely determined to thwart Iran's nuclear programme. So the threat of an all-out military attack remained – and covert attacks did happen. In 2010 the Stuxnet computer virus struck Iran's nuclear facilities, and between 2010 and 2012 four Iranian scientists linked to the nuclear programme were murdered.

76   See http://www.democrats.com/node/21955 Accessed 17 September 2013.

Most commentators assumed these attacks were launched by Israel, or by the USA and Israel.

Inside Iran the conservative faithful (perhaps 15–20 per cent of Iran's population) generally warmed to Ahmadinejad thumbing his nose at Israel and the West. However, the majority of Iranians felt deeply embarrassed – especially over the Holocaust denial – and fearful about the prospect of another war.

All Iranians pride themselves on their history of tolerance, a pride clearly seen in 2010 when nearly 500,000 people[77] visited an exhibition of the "Cyrus Cylinder" on which Cyrus the Great, who ruled Iran from 559 to 530 BC, had authored the world's first declaration of human rights. This tradition of tolerance has especially had an impact on Jews, for it was this same Cyrus who had supported the Jews in their desire to return to their land, and brought their Babylonian captivity to an end. Many did not return. They stayed in Iran where they were treated with respect and became one of the largest diasporas in the Middle East.[78] By playing the cheap anti-Semitic card saying that cunning Jews had invented the "myth" of the Holocaust to bolster support for their claim to Palestine, President Ahmadinejad betrayed this tradition of tolerance. To then host neo-Nazis and white supremacists as Iran's guests was to poison the betrayal even more. The stance was possibly revolutionary; it was not Iranian.

Iranians are also extremely proud of their education. School is compulsory; more than 3 million go on to study at over 100 universities and these graduates often make their mark on the world stage. Iran's scientific community is placed fifteenth by the Scopus ranking agency and the output of Iranian scientists is more than those from some European countries.[79] Being

77   See http://www.economist.com/news/books-and-arts/21573955-show-tests-limits-cultural-politics-diplomatic-whirl Accessed 18 September 2013.

78   Under the last Shah there were 85,000 Jews in Iran.

79   http://www.iranreview.org/content/Documents/Scientific-Technological-Achievements-of-Iranians-3.htm Accessed 18 September 2013.

seen as educated is important for Iranians and to label someone *bisavad* (without education) is very insulting. So for the official spokesman of the nation to call the Holocaust a myth was deeply shameful because even the casual researcher on the Google search engine can see there is evidence to prove Jews were murdered on an industrial scale in Nazi-occupied Europe. Ahmadinejad was declaring to the whole world that he – and so by definition all his supporters – were *bisavad*: uneducated. This caused deep resentment.

President Ahmadinejad's Holocaust denial also caused a hostile reaction among Iran's politicians. The MP for Iran's Jews, Morris Motamed, was of course furious. The conference, he said, "hurts all Jews… who are very sensitive about this red line in their history, the biggest catastrophe ever".[80] Reformists were outraged. Former president Mohammad Khatami called the Holocaust "a historical reality" adding that "We should speak out if even a single Jew is killed."[81] Respected academic and journalist Ahmad Zeidabadi said that, "His [Ahmadinejad's] comments have seriously tarnished the image of a great nation in the world."[82] Another journalist, Davoud Bavand wrote, "His words don't fit with those of a responsible president."[83]

Even fellow hard-line conservatives were critical. University professor Mahmoud Kashani chided Ahmadinejad for "creating tension in foreign relations"; Hamid Reza Taraqi, leader of the Islamic Coalition Society, said, "The president has to choose his words carefully"; and the Baztab website, linked to the Revolutionary Guards, called Ahmadinejad's foray into Holocaust denial as "adventurism at the cost of national interests". The website also reminded readers that Ayatollah

80   http://www.ft.com/cms/s/680910ec-8985-11db-a876-0000779e2340 Accessed 18 September 2013.
81   http://news.bbc.co.uk/1/hi/world/middle_east/4763494.stm Accessed 18 September 2013.
82   Naji, p. 161.
83   Naji, p. 156.

Khomeini had never doubted the reality of the Holocaust.[84]

The hostility was not limited to comments from prominent individuals. Parliament was enraged by the Holocaust denial conference and two weeks after the event insisted on holding a closed-door session with Foreign Minister Mottaki. He met with a barrage of criticism and the meeting ended with a unanimous verdict: the conference had undermined Iran's standing at a critical time.

Meanwhile Iran's government's response to the military threats emanating from Tel Aviv and Washington as a result of Ahmadinejad's style of diplomacy was belligerent. The tone is typified in a speech to the armed forces by the Supreme Leader in November 2011. Ayatollah Khamenei said:

> We will answer threats with threats… Anybody who thinks of attacking the Islamic Republic of Iran should be ready to receive hard slaps and an iron fists from our armed forces… And America, its allies, and its guard dog… the Zionist regime should know that the response of any aggression, attacks or even threats against the Iranian nation will be a response that will make them collapse from within.[85]

The government was bullish, but anecdotal evidence shows there was no enthusiasm for a war; indeed there was fear. Pundits were talking about a conflict being inevitable; there were stories of people stocking up with food; some were even planning an escape route.[86] There was not just fear of an attack, but also fear about how a war would increase internal oppression. In December 2011 a labour union sent a letter to Amnesty International warning against a war. The letter

84   Naji, pp. 160–62; 175.

85   http://www.shiatv.net/view_video.php?viewkey=0e91d8b47c6f97db21f7 Accessed 18 September 2013.

86   http://www.washingtonpost.com/world/middle_east/leaders-are-defiant-but-many-iranians-fear-war/2011/12/08/gIQAHVdMrO_story.html Accessed 18 September 2013.

bluntly stated, "There would be no room for campaigning for human rights when cities are bombed and civilians slaughtered."[87]

In the run-up to the 2013 presidential elections solid evidence emerged that the prospect of war was deeply unpopular among Iranians. During televised debates between the contenders every candidate agreed that the incoming government must defuse the tension with the West. War was to be avoided at all costs. These contenders knew what their electors wanted. The proof of this was when they gave most of their votes to the man with the best credentials for dealing with the crisis with the West: the seasoned diplomat Hassan Rouhani.

The nightmare of Ahmadinejad's economic record

It was not just the crisis in foreign affairs that encouraged the electorate to vote for Rouhani. Closely related to problems on the international stage was another trauma much nearer to home: the crisis in the economy.

For most Iranians Ahmadinejad's record on the economy was a nightmare. During his presidency inflation had soared. When Ahmadinejad took office in 2005 inflation was 12 per cent – lower than the Islamic Republic's 17 per cent average since 1979. With the exception of 2009 and 2010, inflation continued to rise steadily from 18 per cent in 2007 up to 45 per cent in 2013.[88] Some families were struggling to put food on the table;[89] everyone was talking about the nightmare of shopping –

87   http://www.niacinsight.com/2011/12/15/iranian-labor-movement-makes-international-appeal-against-war/ Accessed 19 September 2013.
88   http://www.tradingeconomics.com/iran/inflation-cpi Accessed 19 September 2013. Other sources put the unofficial rate of inflation as being even higher. The anomaly in 2009 and 2010 has been attributed to a worldwide fall in food prices:
89   http://www.bbc.co.uk/news/world-middle-east-16813248 Accessed 20th September 2013.

so much so that in 2012 Iran's chief of police urged broadcasters to refrain from showing pictures of people eating chickens as –"Certain people witnessing this class gap between the rich and the poor might grab a knife and think they will get their share from the wealthy."[90]

This was the sombre summing up of the German international broadcaster Deutsche Welle (DW) about the impact of Ahmadinejad's economy for Iranians published in May 2013:

> **Unemployment, poverty, and inflation have fundamentally changed the lives of many Iranians in the past few years. The country is struggling with a drastic inflation rate, and is hurtling ever deeper into crisis. Prices for basic foods and consumer goods are rising almost every day.**[91]

As well as inflation there was the collapse of Iran's currency. When Ahmadinejad took office in 2005 the Iranian rial was trading at around 10,000 to 1 US dollar. The currency then slowly began to sink and by the autumn of 2011 a US dollar cost over 12,000 rials. In January 2012 there was a further drop with the dollar trading at 18,000 rials. And then in October things went into free fall. In a matter of hours 18 per cent was wiped off the value of the currency, and, as if in a bad dream, Iranians saw that one US dollar cost 35,000 rials.[92] Their currency had lost 80 per cent of its value since the start of 2011.[93] This was a personal catastrophe for many. As traders, savers, and travellers took in the extent of the collapse, so there were angry demonstrations

90   http://articles.chicagotribune.com/2012-07-22/news/sns-rt-us-iran-economy-chickenbre86l08e-20120722_1_chicken-crisis-ahmadi-moghaddam-iranian-women Accessed 19 September 2013. Iranian cartoonists and comedians had a lot of fun with this intervention.

91   http://www.dw.de/the-stranglehold-on-irans-economy/a-16838270

92   A popular joke at this time was: "How many rials are in a dollar? Now, or… now?"

93   http://www.bbc.co.uk/news/business-19786662 Accessed 20 September 2013.

in Iran's bazaars.[94]

Most Iranians blamed the president for their financial hardship for at least four reasons. First, there was the spontaneous spending and interference that wasn't thought through. Whenever the president went on a tour of the provinces – on average, one visit every twenty-three days[95] – he showered largesse on the crowds.[96] In his first year alone he made at least thirteen trips to rural areas where expenditure shot up by 180 per cent.[97] It was the same in his second year. During a visit to South Khorasan, province irrigation projects, petrochemical factories, and improvements on shanty towns all received government cash.[98] Naturally the rural areas liked their new president. Economists back in Tehran were not keen on these spending sprees, written seemingly on the back of a cigarette packet.

Nor were they keen on the president's penchant for announcing policy without consulting senior economists, such as when he ordered banks to drop their interest rates, or raised the minimum wage by 60 per cent.[99] The Management and Planning Organization of Iran (MPO) and senior figures in the establishment, concerned about balancing the books, were vocal critics. They warned that all the cash handouts to these rural projects and the lowering of interest rates would increase liquidity. They were right: it went up by 40 per cent in a year.[100] They warned this would fuel inflation. As we saw above, they

94   http://www.csmonitor.com/World/Middle-East/2012/1004/Iran-s-currency-Why-did-the-rial-tumble-so-precipitously-video Accessed 20 September 2013. This web page has an amateur video showing the demonstration.
95   http://www.brandeis.edu/crown/publications/meb/MEB74.pdf. See p. 2.
96   For a detailed description of one of Ahmadinejad's speeches in the provinces see Naji, pp. 215–19.
97   http://iranian.com/Javedanfar/2006/June/Ahmadinejad/index.html Accessed 20 September 2013.
98   http://www.csmonitor.com/2007/1207/p01s07-wome.html Accessed 20 September 2013.
99   Scott Peterson, *Let the Swords Encircle Me*, p. 317.
100   Ibid.

were right. President Ahmadinejad ignored their advice and dissolved the MPO in 2006.[101] As for raising the minimum wage, this meant that "hundreds of thousands of Iranians were forced out of work by employers who could no longer afford them".[102]

Then there were the cash handouts to ease the pain of cutting the state subsidies on basic items. Since 1980 the Islamic Republic has subsidized petroleum products, some medicines, essential foodstuffs, and utilities (water, gas). By the 1990s economists and senior politicians realized the cost of the subsidies (between $70 and $100 billion per annum[103]) was unsustainable.

Initially President Ahmadinejad was reluctant to cut them, but having to use vulnerable government funds to import petrol (due to a lack of modern refineries), which was then given to the public at ten cents a litre, focused his thinking.[104] So did the estimated cost of $30 billion in energy wasted each year due to its cheap price.[105] In 2008 the president drew up plans to cut the subsidies and these won the general approval of the International Monetary Fund.[106] The implementation of the subsidy cuts in early 2011 went smoothly – there were no disturbances – and there were reports that previously subsidized items were being used more carefully.

The problem came from the cash handouts the government gave to ease the pain of cutting the subsidies. About 70 million

101   The MPO was re-launched by President Rouhani in September 2013. See http://www.al-monitor.com/pulse/originals/2013/08/iran-planning-agency-revived-rouhani.html Accessed 20 September 2013.
102   *Let the Swords Encircle Me*, p. 317.
103   http://iranprimer.usip.org/resource/subsidies-conundrum Accessed 20 September 2013.
104   "Tough economic realities apparently changed his mind" – see http://iranprimer.usip.org/resource/subsidies-conundrum Accessed 20 September 2013.
105   http://www.nytimes.com/2011/01/17/world/middleeast/17iran.html?pagewanted=all&_r=0 Accessed 20 September 2013.
106   http://www.imf.org/external/pubs/ft/wp/2011/wp11167.pdf Accessed 20 September 2013. This report is generally positive about Ahmadinejad's policy.

Iranians became eligible for a payment of $40 a month[107] at a cost to the government of an estimated $59 billion. This was an expensive sweetener, so much so that the fiscal burden to the government actually increased.[108] Worse, this injection of cash into the economy, along with the general rise in prices across the economy due to subsidies ending, were two more factors that fuelled inflation to soar to over 30 per cent (some say it was much higher) thus wiping out any benefit of the handout. After less than a month in power President Ahmadinejad's successor decided to end the handouts. In the public mind they – and the inflation they partially caused – belonged firmly to the Ahmadinejad era.

Another issue that will stay in the public mind is that of corruption. For it was on the watch of President Ahmadinejad – the anti-corruption candidate – that Iran's worst banking scandal in history erupted. In September 2011 the story broke that an unknown businessman, Mahafarid Amir Khosravi, had obtained seven fraudulent letters of credit worth $2.8 billion from the Saderat, Saman, Sepah, and even Melli Bank, Iran's oldest and most respected financial institution. The money was poured into Mr Khosravi's business, Arya Investment Development Company. It has not come back.[109]

The scam severely damaged President Ahmadinejad. Day after day Iranians were reading about massive corruption and there in the background was President Ahmadinejad and his friends with their hands on most of the levers of patronage and influence. Accusations were inevitable. With the Holocaust and 9/11 President Ahmadinejad had made Americans and Jews suffer by treating the dark whispers of conspiracy theorists as facts; now he was declared corrupt and guilty by the same logic of conspiracy he had used on others.

107   http://www.ft.com/cms/s/0/9313c7c4-70e8-11e0-962a-00144feabdc0.
html#axzz2fQIpeS4E Accessed 20 September 2013
108   http://www.brandeis.edu/crown/publications/meb/MEB74.pdf Accessed 20
September 2013, see p. 4.
109   Mr Khosravi was executed in May 2014 for his involvement.

The conspiracy case seemed convincing. How could his aides not have known about such a massive scam? When President Ahmadinejad came to power he had "replaced the top management of the banks",[110] which meant that the national banks that made the loans were managed by men he had appointed. And those loans were checked by the Money and Credit Council, a government agency of Ahmadinejad appointees. For the conspiracy theorist it was obvious: at least Ahmadinejad's aides must have known what was going on.

But then the spotlight began to fall on Ahmadinejad himself, the man elected as the enemy of corruption. Accusations began to appear that the president's chief of staff and closest ally, Esfandier Rahim Mashaei, had filled the Money and Credit Council with his own men.[111] That explained the lax regulation. Then there was a leaked letter proving that Mashaei had signed for a company to buy up a state business without first going through all the normal procedures.[112] This took things very close to Ahmadinejad, for he had pushed through policies to sell off government enterprises to the "workers", and to make this easier he had forced the banks to offer loans to favoured groups with lower interest rates. At his populist rallies these policies sounded good: Ahmadinejad, the workers' Robin Hood, was going to grab the wealth of the corrupt insiders who had prospered under his predecessors, Rafsanjani and Khatami, and pass the treasure onto the pious poor. Now the banking scandal was painting another picture: Ahmadinejad – or at least his aides – was presiding over a system that gave stolen money to his friends so they could buy state-owned businesses at knock-down prices.

Many people, not just in the streets, but also in the corridors

110   Naji, p. 231.
111   http://www.pbs.org/wgbh/pages/frontline/tehranbureau/2011/10/in-a-nutshell-irans-massive-banking-scandal.html Accessed 23 September 2013.
112   http://www.theguardian.com/world/2011/sep/15/iran-president-mahmoud-ahmadinejad-scam Accessed 23 September 2013.

of power, believed the conspiracy theory and Ahmadinejad's team got caught up in the intense backlash caused by the scam. Of the thirty-nine people arrested over the fraud, analysts said many were linked to "appointees of Mr Ahmadinejad's administration".[113]

A lot of MPs in parliament were convinced the administration was guilty. In November 2011 there was a motion to impeach Ahmadinejad's Economic Minister, Shamseddin Hosseini. He survived, but the vote showed how bruised Ahmadinejad was: 141 voted against the impeachment, but with 93 in support and 10 abstentions.[114]

But it got worse. There was a petition demanding that President Ahmadinejad himself appear before them to explain his record on the economy. This of course would include the banking scandal. Humiliatingly for Ahmadinejad this was the first time a serving Iranian president had been forced to appear before the country's law-makers. While it was never proven that Ahmadinejad had had any involvement in the banking scandal, the association with corruption still created a negative impression.

Inflation, collapse of the rial, corruption – these are the words cemented in the public mind when it comes to thinking about President Ahmadinejad and the economy.

And there is one more – sanctions. The Islamic Republic is no stranger to sanctions, especially from the US. In response to the American hostage crisis of November 1979 the US froze Iranians' assets, and banned some imports from Iran. Then there were no sanctions until the mid-1990s when President Clinton, concerned about reports of a nuclear programme and Iran's support for Hezbollah, put limits on how much US companies could invest in Iran's energy sector. These were sanctions Iranians could live with.

113   http://www.nytimes.com/2012/07/31/world/middleeast/iran-sentences-four-to-death-over-billion-dollar-bank-fraud.html Accessed 24 September 2013.
114   http://www.businessweek.com/news/2011-11-02/iranian-economy-minister-survives-impeachment-over-banking-fraud.html Accessed 24 September 2013.

There were no new sanctions until Ahmadinejad took office in 2005. Then the flood began. The new sanctions came not just from the US, but the UN, the EU, Switzerland, Canada, Australia, India, Japan, and South Korea. The nine sets of sanctions from the US amounted to almost a total ban on all economic activity with Iran.[115] As well as banning the import of oil, the EU sanctions also hit Iran's tankers as it barred them from using European insurance providers – and, crucially, they stopped Iranian banks from using SWIFT,[116] the international network for transferring funds electronically. The combination of US and EU sanctions means that Iran's economy was frozen out of the international trading system.

It was the ordinary people who felt the impact of the sanctions and the sanctions fuelled inflation because, all along the supply chain, Iranian traders struggled to import goods, not because they did not have money, but because sanctions had blocked up their channels of payment. For example, the price of chicken suddenly soared by 60 per cent in 2011 because farmers could not get the feed needed as payments were normally made in US dollars. And then there was the collapse in the currency, discussed above. Until this set of severe sanctions Iran had stabilized the currency by pumping in petrodollars. But now sanctions were drying up those petrodollars, partly because Iran was selling a lot less oil, but mainly because Iran was now excluded from the international banking system, which operated in dollars.[117]

Experiencing the economic misery caused by the sanctions, Iranians blamed the West – and President Ahmadinejad. For the

115 This became so intense and retailers so fearful of breaking the sanctions that an Iranian US citizen visiting an Apple store in Alpharetta, Atlanta in the USA and being overheard speaking Farsi was not allowed to buy an iPad. See http://www.wsbtv.com/news/local/customer-apple-store-denied-me-ipad-speaking-farsi/nPY4p/
116 Society of Worldwide Interbank Financial Telecommunication.
117 Specifically US sanctions persuaded the Dubai-based Noor Islamic Bank to stop clearing the money for Iran's oil exports in November 2011. See http://www.bbc.co.uk/news/business-19800532

sanctions were a direct result of his defiant approach. Previously, under President Khatami, Iran agreed to halt its production of enriched uranium and allow the IAEA (International Atomic Energy Agency) inspectors free access to all their nuclear facilities. The result: no crippling sanctions.

The populist Ahmadinejad saw the nuclear issue as a patriotic, even a religious one. It was this approach that led to a new wave of sanctions. He publicly mocked the pliant approach of Khatami's negotiating team led by Hassan Rouhani (his successor as president in 2013): "Those who are handling the talks are terrified, and before they even sit down at the negotiating table they retreat 500 kilometres."[118] Ahmadinejad's aides were just as critical, comparing Hassan Rouhani and his fellow diplomats to those who had signed the 1828 Turkmanchai Agreement whereby Iran lost swathes of territory to Russia. Such cowardly negotiators were "internal traitors" ready "to sell Iran down the river to its imperialist enemies."[119]

In 2005, President Ahmadinejad spelt out his hard-line stance during his first visit to the UN General Assembly. In side meetings he shocked diplomats by calling three of Europe's foreign ministers "lackeys" of the US[120] and offering Iran's nuclear knowledge to other countries.[121] In his speech he slammed the West's opposition to Iran's nuclear programme as being the imposition of "nuclear apartheid" and threatened to pursue atomic weapons if the attempts to stop Iran developing nuclear technology continued. He also had an odd plan for trying to ease the West's concerns over the programme. It was for South Africa, whose government had not been consulted, to work with Iran on developing enriched uranium on Iranian soil.

118 Naji, p. 122.
119 Naji, p. 124.
120 Naji, p. 127.
121 http://www.telegraph.co.uk/news/1498456/Iran-to-share-nuclear-technology-with-Islamic-countries.html Accessed 30 September 2013.

Perhaps while electioneering in the provinces of Iran this abusive language, defiant threats, and references to colourful but fanciful international schemes went down well with Ahmadinejad's largely local audiences – not so in New York. The audience here was alarmed by the threat, and unimpressed by the South African plan. The response was a determination to report Iran under President Ahmadinejad to the Security Council. Sanctions were now on the horizon.

Despite this, President Ahmadinejad's tone remained defiant, not least because the patriotic ticket can always fire up a crowd. So in April 2006, just a few months after his appearance at the UN, he announced to a delighted crowd in Mashad that Iran had joined the nuclear club,[122] and would enrich uranium to more than the 3 per cent needed for nuclear energy. There were celebrations up and down the country and some school children were given yellow (the colour of uranium) cake to eat. Both President Ahmadinejad and the Supreme Leader told the leaders of Kuwait and Sudan respectively they would share Iran's nuclear know-how.[123]

It seemed Iran's government was goading the international community to take action. And take action they did. On Christmas Eve 2006 the UN Security Council unanimously agreed to impose economic sanctions on Iran. So the new wave of sanctions began. And the more they came and battered Iran's economy, the more defiant and shrill President Ahmadinejad became. He called the 2006 resolution from the Security Council "a useless scrap of paper" and "unlawful".[124] His officials agreed and talked of building another 3,000 centrifuges to speed up the enrichment of uranium.

In speech after speech President Ahmadinejad told cheering crowds about Iran's "undeniable rights" to nuclear technology.

122 http://www.theguardian.com/world/2006/apr/12/iran.topstories3 Accessed 30 September 2013
123 Naji, p. 127.
124 Ibid., p. 129.

He wrapped himself up so entirely in the patriotic flag that it was impossible for him now to negotiate with the UN. He had shouted himself into a corner and here he remained until he left office in 2013. The policy was nuclear or bust: the 2013 election proved that most people believed it was bust. Hence they elected Hassan Rouhani, the former nuclear negotiator, labelled a coward by Ahmadinejad.

On hot steamy nights the crowds had lustily cheered for Madame Nuclear, but in the grey cold morning they woke up to rising prices and a crashing currency. Madame Nuclear could spike the emotions, but she couldn't pay the bills, nor could her crowd-pleasing orator. Again President Ahmadinejad had not thought things through. Creating a dogma that pleased the crowd and being surrounded by sycophants who only cheered the rhetoric, he failed to see the inevitable economic cul-de-sac that would result in cutting off Iran from the world economy.

The open sore: Ahmadinejadism in the name of Islam

Women being arrested for wearing nail polish: this was upsetting; hearing your president deny the Holocaust: this was embarrassing; being unable to buy some chicken for the weekend meal: this was painful. Cultural repression, international isolation, economic misery: for the vast majority of Iranians this is what Ahmadinejadism represented.

Back in 1979 Ayatollah Khomeini had announced the start of the "Government of God". So by 2005 the relationship between Iran and her national religion was already bruised because in the name of that religion Iranians had experienced so much violence, especially – as we have seen – under

Ayatollah Khomeini.[125] Now President Ahmadinejad was again emphasizing that the Shia faith was the state. The message received, especially in the provinces, was that if you support the president you are supporting Islam and hastening the return of Mahdi; if you do not support him, you are an enemy of Islam.

And as with Ayatollah Khomeini this divisiveness forced Iranians to make a choice. Some bought the whole package. Ahmadinejad and Islam were one, and worthy of support and any problems Iran was experiencing was due to the malign interference of foreign powers. Many, though – including senior ranks in the establishment – tried to separate the package, peeling away Ahmadinejad from their religion. This solution was not entirely satisfactory as it implied that all the fervent supporters of Ahmadinejad were not true believers. But they certainly appeared to be. And finally there were those who rejected the whole package. Ahmadinejad had positioned himself – somewhat cheekily since he had no clerical qualifications – as the heir to Ayatollah Khomeini, the man who would ensure that Iran was truly revolutionary.

Already by 2005 many were rejecting Iran's religion because of what had happened in Iran as a result of Khomeinism. Now a new generation was presented with its child, Ahmadinejadism. Again they were being asked to make a decision about their national religion. And again many decided that since Ahmadinejadism belonged to Islam, they were unable to equate this with God. The shadow between the rhetoric and the reality was too dark. Hence the impact of Ahmadinejad on Iran was to widen the wound that already existed between her people and her religion.

Many did not take this decision when Ahmadinejad left office in 2013, but when the wound became viciously infected

---

125   The number of executions increased dramatically under Ayatollah Khomeini. From 1971 to 1979 there were 100 executions under the Shah; from 1981 to 1985 there were over 7,000 under Ayatollah Khomeini; see Peterson, p. 52.

after the disputed presidential elections of 2009. For many of the younger generation already deeply disillusioned by the religion touted by Ahmadinejad, this disillusionment turned to outright rejection when they witnessed the violence of the summer of 2009.

It is to this bloody tale we now turn.

CHAPTER 4

THE 2009 ELECTIONS: THE WOUND INFECTED

On 20 June 2009 a mobile phone filmed a young girl dying of a bullet wound. This amateur footage was then uploaded onto the internet. Millions watched.[126] So it was that the death of 26-year-old Neda Agha-Soltan became "probably the most widely witnessed death in human history".[127]

Neda Agha-Soltan was shot dead while walking down Karegar Street in Tehran. She had joined a protest against the official result for the presidential elections that had declared Mahmoud Ahmadinejad the winner.

At the scene was Dr Arash Hejazi, a physician who is now a respected publisher.[128] He described what had happened when the crowd thought they had found the gunman:

> I realized that a crowd was pulling someone towards us, and the person was shouting that "I didn't want to kill her," and the people had started beating him, throwing him on the ground. They took off his clothes, his shirt.
>
> And then some other part of the people got involved and said, "No, we don't want to beat him; we are not like these killers." He was still shouting: "I swear to God that I didn't want to shoot her. I didn't want to kill her."
>
> I wanted to see what happens next, because I was really

126 Two uploads onto YouTube have had over 1 million views each.
127 http://content.time.com/time/specials/packages/
article/0,28804,1945379_1944701_1944705,00.html Accessed 2 October 2013.
128 http://gazeofthegazelle.com/about-arash-hejazi/ Accessed 4 October 2013.

furious…

Then they started discussing what they should do with him. They searched his body; they took out his wallet; they took out his ID card and started shouting, "He is a Basij member; he is one of them," and started swearing and cursing.

They couldn't really hurt him there because it didn't make sense to hurt him.

And so all of a sudden in the chaos, they decided to release him, and they took his ID cards and released him.[129]

The Basij: a religious organization

Dr Hejazi's account virtually proves that the killer of Neda Agha-Soltan was a member of the Basij.[130] A brief look at the Basij will then show that the fatal bullet was essentially a religious bullet. The Basij is a very large volunteer militia, with at least 90,000 in full-time service, 300,000 reservists, and well over 1 million ready to be mobilized[131] – all dedicated to defending the values of Iran's Shia faith. The militia operates under the authority of Iran's Revolutionary Guards, whose commander reports directly to the Supreme Leader, Ayatollah Khamenei, Iran's most senior religious leader.

The training of the Basij is extensive and religious. Every member of the Basij must attend a fifteen-day general training course where for eighteen hours a day "Basij ethics" are studied,

129   http://www.pbs.org/wgbh/pages/frontline/tehranbureau/deathintehran/
interviews/hejazi.html Accessed 2 October 2013.

130   In the aftermath of the murder, news agencies in Iran put out stories suggesting
that Neda Agha-Soltan's murder was part of a CIA or BBC plot. When strung together
these clichéd xenophobic conspiracy theories appear comical. See http://www.
persianumpire.com/2009/08/15/a-straight-story/

131   Estimates of the total number of Basij vary widely. In 2002, the Iranian press
reported that the Basij had between 5 million to 7 million members. By 2009, IRGC
(Iran's Revolutionary Guards Corps) human resources chief Masoud Mousavi claimed
to have 11.2 million Basij members. But a 2005 study by the Center for Strategic and
International Studies, a Washington think-tank, put the numbers as I have stated
above. http://www.pbs.org/wgbh/pages/frontline/tehranbureau/2010/10/iran-primer-
the-basij-resistance-force.html#ixzz2gfh4Lt7b Accessed 3 October 2013.

as well as the "Major Islamic Commandments". Active service demands a forty-five-day programme, and for those who want to move up the ranks there is a specialist course that lasts a month. There are also regular refresher courses that can last between five and fifteen days. And since 2008, to strengthen the ideological mindset of the Basij, "Tadavom" ("continual") training was introduced.[132] The actual teaching usually happens at a mosque, which serve as Basij bases throughout Iran. Some of the Tadavom training is through correspondence.

All of this training comes under the supervision of the Office of the Representative of the Supreme Leader's Office.[133] This office prepares the courses and the textbooks that are then checked by the Centre for Islamic Research based in Qom to ensure they are in line with orthodox Shia Islam. The content of their training makes it clear that the ideology that inspires them is Islamic. Of the seven basic courses each member must study, five are wholly religious: the fundamentals of belief; Islamic ethics and education; Islamic commandments; familiarity with the Koran; and the history of Islam.

One of the most important newer programmes used for the Tadavom training of the Basij is the Righteousness (Salehin) Plan. It was launched in June 2008 in 5,000 Basij bases and has been very successful. By 2010 there were 17,000 classes studying the course. The content of the seminars is based on Ayatollah Khomeini's sermons and edicts, and, on his advice, most of the textbooks used are based on lectures by the late Ayatollah Motahari.[134] Ayatollah Motahari, in his many lectures,

132   Dr Saeid Golkar, "The Ideological-Political Training of Iran's Basij", 2010. http://www.brandeis.edu/crown/publications/meb/meb44.html Accessed 7 October 2013.
133   Ibid.
134   Ayatollah Motahari was a close associate of Ayatollah Khomeini. From 1944 to 1952 he studied in Qom, and for the next twenty-two years he taught philosophy at the University of Tehran and lectured at the Hussein Institute. It is mainly from these lectures that more than sixty books have been published since 2008. He was assassinated by left-wingers in May 1979. When Ayatollah Khomeini heard the news of his death he said, "I have been deprived of a dear son of mine. I am lamenting upon the death of one who was the fruit of my life." www.iranchamber.com/personalities/

argued that Islam should never be mixed with any Western, materialistic, or atheistic system of thinking.

The Office of the Representative of the Supreme Leader's Office also appoints the several thousand lecturers who teach the courses. They are usually clerics or senior members of the Revolutionary Guards. Bodies such as the Imam Khomeini Education and Research Institute, directed by Ayatollah Mesbah-e Yazdi, will supply students to teach courses for the Basij.

The Supreme Leader and other senior ayatollahs believe this religious training is important as they rely on the Basij as a militia that will uphold Islamic values. So in Ardebil in July 2000 Ayatollah Khamenei told a group of candidates, "When it is a matter of the rule of God's religion… the Basij will be there."[135] He made the same point in November 2005, pointing out the importance of the Basij's own faith. "The stronger the Basij become, the more secure our country will be in the future…" He went on to underline the importance of their personal religious faith: "The reason for the success of the Basij is its members' faith and trust in God."[136]

The late Ayatollah Ali Meshkini, who chaired the influential Assembly of Experts, also emphasized the religious nature of the Basij: The "founding of the Basij units [is] a blessing from God and proof of His love for the Islamic Republic of Iran".[137] Ayatollah Ahmad Jannati has been at the centre of Iran's religious establishment for over thirty years. In 1980 he was appointed by Ayatollah Khomeini to the Guardian Council – the body that checks all parliamentary legislation – and has been the chairman since 1998. He too sees the Basij as being

mmotahari/morteza_motahari.php#sthash.Ebj81Qlv.dpuf Accessed 7 October 2013. He was known as the theoretician of the Islamic Republic http://www.aawsat.net/2014/05/article55332765

135   http://www.memri.org/report/en/0/0/0/0/0/0/0/1594.htm#_edn2 Accessed 3 October 2013.

136   Ibid.

137   Ibid.

pivotal to Iran as a religious state. Leading Friday prayers in December 2005 he said that Iran could become: "a powerful state in the coming years… thanks to Islam, to the revolution, *and to the Basij culture*"[138] (author's italics).

The Basij, then, is wholly identified with Iran's national religion and its most senior religious leaders: it was founded by Ayatollah Khomeini; it is inspired by the teachings of Ayatollah Mothari; their training is supervised in detail by Ayatollah Khamenei's office; the contents of the syllabi checked by religious scholars in Qom. It is this militia that played a prominent role dealing with the protests that erupted after the disputed presidential elections of 2009.

Neda Agha-Soltan was not their only victim. All the evidence from eyewitnesses and even official reports show a canvas where thirty to eighty people were murdered,[139] 5,000 arrested and imprisoned,[140] hundreds injured in beatings,[141] some even raped (in prison),[142] and at least eleven sentenced to death. It is a canvas drenched in violence, and, as with Neda Agha-Soltan, the source of the violence was usually the Basij.

The rigged election

The presidential elections were held on 12 June 2009. The main challengers to the incumbent, Mahmoud Ahmadinejad, were all senior politicians. The more conservative-minded Mohsen Rezaee had formerly been the commander-in-chief of Iran's Revolutionary Guards; of the less conservative-minded[143]

138   Ibid.
139   http://www.theguardian.com/world/blog/2009/jul/29/iran-election-protest-dead-missing Accessed 8 October 2013.
140   *From Protest to Prison*, Accessed 8 October 2013.
141   http://www.amnesty.org/en/news-and-updates/news/arrests-and-killings-rise-election-protests-grip-iran-20090617 Accessed 8 October 2013.
142   http://www.telegraph.co.uk/news/worldnews/middleeast/iran/8102358/Rape-in-Irans-prisons-the-cruellest-torture.html Accessed 8 October 2013.
143   When a politician in Iran is not a hard-line conservative it is easy to assume they are "Reformist". However, neither Mousavi nor Karroubi were signed-

candidates, Mehdi Karroubi had been a speaker for parliament (1989–92), and Mir-Hossein Mousavi, a former prime minister (1981–89). They were serious capable men.

Mir-Hossein Mousavi attracted a lot of support. In Tehran thousands came out every night, sporting something in green, the colour of the Mousavi campaign. And support for Mousavi was not limited to the capital. Author and Iran expert Scott Peterson reported on a visit of Mousavi to Birjand, a small city and conservative stronghold in the east, which had earlier greeted President Ahmadinejad like a "rock star". According to Scott Peterson, "Mousavi was mobbed in Birjand from the moment he stepped out of the airport terminal." Peterson had no doubt what was fuelling the support. "These new Mousavi adherents… were angry over the tanking economy and the president's failure to fulfil extravagant promises."[144] Iranian-born Canadian journalist Maziar Bahari[145] found likewise:

> In dozens of interviews… I found that many lower-income people also supported Mousavi for the same reason the middle classes did. Rampant corruption… and Iran's status as an international pariah…[146]

Evidence that Mousavi would win many votes came not only from the size of the rural and urban crowds but even from the government itself. Maziar Bahari had a friend, Amir, who had

up supporters of the former president Mohammad Khatami or the writings of Abdolkarim Soroush, the intellectual inspiration of the movement. Like the Reformers they were critical of Ahmadinejad and especially the role of the judiciary, but it is still not easy to give them the label "Reformist" as usually this means someone who wants to fundamentally alter the character of the Islamic regime.

144   Peterson, pp. 473–74.

145   Maziar Bahari reported for Newsweek from 1998 to 2011, and has contributed to numerous TV channels including BBC, Channel 4, and HBO. Bahari was in Iran during the 2009 elections with an official press card to work as a journalist. In the protests that erupted after the election Bahari was arrested and imprisoned at Evin for over four months where he endured hours of interrogation.

146   Maziar Bahari, *Then They Came for Me*, p. 25.

worked for the Ministry of the Interior. In the run up to the 2009 election this friend still had reliable contacts there. According to these contacts the Ministry of Intelligence had conducted a secret poll across Iran: "The poll... predicted that Mousavi would win the election with sixteen to eighteen million votes to Ahmadinejad's six to eight million."[147]

This is not the only evidence that the government expected Mousavi to win. A source close to Ayatollah Khamenei told Lindsey Hilsum, a senior journalist with the British broadcaster Channel 4, that private polling for the Supreme Leader's office had shown that Mousavi would win by a two-to-one margin.[148]

According to the Ministry of the Interior, 85 per cent of those eligible to vote – 39 million people – turned out on election day. This was a record for a presidential election in the Islamic Republic. One reason for the impressive numbers according to the opponents of Ahmadinejad was that the more people who voted, the less opportunity the security forces had of cheating.[149] This fear of cheating produced rumours. In the Mousavi camp there was one rumour that officials would give them pens with disappearing ink, and in the Ahmadinejad camp there was the same rumour except it was the Americans who had smuggled in pens with disappearing ink. So lots of voters brought their own pens to the polling booths.[150]

It turned out that the cheating proved to be less subtle than pens with disappearing ink. It was in fact brazen and brutal. Even as evening fell veteran watchers of Iran's presidential elections noticed disturbing signs. Polling stations that had run out of ballot forms were not re-supplied; despite the large queues, some of the polling stations closed early. The Ministry of the Interior buildings where the results would be announced turned into a fortress. Cranes lowered concrete barriers to block

147 Ibid., p. 37.
148 Peterson, p. 489.
149 Ibid., p. 495.
150 Ibid., p. 500.

all access and in front of them there were "three rows of police cars, all with their lights flashing".[151]

The most disturbing indication of outright interference happened at around 5.30 in the afternoon, three-and-a-half hours before the polling stations were due to close. The Fars News Agency website, aligned with the government, announced that Ahmadinejad had won the election by 20 million votes.[152] The government apparently knew the result of the election before the voting had even finished. This is proof enough that there had been no counting of votes, simply an announcement – but there was more evidence. A member of the Basij told a Channel 4 journalist that they were told to take ballot boxes back to the Ministry of the Interior, even if they were uncounted.[153] The announcement on the Fars News Agency site was taken down, but then just three hours after the polling stations were meant to close down the Ministry of the Interior made the official announcement. It is difficult to see how so many votes could have been counted so quickly. And, in past presidential elections, there has been a lot of variation in the percentages won by the contenders in different areas of the country. But in this election there was a "suspicious consistency".[154] Whenever a result was announced, Ahmadinejad had won by a two-to-one majority. Furthermore in previous elections there had always been a significant swing in a candidate's home province, but Ahmadinejad had also won by a two-to-one majority even in Mousavi's home town of Khamaneh in the province of East Azerbaijan.

It seems as if somebody had been told that Ahmadinejad should win by two-to-one across the country and had simply put a formula into the computer to produce this result. The fact that nobody bothered to ensure there was some variation

151   Ibid., p. 504.
152   Bahari, p. 53.
153   Michael Axworthy, *Revolutionary Iran*, p. 403.
154   Ibid., p. 402.

to avoid suspicion shows how brazen the cheating was. The cheating could be so brazen because officials knew the reaction to any protests would be brutal.

Basiji violence against protestors

After the results were announced on the evening of 9 June, so the protests began. The response from the Basij was indeed brutal. Eyewitness Scott Peterson watched them attack a group of protesters, with batons, kicking and punching and blasting with pepper spray: "I saw on one man's upper arm the imprint of the sole of a boot where he had been kicked."[155] The peaceful protests and the brutal response from the Basij continued the next day. Maziar Bahari got caught up in the violence:

> I pushed my way through the crowd toward an officer and shouted to him that I needed to get to a shop on the other side. He shouted back at me to move on, but just as I began to pull away, a plainclothes officer came from behind me and kicked me hard in the back. He then pushed me toward the line of anti-riot police. I fell onto one of the officers who instantly kicked me and struck my arm with his club.[156]

Shortly after this Bahari came across a sixteen-year-old boy, Reza, who had been returning home from a language school who was, "semiconscious, and his blue short-sleeved shirt was drenched in blood". The author found out that Reza had been struck for simply being where he was, and when he had fallen to the ground, "a plainclothes intelligence officer kicked him in the head".[157]

The size and anger of the protest in Tehran grew the next day (Sunday 14 June), especially after Ahmadinejad had

155   Peterson, p. 505.
156   Bahari, p. 60.
157   Ibid., p. 62.

referred to Mousavi supporters at a press conference as *khas o khashak* ("dust and dirt"). The mindless brutality of the Basij also grew, as Bahari witnessed.

> The city was quickly sinking into bedlam. Gangs of anti-riot police on motorcycles roamed the street… A driver on Beheshti Avenue honked his horn in protest when policemen on motorcycles blocked his way. Within an instant, three or four cops got off their bikes and smashed the car's windows with their clubs… policemen dragged him (the driver) out of the car and to the pavement where another officer started slapping him.[158]

Bahari was to witness worse brutality:

> As I walked wearily along Vali Asr Avenue that evening I saw four or five officers beating an old woman with a club because she'd protested that they were blocking the entrance to her house. The woman collapsed with the first blow… As I saw the club hitting the woman's backside, I felt her pain in my body as well. It was the same kind of electric instrument I'd been hit with the day before.[159]

The next day, Monday 15 June, between 1 and 2 million people rallied for Mousavi in Tehran. The vast crowd stretched for miles from Freedom Square to the south of the city. This is when the Basij shooting began. At dusk, outside a Basij base, the crowd, possibly provoked, tried to climb over the perimeter fences. In response gunmen started shooting from the roof. One witness told Scott Peterson, "They shot three people in front of my eyes…" Another witness told Peterson of a gunman who fired about three hundred bullets from the rooftop – roughly half into the air and the other half into the crowd.[160]

158 Ibid., p. 67.
159 Ibid., p. 68.
160 Peterson, p. 518.

Maziar Bahari also witnessed this Basij shooting:

> Before long the Basijis stopped firing warning shots and began shooting indiscriminately into the crowd of protestors. The two Basijis on the roof did not seem to care if the people they were shooting at were attackers or passersby. One man in his early twenties was shot as he tried to leap over the fence…The boy's slim body dropped onto the fence as soon as the bullet entered his body. He went into cardiac arrest and slowly rolled over onto the ground… Another man was shot in the head while trying to kick down the door of the base.[161]

All this and more was filmed by Maziar Bahari and broadcast around the world on *Channel 4 News*.

The protests continued frequently until the end of July and then intermittently into the winter. There were large demonstrations across the country on 27 December. The reaction from the Basij was as brutal as ever. It was witnessed by a Norwegian student who got caught up in the violence:

> A young boy was laid down in front of me. One of the Basijis held my head and told me to look. They held his arms and foot and they had a stick or baton and were beating his knees. I saw his eyes and heard the sound of blades… After this, one of the female demonstrators was saying something… they forced a baton into her mouth, penetrating her mouth – she was screaming in pain.
>
> At one point there was a small bus on fire, people were trying to get out. When they tried to get out they were shot at. Some of them did not get out.[162]

161 Bahari, p. 78.

162 *From Protest to Prison: Iran one year after the election*, Amnesty International, 2010, http://www.amnesty.org/en/library/asset/MDE13/062/2010/en/a009a855-788b-4ed4-8aa9-3e535ea9606a/mde130622010en.pdf

Officially nine people were murdered on the streets that day, including the nephew of the presidential candidate Hussein Mousavi. During all the protests thirty-two people definitely lost their lives. There is certainty about this number because the report of each death is corroborated,[163] and the government itself confirms that thirty people were killed.[164] However it is very likely that more died, not least because doctors were given strict reports not to record any deaths as being due to street violence. The Revolutionary Guard put the order in an urgent memo to the Ministry of Health: "The disclosure of medical documents to all injured patients of recent events is strictly prohibited."[165] However, estimates have been made. Relying on reports from within Iran, the UK's *The Guardian* newspaper put the number of dead at eighty[166] and another agency states that relying on uncorroborated reports 157 were killed,[167] which added to the thirty-two who definitely died brings the total to 189 deaths. Even if the number was "only" thirty, since it is clear that some of these deaths were caused by the Basij firing on unarmed protesters, this still cements the Basij – and their religion – with violence in the public mind.

Torture, rape, and death in the prisons

The beating and shooting was not the only violence. The Basij and other security agents arrested and imprisoned thousands of people. In one month after the election there had been over

163   Iran Tracker has a detailed list of the incidents that occurred during the protests, and records the number of deaths which can be corroborated as thirty-two. See http://www.irantracker.org/analysis/unrest-iran-protests-arrests-and-deaths-source-data Accessed 9th October 2013

164   http://www.theguardian.com/world/blog/2009/jul/29/iran-election-protest-dead-missing Accessed 9th October 2013

165   Peterson, p. 536.

166   http://www.theguardian.com/world/blog/2009/jul/29/iran-election-protest-dead-missing Accessed 9 October 2013

167   http://www.irantracker.org/analysis/unrest-iran-protests-arrests-and-deaths-source-data Accessed 9 October 2013.

2,500 arrests just in Tehran;[168] Amnesty International states that during the unrest over 5,000 were arrested across the country.[169] Those who were arrested include those taking part in the demonstrations and many others who had connections with the political opponents of President Ahmadinejad.

Conditions in the prisons were grim because of the intense over-crowding. Christian prisoners Maryam Rostampour and Marzieh Amirizadeh Esmaeilabad, jailed since March 2009, witnessed the sudden influx of new inmates:

> As the postelection protests intensified, the prison became more crowded than ever... Women were jammed so tightly into the cells that there was scarcely room to move at night. The air became even more stale, and the smell of so many bodies in close quarters was sickening.[170]

Prisoners endured much more than crowding; according to "numerous reports" collected by Amnesty International torture and mistreatment was widespread.

> Methods of torture and other ill treatment frequently reported include severe beatings, using hands, feet or cables; electric shocks; confinement in tiny spaces; hanging upside-down by the feet for long periods; rape of both men and women, including with implements; death threats, including mock executions; exposure to constant light; threats to arrest and torture family members; actual arrest of family members; deprivation of light, food and water; and denial of medical treatment.[171]

One of the "numerous reports" concerns Ebrahim Sharifi, a computer engineer student who worked for Mehdi Karrubi

168   *From Protest to Prison* Accessed 9 October 2013.
169   *From Protest to Prison* Accessed 9 October 2013.
170   Maryam Rostampour and Marziyeh Amiridazeh, *Captive in Iran*.
171   *From Protest to Prison,* p. 34, Accessed 9 October 2013.

during the election campaign. Ebrahim Sharifi was arrested on 23 June, returning from a language class held at the Italian Consulate. He said, "Someone grabbed me from behind, tied my hands, and blindfolded me. He pushed me to the floor of the car."[172]

Ebrahim Sharifi was taken to a detention centre and beaten for four days. While beating him the guard would call out, "Ya Hossein" or "Ya Zahra"[173] (the names of Muslim saints). On the fourth day a noose was tied round his neck and he endured a mock execution. The guards took the noose away saying the Supreme Leader had forgiven him. But Ebrahim Sharifi's suffering was not over:

> Someone kicked me in the stomach and I fell on the ground. He kept kicking me in the stomach. Then he told someone: "Go and make [him] pregnant." He kept kicking me. I was throwing up blood and my stomach was injured. He pulled me to another room and tied my hands to the wall.

Ebrahim Sharifi was raped. "I think that a person did it, but I can't be sure whether it was done by that individual or whether he used something."[174]

Maryam Sabri was also raped. Forty days after the murder of Neda Agha-Soltan she had gone to Tehran's main cemetery to mourn, as is the custom in Iran. While there around 100 Basij guards broke up the group of mourners and 21-year-old Maryam Sabri was arrested. In prison she was periodically interrogated and beaten by "ski-mask wearing guards". During the first three interrogation sessions she refused to cooperate. During the fourth the male guard raped her:

172 http://www.payvand.com/news/09/sep/1243.html Accessed 9 October 2013.
173 Peterson, p. 562.
174 http://www.payvand.com/news/09/sep/1243.html Accessed 9 October 2013 Ebrahim Sharifi talks about the rape here: http://www.youtube.com/watch?v=hZJsuInaFOs

He said, "OK, fine. You wanted your vote? I am here to give your vote back. I will give you your vote now and you can see if it is any good." I felt him grab my shoulders. He had never grabbed me this hard while he beat me. He got me up from the chair and took off my clothes by force. I was screaming and crying. I begged him."[175]

Before being released Maryam Sabri was violated five times. In a report in the UK's *The Times* newspaper a total of thirty-seven young men and women in Tehran alone claimed to have been raped by their captors.[176]

People also died in prison. Amir Javadifar, a 24-year-old student from Qazvin was beaten up during a protest on 9 July and then arrested. Later doctors confirmed that he had minor injuries to his elbow, jaw, and nose. The next day he was taken to Kahrizak prison. On 25 July his family were asked to come and identify his body. A cellmate of Amir Javadifar at Kahrizak later spoke of how 160 inmates were crowded into a room designed for twenty with hardly any ventilation: "It was very hot. There was a very small air vent, and at night the smell of gasoline came in. There were no windows. We banged on the door to get air, and instead, we had gasoline through the vent..."

It seems likely that Amir Javadifar died after being beaten on 14 July. The same cellmate describes that difficult day:

Around 12:00 p.m., they took us to the courtyard. They made half of us crawl on our hands and knees around the courtyard while carrying the other prisoners on our backs. The ground was so hot, we were burning. After five minutes, I only saw blood on the ground from other people's knees and hands... We circled the courtyard maybe twenty or

175   http://www.iranhrdc.org/english/english/publications/reports/3161-violent-aftermath-the-2009-election-and-suppression-of-dissent-in-iran.html?p=19#. UlV3s9I3suc Accessed 9 October 2013
176   Peterson, p. 569.

> twenty-five times. If we stopped, they beat us... Several
> people were unconscious. Officials could see that we may
> not survive... A person named Javadifar was thirsty and
> had trouble eating. They kept beating him.

These prisoners were then transferred to Evin. By the end of the journey Amir Javadifar was dead. The cellmate continues, "Javadifar had lost consciousness... We had to carry him [to a bus]... He died in the bus. We saw his body in the [Evin] courtyard." [177]

The Iranian authorities acknowledge that two other prisoners died after their ordeal in Kahrizak prison.[178] Eighteen-year-old Mohammad Kamrani was also arrested on 9 July during the protests. His family were informed of his release on 15 July, but when they went to meet him, they were told he was in a hospital. Mohammad Kamrani died the next day.[179]

The other prisoner who died was Mohsen Ruholamini, also arrested in Tehran on 9 July, and then sent to Kahrizak prison. His case created a lot more publicity because he was the son of Abdolhossein Ruholamini, a senior official in the Ministry of Health and an adviser to the Conservative presidential candidate, Mohsen Rezai. Through a close friend to the family, Abdolhossein Ruholamini let it be known that his son had been severely beaten:

> When I saw his body I noticed that they had crushed his
> mouth. My son was an honest person. He wouldn't lie. I'm
> sure that he's given correct answers to anything they'd asked

177   http://www.iranrights.org/english/memorial-case-61251.php Accessed 10 October 2013.
178   The deaths of Amir Javadifar, Mohammad Kamrani, and Mohsen Ruholamini are confirmed by Mehr, a semi-official news agency in Iran see http://www.payvand.com/news/12/jul/1182.htm
179   http://www.iranhrdc.org/english/english/publications/reports/3161-violent-aftermath-the-2009-election-and-suppression-of-dissent-in-iran.html?p=20#. UlaKGNI3suc Accessed 10 October 2013

him… They probably couldn't stand his honesty and beat him until he died under torture.[180]

Ramin Aghazadeh Ghahremani and Abbas Nejati-Kargar were also detainees in Kahrizak prison at this time and their families maintain that they also died after their release as a result of injuries suffered there.[181] If these families are correct this would mean five Iranians died in custody after being arrested during the protests.

The death of Mohsen Ruholamini and the reports of rape and torture in the prisons were at first ignored, but as the families of victims kept on talking, the outrage became so intense that Ayatollah Khamenei intervened and ordered the closure of Kahrizak in late July 2009.[182] At the same time a parliamentary enquiry was set up to investigate the abuses.

Show trials, death sentences, and executions

Some of those arrested also endured humiliating show trials held from 1 August through to 15 September 2009. On Saturday 1 August, about a hundred protesters, some linked to Iran's Reformist movement, were brought into a televised courtroom to make public confessions of their crimes against the state. Among them was Mohammad Ali Abtahi, a former vice president during the Khatami years, whose wasted body shocked his wife when she saw her husband on television. In court Mohammad Ali Abtahi and others confessed to involvement in a plot with foreign agents and their media to overthrow the Islamic Republic. Their families were certain these confessions were obtained after torture.

180   http://www.pbs.org/wgbh/pages/frontline/tehranbureau/2009/08/official-leak-rouholamini-tortured-to-death.html Accessed 10 October 2013.
181   http://www.hrw.org/news/2012/09/27/iran-bring-notorious-abuser-justice Accessed 10 October 2013.
182   http://news.bbc.co.uk/1/hi/8172516.stm Accessed 13 December 2014.

Maziar Bahari's own experience, detailed in his book *Then They Came for Me* proves that the confessions were made after torture. He had been arrested on 21 June and kept mainly in solitary confinement. He had been taken blindfolded almost every day to be interrogated and beaten by a man he called "Rosewater", because of his smell. Before the trial "Rosewater"[183] made it very clear what was meant to happen. This is what he said to Bahari:

> "Listen you bacheh khoshgel – you pretty boy – you either name everyone on the list I gave you and apologize to the supreme leader for breaking his heart, or you're going to be sentenced today and executed a few days from now." He slapped me on the head again and opened the door. "It's your choice to live and see your mother, or die for Mousavi and Rafsanjani." He shut the door behind him.[184]

Due to international pressure Maziar Bahari was eventually released on a bail of $300,000 in October. He left the country. In May 2010 the court sentenced him to thirteen years' imprisonment and seventy-four lashes for "conspiring against the state".

Mohammad Ali Abtahi was less fortunate. He was given a six-year custodial sentence and then released "temporarily" on bail for $700,000.[185] Others too have been released on bail,[186] but it is estimated that even in 2013 there were still over eighty in

---

183 The film about Maziar Bahari's ordeal is called *Rosewater*, directed by Jon Stewart.
184 Bahari, p. 225.
185 http://www.theguardian.com/world/2009/nov/22/mohammad-ali-abtahi-iran-protests-jailed Accessed 11 October 2012.
186 A list is here: http://www.iranhumanrights.org/2010/03/heavy-bails-releasing-the-prisoners-or-new-hostage-taking-by-the-judiciary/ Accessed 11 October 2013. This site considers that the word ransom is a better word than bail for the figure demanded by the judiciary when negotiating the release of political prisoners.

prison who were arrested during the 2009 election protests.[187]

Seven young men at the show trials of August were even less fortunate. They were sentenced to death for the crime of *Moharebeh* – enmity against God. Mohammad Reza Ali-Zamani, Arash Rahmanipour, Naser Abdolhosseini, Hamed Rouhinejad, Ayoub Porkar, Reza Khademi,[188] Amir Reza Arefi, and Ahmad Karimi[189] were nearly all young men, accused of having links with royalist or socialist Islamic groups seeking the overthrow of the regime. In the context of these trials there was much unease over these sentences within Iran and around the world. The men were found guilty on the basis of confessions, which, as seen in the case of Maziar Bahari, were almost certainly made under duress. Another alarming irregularity is that five of the condemned men (Mohammad Reza Ali-Zamani, Ahmad Karimi, Hamed Ruhinezhad, Arash Rahmanipour, and Amir Reza Arefi) were all arrested and in prison before the election protests began. Nasrin Sotoudeh, the lawyer for Mohammad Reza Ali-Zamani, who was herself later arrested and imprisoned, was dismissive of the charges against her client: "He was arrested in Farvardin [the Iranian month covering March–April] – before the election – and charged with co-operation with the Kingdom Assembly… He confessed because of threats against his family."[190]

Most of these death sentences were commuted to long prison sentences, but two of the condemned men were executed. At dawn on 28 January 2010 Mohammad Reza Ali-Zamani (aged thirty-eight) and Arash Rahmanipour (aged

187   http://www.telegraph.co.uk/news/worldnews/middleeast/iran/10328961/
Iran-pardons-80-political-prisoners-on-eve-of-President-Rouhanis-visit-to-US.html
Accessed 11 October 2013
188   "Violent Aftermath: the 2009 Election and Suppression of Dissent in Iran"
published by Iran Human Rights Documentation Centre, Connecticut, USA, section
5.6. http://www.gozaar.org/english/articles-en/A-Report-on-Political-Prisoners-in-
Iran.html Accessed 11 October 2013
189   http://www.gozaar.org/english/articles-en/A-Report-on-Political-Prisoners-in-
Iran.html Accessed 11 October 2013 and http://ireport.cnn.com/docs/DOC-410354
190   http://news.bbc.co.uk/1/hi/8484478.stm Accessed 11 October 2013.

twenty) were hanged in Evin prison. Amnesty International and other human rights agencies led a chorus of international criticism, concluding that the two were "unfairly convicted", and "unjustly killed".[191]

One year after the protests Iran's streets had been numbed by violence. Protesters were to be seen no more, their will broken by the ruthlessness of the crackdown. In public everyone had to subscribe to the official version of events: Mahmoud Ahmadinejad had legally won the election by a two-to-one majority,[192] but foreign powers using Reformist politicians and agents of the foreign media intent on overthrowing the Islamic Republic had incited people to stage demonstrations.[193] The plot had failed, the conspirators rightly punished.

In this showdown between the Reformists and Conservatives, the Conservatives had again won. But there was a price for this victory: a haemorrhaging of political and spiritual legitimacy.

Haemorrhaging of political legitimacy

Political legitimacy drained away because satellite TV, the internet, and close ties to the diaspora meant the majority of Iranians had access to evidence that wholly rejected the official political story outlined above. The version of events that the evidence points to is summarized here.

The authorities knew that Mousavi was on course to win the election. A decision was then taken to ensure that Ahmadinejad was the outright winner;[194] and to prepare the Basiji to deal

191   http://www.amnesty.org/fr/node/15194 Accessed 11 October 2013
192   http://www.irantracker.org/analysis/iranian-presidential-election-news Accessed 17 December 2013.
193   https://www.fas.org/sgp/crs/mideast/R40653.pdf See p. 1. Accessed 18 December 2013.
194   A former member of the Basiji told the British TV journalist Lindsey Hilsum: "We had received orders… that Mr Khamenei has Mr Ahmadinejad in mind for the presidency and so he must be announced as the winner." See Peterson, p. 524. This

with any hostile reaction.[195] Ayatollah Khamenei authorized the arrests of people he called "seditionists" with links to foreigners.[196] From eyewitnesses on the streets[197] it is clear the Basiji had been given permission to use as much violence as deemed necessary to defeat the protesters. This included killing, as confirmed by a Basiji who talked to Scott Peterson: "It was very hard. If there was an issue with killing, it was explained that the killing was for a cause and was a good deed."[198] To justify the violent crackdown on the protests Ayatollah Khamenei accused the Western powers of orchestrating the disturbances at the Friday prayers on 19 June 2009, so condemning the protestors as enemies of Iran in league with the USA, UK, and Israel.[199] The Revolutionary Guards then set about acquiring confessions from arrested politicians and journalists to prove that a Western conspiracy was behind the protests.[200]

In the official version of events the brutal repression of the protestors was necessary to deal with the threat of Iran's foreign enemies orchestrating the "soft" overthrow of the Islamic

decision was taken against a background whereby the Supreme Leader and other senior figures in the ruling elite, including the head of the Revolutionary Guards, were convinced that America was funding a "soft" cultural invasion of Iran and the government would face a similar fate to the autocracies of the former Soviet Union unless decisive action was taken. See Peterson, Chapter 6, for excellent detail on this.

195   General Moshafagh, a senior official in the Revolutionary Guards, told a seminar of clerics in Mashad that there had been planning to deal with any "sedition" following the election. See http://www.payvand.com/news/12/jan/1006.html Accessed 12 December 2013

196   By confirming that the arrests of political and civil activists were on orders of Ayatollah Khamenei, Herandi, who at one time was the chief editor of the right-wing Kayhan newspaper and is now the adviser to the IRGC commander, said, "The wise view of the leader was that the leadership of the sedition was outside the country. He believed that the channel that connected the seditionists to the outside world had to be discovered. This led to the arrest of a group of individuals 90 per cent of whom were subsequently released with warnings and only 10 per cent were interrogated and prosecuted." See http://www.payvand.com/news/12/jan/1006.html Accessed 12 December 2013.

197   See evidence pp. 83–86.

198   See Peterson, p. 534.

199   http://www.theguardian.com/world/2009/jun/19/iran-elections-ayatollah-ali-khamenei Accessed 12 December 2009.

200   See especially Chapter 14 of Bahari's *Then They Came for Me*.

Republic. There is a patriotic logic to the violence. However, in the political story supported by the evidence that threat of a foreign conspiracy was a threat that was created purely by the hardliners.

Their use of the "foreign infiltrator" sounded particularly threadbare when the abuse at Kahrizak detention centre became public knowledge. President Ahmadinejad's first reaction was to blame "foreign plots".[201] However, the idea that foreign agents would be able to operate in government prisons surrounded by the regime's most loyal supporters was stretching people's belief in the reach of the West's spies beyond its limits.

Ironically President Ahmadinejad's desperate attempt to deflect decent people's anger away from the criminal officials responsible for the abuse actually underlined just how implausible the whole political story of the government was. For if it was extremely unlikely that foreign agents would have been able to rape prisoners in Iran's jails, so too it was extremely unlikely that foreign agents would be able to arrange for 1–2 million protestors to march in Tehran, as they did on 15 June 2009.

It was obvious to nearly everyone that the "foreign infiltrators" were a creation of the hardliners. Their political story unravelled. With no "foreign infiltrators" all that was left was a leadership willing to sanction election rigging, beatings, torture, and rape to preserve power. Their political legitimacy had drained away.

This haemorrhaging of the government's political legitimacy was announced by one of the most senior clerical figures in Iran and the Shia world: Ayatollah Montazeri, the one-time deputy to the Islamic Republic's founder, Ayatollah Khomeini, who was later demoted and ended his days under house arrest. Ayatollah Montazeri declared that Iran under

201   http://www.pbs.org/wgbh/pages/frontline/tehranbureau/2009/08/official-leak-rouholamini-tortured-to-death.html Accessed 12 December 2013.

Ayatollah Khamenei was neither Islamic nor a republic – but in fact a military regime. Recognized as being clerically more senior than Ayatollah Khamenei he then used his authority as a Grand Ayatollah to issue several fatwas against the Supreme Leader for the injustices that prevailed in Iran since the 2009 elections.[202]

The fatwas were ineffective. The Supreme Leader remained in office and he also remained faithful to the same political script that Ayatollah Montazeri had denounced as lacking legitimacy. In the autumn of 2010 Ayatollah Khamenei made a much-publicized visit to Qom to reassert his authority over the clerical community that had also been divided over the issue of the 2009 elections. Here he made an important speech using the same script: Iran was under attack from the West who were using "mercenaries and lackeys inside the country" and supporting "promiscuity", "fake mysticism", and "a network of house churches" in a soft-war to undermine the Islamic Republic.[203]

The haemorrhaging of political legitimacy due to the 2009 elections, even when announced by the likes of Ayatollah Montazeri, did not seem to have any impact on political life. The discredited story that had foreign agents raping prisoners in Iran's jails seemed to be back on the front page, justifying more injustice.[204]

But in fact 2009 stayed in many people's minds, especially those of the politicians. As the new presidential election approached in 2013 it became clear that none of the candidates, all vetted by the Supreme Leader, were ready to use the old political script of a pure revolution being betrayed by seditious

---

202   http://www.pbs.org/wgbh/pages/frontline/tehranbureau/2009/07/grand-ayatollah-montazeris-fatwa.html Accessed 13 December 2013.

203   http://english.khamenei.ir/index.php?option=com_content&task=view&id=1369

204   After Ayatollah Khamenei's speech in Qom in October 2010, the level of persecution against Christians increased. See Chapter 8.

supporters of foreign interests. This script had remained on stage by force, but the shame of the crackdown was still fresh in people's minds:[205] the script had no legitimacy.

Hence, all the candidates distanced themselves from this script. And in the run-up to the election a barrage of criticism from along the political spectrum fell on the script's main star, President Ahmadinejad. During the robust TV debates the candidates disagreed on many areas of policy; but they all agreed that President Ahmadinejad's record in office had been a disaster.[206] The Supreme Leader, the media, and the judiciary all aligned to the hardliners who had supported President Ahmadinejad. Now they remained silent. They offered the discredited president no help. The haemorrhaging had had an impact.

During the TV debates there was another issue on which all the candidates agreed. Iran's foreign policy had to change. There needed to be some sort of accommodation of the West. This was a stance that would rip out the heart of the 2009 script, the whole momentum of which relied on constant references to the danger of "foreign plots". But now, instead of scaremongering about "foreign plots", all the contenders advocated diplomacy with the West; gone was the xenophobic isolationism, the hallmark of Ahmadinejad's foreign policy.

Again the Supreme Leader remained silent. When Hassan Rouhani, the candidate who had campaigned on talking with the West, was then elected president, there was no repeat of the official intervention and cover-up that had marked the elections of 2009. The Supreme Leader supported the people's choice. A

205   Candidate Mohammad Reza Aref said on TV, "I don't want to open the case of 2009, but I silenced myself for four years and I was in pain." http://articles. washingtonpost.com/2013-06-07/world/39810369_1_ali-akbar-velayati-nuclear-case-saeed-jalili Accessed 16 December 2013.
206   "Among the candidates, points of agreement were few and far between but all eight men agreed on one point: that the 8-year record of sitting President Mahmoud Ahmadinejad had been a disaster for Iran…" http://edition.cnn.com/2013/06/11/ opinion/iran-election-foreign-policy/ Accessed 13 December 2013.

few weeks later when Rouhani addressed the United Nations in New York the newspapers talked about an Iranian "charm offensive". Journalists had one very important question: did the new president have the Supreme Leader's authority to negotiate? The answer was a very confident "Yes".[207] Then in November President Rouhani's foreign minister, Mohammad Javed Zarif, spearheaded a diplomatic breakthrough in talks with the West over Iran's nuclear programme. Ayatollah Khamenei thanked the diplomatic team.

On many occasions in the past Ayatollah Khamenei has made it clear he does not believe in talking to the US. Not only are the crimes against his country too many[208] but, more importantly, he has always believed that Washington is determined to bring about regime change in Iran. He has been entirely committed to the "foreign plots" script. So in 2000 in a speech to officials the Supreme Leader said this: "An all-encompassing plan has been arranged to collapse the Islamic Republican system." In public he referred to this plan to explain the 2009 protests. Speaking in June 2011 he said, "This revolution is alive, for it defends itself and indeed prevails and wins. This is certain, as you saw happen in 2009."[209]

As for the sanctions, in this paradigm they were not to be seen as being primarily about Iran's nuclear programme, but about Washington and Tel Aviv's main concern: ending the Islamic Republic. In August 2011 Ayatollah Khamenei said, "Although the excuse for the sanctions is the issue of nuclear energy, they are lying... the enemy's real goal is to hurl the

207   http://www.washingtonpost.com/blogs/worldviews/wp/2013/09/18/two-great-signs-and-a-dubious-one-from-iranian-president-rouhanis-first-western-interview/ Accessed 17 December 2013.
208   These crimes have occurred in Ayatollah Khamenei's speeches: the ousting of Mossadeqh; supporting the Shah (in whose prisons he languished); not letting the Shah be tried; freezing Iran's assets; supporting Saddam Hussein in the Iran–Iraq war; instigating sanctions against Iran. See Akbar Ganji, "Who is Ali Khamenei?" September/October 2013, especially pp. 5–9.
209   See Ganji, "Who is Ali Khamenei?"

Islamic Republic to the ground."[210]

Given Ayatollah Khamenei's consistency in maintaining that Iran is under threat from "foreign plots", it is unlikely he has jettisoned this view of world affairs. Indeed, in November 2013, the month of the Geneva talks, the Supreme Leader warned all the Muslims of the Middle East to be on their guard against "plots" to undermine Islam.[211]

Yet Ayatollah Khamenei has given permission for the Islamic Republic to talk to America, the source of all the plots. The probable answer to this contradiction is a case of political pragmatism due to the script losing its legitimacy. In 2009 Ayatollah Khamenei backed President Ahmadinejad using the "foreign plots" script. The script was first torn apart by the ruthless crackdown, with the Supreme Leader acknowledging there had been rapes and abuse in Iran's prisons. And then the script was shredded by another four years of ideological xenophobic religious nationalism that left Iran on the verge of economic collapse, threatened with military attack, and Iran's people deeply resentful.

In 2013, during the last TV debate between the presidential candidates, the Supreme Leader's ally, Saeed Jalili, was torn apart for his ideological stance on the nuclear issue by the arch Conservative, Ali Akbar Velayati, a former foreign minister under Ayatollah Khomeini. This was a defining moment in the election campaign, and it became more defining when the Supreme Leader chose to stay silent.

For whatever his own personal beliefs, it is likely Ayatollah Khamenei had come to a pragmatic conclusion. The ideological stance epitomized by Jalili neither had the support of the masses groaning under sanctions, nor many senior figures such as Velayati in the ranks of the establishment. While the Supreme Leader might still have faith in the "foreign plots" script, it was

210   Ibid., p. 8.
211   http://english.farsnews.com/newstext.aspx?nn=13920905000673 Accessed 16 December 2013.

abundantly clear from the election campaign that this script had no legitimacy. Politically, it was not working. To stay with this script meant risking public outcry on the streets, and bitter division among the politicians. And so Ayatollah Khamenei made a political calculation: staying with the old "foreign plots" script for Iran was too dangerous for the survival of the regime.

Haemorrhaging of spiritual legitimacy

The late Ayatollah Montazeri's[212] scathing verdict on the 2009 elections was double-edged. He said that Iran under Ayatollah Khamenei was neither Islamic, nor a republic. It might be that the Supreme Leader's support for the democratically elected (but vetted) President Rouhani will be able to dull the sting of the second charge. The fact that Rouhani is now president, and not Jalili, shows that when the Iranian constitution is respected, the colour of power changes.

Crossing out Ayatollah Montazeri's second verdict is more problematic, not least because the stakeholders are not agreed on what "Islamic" means. In his answers to an enquirer, Ayatollah Montazeri spelt out what Islamic was not: killing innocent people; stopping public protests; imprisoning protestors; forcing confessions; controlling information; slandering protestors as traitors; and ignoring people's votes.[213] However Ayatollah's Montazeri's judgments go to the heart of Iran's problem when it comes to the word Islamic. For according to Iran's constitution Islamic is whatever is the judgment of the Supreme Jurist, Ayatollah Khamenei. Hence all that has happened with Ayatollah Khamenei's permission, such as the imprisonment of the protestors, is Islamic.

212   Ayatollah Montazeri died on 19 December 2009, just two months after criticizing Ayatollah Khamenei's policies after the election protests. Hundreds of thousands attended his funeral.
213   See http://www.pbs.org/wgbh/pages/frontline/tehranbureau/2009/07/grand-ayatollah-montazeris-fatwa.html Accessed 16 July 2013.

And that is why the election and crackdown of 2009 has also caused a spiritual haemorrhaging. Some agree with Ayatollah Montazeri that what happened was not Islamic. But in the public mind it is not so easy to separate religion from the events of 2009 and simply say: this was not "Islamic". For at every stage of the 2009 journey, men steeped in Shia Islam are involved. The decision to interfere in the election and respond robustly to the expected reaction came from senior clerics. In his speech on Friday 19 June Ayatollah Khamenei supported the crackdown, as did other senior clerics. In January 2010 Ayatollah Jannati urged the authorities to continue to execute protestors until all the demonstrations ended.[214] The Basiji, who beat up some people in the street and shot others, were men who had gone through training that was predominantly religious: they met in mosques; studied textbooks written by Ayatollah Motahari; and were lectured by teachers appointed by Ayatollah Khamenei's office. The rape and torture of protestors and the show trials where people like Maziar Bahari made confessions on the threat of death happened in a judicial system presided over by the Islamic cleric Ayatollah Sadeq Larijani.

Before the summer of 2009 the spiritual legitimacy of the Islamic Republic was wounded. By the autumn it was infected. While the deceit of the rigging of the election angered, it was the violence that poisoned Iran's religion:[215] the murder of Neda Agha-Soltan and others by Basiji gunmen, the rapes of Maryam Sabri and others by Basiji prison guards, the deaths of Mohsen Ruholami and others due to Basiji torturers.

While being raped by two Basijis on 21 June 2009 "Ardeshir" asked himself an obvious question: "All I could think of was...

214   http://www.voanews.com/content/iranian-cleric-calls-for-more-executions-83044532/111811.html Accessed 17 December 2013
215   "Iranians began to ask how a regime that claimed divine sanction could be so brutal" was Scott Peterson's conclusion (who was there during the elections). See Peterson, p. 560.

why these people who claim to be the most religious in our society can do such things."

When he was released, Ardeshir's question became sharper. He was told, "Everything that has happened has been *religiously* sanctioned by the Leader" (author's italics).[216]

The conclusion of Ardeshir and hundreds of thousands of other Iranians who have seen so much from the Basiji is to reject their religion. It is impossible for Ardeshir to connect the idea of the Basiji's faith with God. Their brazen brutality has been too much.

This is the background, painted in the previous three chapters, on which the new Iranian church is growing. It is not difficult to see how the impact of Ayatollah Khomeini in particular and that of the former President Ahmadinejad soured the feelings of these Christians towards the religion of their birth.

However, before moving on to look more closely at the house-church movement in Iran, there is another part of the background that needs some explanation. It is this: the attraction Iranians have to Jesus Christ.

---

216   See Peterson, p. 566.

CHAPTER 5

WHY IRANIANS ARE ATTRACTED TO JESUS CHRIST

The Ahmadinejad years weakened Islam's legitimacy in Iran. But why the attraction to Christianity in particular, especially given its associations?[217]

There are the mysteries of God's sovereignty and intercession – in recent years there has been much prayer for Iran.[218] However, there also seems to be something in the make-up of the Iranian character so that, when there is a decision to walk away from the religion of their birth, Christianity has a peculiar pull.

Ask an Iranian why they are attracted to Christianity and the answer is often very simple: Jesus Christ. Speaking with Iranian Muslims who have been Christians for over twenty-five years it is impossible for this author not to conclude that Iranians have an instinctive love for Jesus Christ.

According to Islam, Jesus' role is only that of a prophet, though nevertheless a special prophet. It is the number of references in the Koran makes Him special: out of 114 chapters, fifteen of them make references to Jesus. So from the Koran the faithful Shia Muslim learns about Jesus' birth, miracles,

217 See Chapter 1.
218 Both Iran's politicians and its church have been in the headlines, thus prompting Christians to get on their knees and pray. In 2006 Elam Ministries launched a forty-day campaign for intercession for Iran. This went around the world. Then in 2009 the agency produced the prayer guide, *Iran 30*. To date there are over 200,000 in print in five languages. Other prayer agencies have also been active.

mission, and even his death.[219] Perhaps more significant are the associations that Jesus brings to mind, not just in the Koran, but also in the Hadiths (the traditions ascribed to Mohammad) and the Islamic religious literature. Respected academic Professor Tarif Khalidi,[220] translator of the Koran and author of several titles on Islam, sums up the special image Jesus has within this Islamic context in this way:

> He (Jesus) is a miracle of God, an *Aya*. He is the prophet
> of peace. He is… a word and a spirit of God… Now if one
> adds to this the other images that he projects in the Islamic
> literary tradition[221] – the ascetic, the prophet of the heart,
> the gentle teacher of manners, the mystic, the lord of nature,
> the healer of spiritual ills – one arrives at a description
> of him, which in a sense complements that of the Four
> Gospels.[222]

Numbed by the violence of the Islamic Republic it is perhaps not surprising that Iranians from within their own Islamic context tend to first turn towards Jesus. For according to Professor Khalidi, it was Jesus who left a legacy of "gentleness, compassion, and humility",[223] so that "in his Muslim habitat, Jesus became an object of intense devotion, reverence, and love".

This image of the loving spiritual mystic and healer has been reinforced by some of Iran's great poets, such as Ferdowsi (940–1020), author of Iran's national epic the *Shahnameh* ("The Book of Kings"); or the mystic Rumi (1207–73) who is known

---

219   Sara Afshari, "An Examination of the Growth of Christianity", p. 17, footnote 30.
220   In 1996 Professor Tarif Khalidi was appointed a Fellows at King's College, Cambridge; he currently holds the Sheikh Zayed Chair in Islamic and Arabic Studies at the American University of Beirut in Lebanon.
221   In *The Muslim Jesus* Tarif Khalidi gives a detailed account of statements about Jesus in Islamic literature from the eighth to eighteenth century.
222   http://www.jerusalemquarterly.org/images/ArticlesPdf/15_gospel.pdf Accessed 13 May 2014.
223   Khalidi, p. 15.

to many simply as "The Master"; or Ali Khaghani (1121–90) whose mother was Christian; or Hafiz (1207–73) from Shiraz, probably the country's most famous and popular lyricist.

These poets all refer to Jesus in words that portray Him as more than an average prophet.

So Ferdowsi refers to Christ as the one who brings back the dead:

> *Like Jesus whose voice called the dead back to life,*
> *I've wakened dead heroes of struggle and strife.*

Rumi presents Jesus as the friend of the afflicted:

> *The house of 'Isa [Jesus] was the banquet of men of heart*
> *O afflicted one, quit not this door.*

And Hafiz tells his readers that to be like light, they must follow Christ:

> *If thou like Christ, be pure and single-hearted*
> *Who once ascended far beyond the sky,*
> *Thy life will shine with beams of light, whereby*
> *The sun will brighten by thy light imparted.*

It is interesting that one cannot find in the writings of these poets similar references to other religious leaders.

It should be stressed that the reputation of these artists is truly massive in Iran. Their poetry is often quoted and their shrines are visited frequently. Indeed, they, and other famous Iranian poets,[224] exercise a huge influence over Iranian culture. Their poetry amounts to what is an alternative canon of Scripture.

---

224 Other famous poets include: Ghazali (1059–1111), Attar (1130–1221), Khayyam (1048–1131), and Saadi (1210–91). Modern writers would include: Ahmad Shamlou (1925–2000), Sohrab Sepehri (1928–80), Mehdi Saless (1928–91), and Forough Farrokhzad (1935–67).

Like Scripture, Persian poetry is memorized,[225] quoted in conversation to make a point, consulted (randomly) to predict the future,[226] and during the Persian New Year (No Ruz) many families will place not a copy of the Koran or a Bible on the special table they prepare to welcome in the spring, but instead use a copy of their favourite poet, usually Hafiz. This reverence for poetry was clearly seen in 2000 when Ahmad Shamlou died. Thousands crammed into Tehran's streets to watch his hearse pass, many wishing him a final farewell by quoting his poetry.[227]

Hence for Jesus to be treated with such esteem by Iran's greatest poets means that nearly every Iranian will also share this admiration. Disillusioned with their own religious leaders, it provides a motivation, arising from within their own culture, for an Iranian to want to learn more about the founder of Christianity.

And once the Iranian begins to explore Christianity, the landscape is not so alien. This is because, ironically, Iran's Shia Islam religion is full of connections to Christianity.[228] The emotional hero for Shias is Hussein, the Prophet's grandson, whom Iranians believe deliberately chose to be martyred for a righteous cause at the battle of Karbala. Every year in a ceremony

225   The author once spent an evening in Iran with four young people who were playing a word game. Divided into two teams, one team quoted a line of a poem, and then the other had to start another line of another poem using the last word of the line their opponents had just quoted. The team who was unable to say the next line lost. You can tell just how central poetry is to Iranian culture by the fact that this game went on for about two hours!

226   Hafiz is the poet of choice. In Iran it is possible to buy a card with a line of his poetry on it from a street vendor for as little as $1. For more excitement there is usually a little bird who will pick out the prophecy. For pilgrims to Hafiz's shrine in Shiraz, having an expert pick out a verse and interpret the meaning is an important part of the visit.

227   http://iranian.com/Features/2000/August/Funeral/index.html Accessed 12 September 2014

228   For a fuller discussion of the connections between the Shia faith and Christianity see Anthony O'Mahoney's 2006 "Catholic–Shia Dialogue: A Christian–Muslim Engagement" here: http://www.theologicalstudies.org.uk/pdf/anvil/23-2_omahony.pdf Accessed 13 May 2014.

known as "Ashura" his violent death is commemorated in street theatre performed in thousands of towns across Iran. It is watched by millions; Hussein's death annually stamped on people's mind. But the Shia story does not end in death. A descendant of Hussein, Mahdi, disappeared in the ninth century. He is now the hidden Imam, alive but unseen, ready – as Ahmadinejad constantly reminded everyone (see Chapter 3) – to give guidance to the faithful. Mahdi is not just alive, he is coming back to restore justice. And the first case of injustice he will deal with is the murder of his ancestor Hussein on the dusty plains of Karbala.

It is not difficult to see how close the Shia story is to the Christian story.[229] Just some adaption is needed. Jesus is the one who truly suffered for righteousness, not Hussein; Jesus, not Mahdi, is the one who is alive but unseen; and Jesus, not Mahdi, will come back to restore justice to the world.

These connections between Shia Islam and Christianity then become more significant in Iran – in contrast to other regions like Lebanon where there are many Shias – because of the influence of Sufism,[230] the mystical side of Islam, and poetry.

Sufism has had a powerful role in shaping the religious identity of Iranians. In Sufism emphasis is placed on experiencing God. Theologically Christianity and Sufism have different foundations. Sufism, rooted in Islam, rejects the divinity of Christ and the cross. And in contrast to the biblical view, there is an emphasis on the existence of a "universal

---

229 For a lucid and comprehensive discussion on this see James A. Bill and John Alden Williams, *Roman Catholics and Shi'i Muslims*. As well as looking at the common theme of redemptive suffering, links are also seen between the treatment of Mary and Fatimeh, the mystics of the two faiths, the attitude to law, and more. Also see the author's *Iran and Christianity*, Chapter 1.

230 Early ascetic Sufis would wear simple woollen garments. The Arabic word for wool is *suf*.

spirit" whereby the "many is one, and the one is many".[231] Then there is the question of whether, when practised, Sufism and its teaching on entering a trance-like state can open doors to the occult.[232] Hence it would be naive to think of Sufism as a friend of Christianity. It is not. It is mystical Islam.

However, most Iranians do not experience Sufism in its religious setting, but in its literary setting. Some of Iran's most famous poets were Sufis: Ghazzali (1059–1111); Attar (1130–1221); Rumi (1207–73); and above all Hafiz (1310–89). And, as seen above, these poets have an extraordinary influence in Iran. The overall impact of Iran's Sufi-coloured poetry is to soften the sharp barbed wire boundaries between Islamic orthodoxy and heresy. This happens in two ways. First of all Iran's poetry deals with universal themes: love, life, death, God. Indeed there is not a single poet in Iran's hall of literary fame that engages specifically with Islam. Second, the poets – especially the Sufi ones – are hostile to religious dogma. It is well known that at Rumi's funeral the coffin was carried by Muslims, Christians, and Jews in recognition that this poet – "The Master" – insisted that all religions led to God. Furthermore he and other Sufis were adamant that dogma must be jettisoned if it prevented an experience of God. So Rumi famously wrote,

If the image of our Beloved is in the heathen temple
Then it is a flagrant error to walk around the Ka'ba.[233]

This radical approach is taken up later by Hafiz:

---

231   See Nader Ahmadi and Fereshteh Ahmadi, *Iranian Islam*, pp. 73–87. They use this phrase in their conclusion.
232   For a full discussion on the practice of Sufism and its impact on mullahs see Roy Mottahadeh's *The Mantle of The Prophet.*
233   The Ka'ba is a large black stone in Mecca which Muslims believe fell from heaven. On the pilgrimage, (hajj) Muslims must go round the Ka'ba several times.

**Dye your prayer mat in wine
If the teacher commands it.**

Poetry is everywhere in Iran. It is a part of people's identity. Iranians do not define themselves solely as belonging to a certain religion. They also see themselves as a part of this poetical tradition that leads them out onto a much more universal and enigmatic landscape where tolerance is more natural than dogma.

The same landscape is opened up by cinema, Iran's other creative passion. Usually the most popular films are the comedies and the action films; however, Iran has a strong tradition for making artistic films and directors such as Abbas Kiarostami, Mohsen Makhmalbaf, and Jafar Panahi are household names. As with poetry, so with films: the landscape is universal, its boundaries enigmatic, and there is no overt engagement with Islam.

Before the days when Iran's relationship with its religion had been sorely bruised, this mystic and artistic aspect of the national character played no part in prising Iranians away from Shia Islam. Indeed, as seen, both the mosque and the poets belonged to the same landscape. An Iranian felt free to walk into the broader and more mysterious land of the poets, but always in the background was the mosque: secure, certain, and easy to return to.

Now that return to the dogmas of the mosque is not so easy for some Iranians. This does not mean that Sufism or Persian poetry and art has suddenly become anti-Islamic. They cast the same shapes over the Iranian landscape as they have always done. What has changed is that some Iranians have become deeply disillusioned with religion. Iran's poetry led them away from the mosque; and now their disillusionment with Shia Islam keeps them walking.

To then argue that these Iranians are going to immediately enter a church is fanciful. They are breathing Rumi's tolerant air where all religions lead to God, so it is unlikely they would want to tie their souls to another dogmatic creed.

However, they might well be more open to considering Christ for at least two reasons. First, as said, there is the honour Jesus is accorded by Iran's poets, and the Sufi poets stress the importance of experiencing God. That is the emphasis of all true Christian preaching: come to Christ, and experience God. And so, for at least the last thirty years, Iranians in Christian meetings all over the world have been coming forward at the end of the sermon, not because they want to discuss theology, but because they want to experience God. It might well be that they have been prepared to make that step by the call of the Sufi poets they learned about in their formative years.

Nationalism is another part of an Iranian's identity that gives them confidence to consider Christ. Unlike Muslim nations such as Saudi Arabia or Pakistan, Iran has a strong non-Islamic identity. Long before the religion of Mohammad existed, Iranians were ruling the greatest empire the world had ever seen. The names of their kings, such as Cyrus and Darius, were respected throughout the world, and honoured in the Bible for their treatment of the Jews.

For thirty years the Islamic Republic has been trying to delete the memory of Iran's empire and monarchy from the national psyche, presenting Iran as solely an Islamic nation. Their task has proved impossible. Iran's royal road is 5,000 years too long to be photoshopped out of history. The ruins of the glorious royal palace of Persepolis still stands; sons are given the names of monarchs; and Iran's most important festival originated in the times of the kings. This is "No Ruz" and the celebrations around 21 March welcome in the New Year. Before this holiday there will be intense spring cleaning and a lot of cooking, especially of sweets; families will set up a "Haft Sin" table with items on it that begin with the Persian equivalent to the letter "S" and represent some aspect of spring and new life; a week before the New Year Iranians will jump through a fire saying, "You take my weakness; I take your strength"; and on the day or night, before the actual hour strikes, the streets will be empty as families gather to greet one another and give *eidi* (money gifts) to the children. Then Iran shuts down for a week as families and friends visit each other.

No Ruz is by far the most important festival in the Iranian year and it has nothing to do with the Shia religion. Every year every Iranian becomes a part of a tradition that tells them there is much more to being an Iranian than just being a Shia Muslim. And it is this perspective that then gives them more confidence to consider Christ. While a part of some of them in an almost tribal way will want to cling to the faith of their birth – "I am Iranian, therefore I am Shia" – there is another part that says, "I am Iranian, and belong to an ancient civilization. I do not have to be a Shia. I can be a Christian."

This dual identity for Iranians (Islamic, non-Islamic) has been active for centuries and has had no significant impact on people's religious faith. As Shia Islam and Persian poetry worked together so too did this Islamic and non-Islamic identity. Now, however, the non–Islamic identity has become important, not because it has increased in any way, but because of the bruised relationship many Iranians have with Shia Islam. It is this disillusionment that activates the significance of an Iranian's non-Islamic identity enabling them to consider the claims of Christ.

There is a final aspect of an Iranian's identity that makes them more open to Christ. It is what Iran historian Michael Axworthy calls their "ease with complexity" due to all the different cultural strands in their history, and their geography, bordered as they are by Arabs, Russians, and the sub-continent.

This so-called "ease with complexity" means that the signed-up members of the Islamic Republic can also be admirers of the West for its achievements. Politicians must chant "Death To America" to shore up the story that Iran is under attack from the West which justifies their authoritarianism. But in private those politicians themselves, and certainly the majority of Iranians, are happy to acknowledge the achievements of the West, and especially America.

As Middle East specialist Scott Peterson writes about Iran, "hidden behind the mullah's mask is the most unashamedly pro-American population in the Middle East." The respected *Smithsonian* magazine agrees: "The paradox of Iran is that it just might be the most pro-American – or, perhaps, least anti-American – populace in the Middle East." After the September 11 attacks on New York this sympathy for America was on full display. Thousands of Iranians spontaneously poured out onto the streets to hold candlelit vigils; on 15 September 60,000 gathered in Tehran's football stadium to pay their respects to the victims.

It is not difficult to see why Iranians in private are at ease with America – and Americans. The two have more in common than one might think. Most Americans are friendly and outgoing; so are Iranians. Americans like big, big houses, big cars, big meals – so do Iranians. Americans have a certain confidence because they know they come from a great country; so do Iranians, for the same reason.

There is more. Money is not a dirty word for Iranians; they like being rich. So they admire the American dream of the penniless immigrant arriving in New York and ending up in a Cadillac. And unlike most Arab countries, where a rigid class system prevails, Iranians, like Americans, are ready to support the outsider who can give the establishment a bloody nose. So, though it was a disaster, they gave their vote to Mahmoud Ahmadinejad, the son of a blacksmith.

There is still more. Unlike the Taliban and Al Qaeda, whose passions are partially fuelled by a blanket hatred of all that is modern, Iranians are devotees of all things new, especially technology. And they recognize that the pioneers are largely from the West, usually America.

There is one other reason why Iranians admire the West: freedom within the rule of law. In recent years Iran has suffered a haemorrhage of its cleverest people. According to the International Monetary Fund some 25 per cent of Iranians with post-secondary education have emigrated abroad.[234] Some are motivated by financial security, but many more dream of a new life not because their standard of living will dramatically improve – often it won't – but because they want freedom and legal protection. It is worth noting to which countries these emigrants go. It is usually America, Canada, or Australia; clear evidence that the admiration Iranians have for the West is not just sentiment. They are willing to vote with their feet.[235]

This respect for the West has an impact on an Iranian's view of Christianity because Iranians tend to see Western countries as being Christian. While the reality is obviously more complex, there is a subconscious connection between the strengths of the West – opportunity to create wealth, technological innovation, social freedom, the rule of law – and Christian values. There is no evidence that this has had any direct impact on Iranians becoming Christians, but it is not difficult to see how, when an Iranian starts to consider other faiths, this connection presents the Christian faith in a favourable light.[236]

234   http://www.al-monitor.com/pulse/originals/2014/01/iran-economy-diaspora-reconciliation-sustainable-progress.html Accessed 1 April 2014.
235   Certainly the devout are concerned about the West's immorality; however, the desire for the rule of law and freedom supersedes these concerns for many. Some Iranian refugees have no choice in where they are sent by the UNHCR (United Nations High Commissioner for Refugees), but most are more than ready to go to one of these countries.
236   There are hardly any examples of Iranians becoming Hindus. Apart from the alien nature of this faith to Islam compared to Christianity, India's caste system and ongoing poverty issues might not appear that attractive.

The brutality of the Ahmadinejad years was the breaking point for many Iranians regarding their relationship with Shia Islam. This chapter has outlined why Iranians are then especially attracted to Christianity: love for the merciful Jesus presented in Islam and their honoured poets; connections between the Christian faith and Shia Islam along with the influence of Sufism; the powerful non-Iranian identity; and finally, despite all the flag burning, respect for the West.

In this equation of disillusionment with Islam and attraction to Christianity women feature prominently. Even a casual observer of Iran's new Christians will notice that there are probably more women than men in the house-church meetings. Footage of one meeting filmed secretly showed there were about fifteen women and just two men. One senior church leader bluntly states that 70 per cent of those coming to faith are women.

This is not surprising. Women have many reasons to spurn the religion of their birth. At every turn the law of the Islamic Republic devalues them. In the law courts their word is worth half that of a man's; in marriage the man can marry up to four wives and have as many temporary ones as he can afford; in divorce the husband is given the custody of the children. In some families manliness is proven by exercising strict control over the female members. The author knows of one husband who, before he became a Christian, would not let his wife have a glass of water without his permission. Control was sometimes enforced by violence.

In other families reputation takes precedence. So, for example, from the age of seven to twelve Mahnaz was repeatedly raped by her cousin. When she eventually mustered up the courage to tell her parents, she was told to keep quiet to protect the honour of her cousin. Legally devalued by their government and sometimes demeaned, or worse, by their family situations, the prospect of becoming a Christian has much to offer: women are of equal value; polygamy is condemned; and the constant example of Jesus Christ – unlike rival religious leaders – was to show respect towards women.

Walking away from the splintered reputation of their national religion, often pushed by tragic events in their personal lives, many Iranians are ready to consider Jesus Christ.

But how does an Iranian Muslim – man or woman – make that journey from being sympathetic towards Jesus Christ to becoming a committed Christian, active in a house church?

That is the question the next chapter will attempt to answer.

CHAPTER 6

HOUSE CHURCHES: FIVE STORIES

For well over ten years there has been talk in Christian circles about what people called the house churches in Iran. It was well known that the Anglicans, Presbyterians, and Assemblies of God churches whose ministry was based in buildings (so sometimes known as "building churches") were facing immense pressure from the government; but, it was said, there was growth among the "house churches".

So Professor Richard Foltz, an expert on Iran's religions, writes: "No new churches have been issued operating licences since the revolution of 1979, but an estimated 40,000 people attend underground churches and estimates of recent converts reach as high as 500,000."

This is the professor's last sentence at the end of a chapter on Christianity in his book *Religions of Iran*.[237] This sort of sentence, and others that appear in articles about Christianity in Iran, invite a lot of questions. The phrases "house church" or "underground church" tell us a little: these are groups of Christians meeting in homes, unbeknown to the government. The curious will have other questions. How did these groups start meeting? How many come to the meetings? What happens at these gatherings? What does the leadership structure look like? How are activities financed? And how are people, disillusioned with Islam and sympathetic to Jesus, drawn into these groups?

237   Richard Foltz, *Religions of Iran*, Oneworld, 2013, p. 124.

A good way to answer these questions and draw a picture of what is meant by the house-church movement is to listen to the stories of Christians who have started, and looked after, house churches. This is what the author did, by interviewing several such leaders. It is then possible to see if there are any common characteristics that warrant some general conclusions about Iran's house church movement. These are just five stories. There are many others.

Each of these five stories is very different. In size some of the churches number less than a hundred; others are much bigger.[238] The leaders have very different backgrounds. Organizational structures vary.

One of the reasons for choosing such diverse groups is to underline that every church group has its own unique story, and so wears the title "house church" very loosely. It is not really possible to talk about a homogeneous movement as if all these churches are the same.

Yet there are connections and similarities that link not just these groups together in Iran, but also show that while the members of these churches are new Christians, they are nevertheless also very much a part of the orthodox and historic body of Christ.

1. Arthur John's story

Arthur John is an experienced older Iranian churchman. He had an encounter with Jesus Christ as a boy and has been a faithful preacher and pastor for many years. He has shared the joys – and all the suffering – of Iran's church. As the hostility of the Islamic Republic towards the church increased, so Arthur's conviction grew that the future of Christianity in Iran was in house churches; Christianity in buildings was dangerous for Muslims, and limiting. The church had no option but to go to people's homes.

238   I have specific figures, but citing big numbers can attract unwelcome attention.

Starting in the late 1990s, Arthur set about constructing a completely new church system. He initially chose about forty potential leaders – both men and women – to train as church planters. It was stressed right from the start that their work was to have absolutely no connection with any established church. There was theological study and there was a lot of personal evangelism. The trainees would wrap up Gospels of Luke and the Jesus film as presents and then go out, usually to shops, chat with the owners, and at the end offer their gift.

Arthur experienced tremendous openness. Often when people realized they had been given a Gospel they would immediately have questions, and so a meeting would be arranged. Through this personal evangelism people came to faith. Looking back at that time Arthur says, "Of ten people witnessed to, six or seven were ready to receive Christ."

Arthur was under no illusions about the severity of the hostility of the government toward Christianity, and especially toward the sort of church he was now attempting to build. He was – and is – extremely cautious. Before each house group began Arthur insisted the students spend a lot of time individually with new believers teaching them discipleship: how to have a quiet time; how to pray; how to witness; basic doctrine. There had to be a deep peace that the new believer's faith was real. Then when the student had five genuine "disciples", there was first discussion with Arthur. Only then was a house church started, if possible in one of the new believers' homes.

At the meeting the student leader would teach the new believers some worship songs. The singing would usually be very quiet, and would not last very long.

Then there was an opportunity for everyone to pray. This was followed by a time of sharing. The new believers would be encouraged to tell the others in the group either about how God had worked in their lives, or a blessing they had received from the Scriptures. Hence, right from the start, the believers were expected to contribute spiritually to the meeting. Then the leader gave a Bible study, so again people were being asked questions and were involved. For the first few meetings the student leaders were free to choose a topic, but then Arthur asked all the groups to study a Gospel. He wanted the foundation of these new churches to be the life of Christ.

In all the meetings there was also a strong emphasis on the importance of witnessing. New members were encouraged to share the Gospel with their families and close friends. Soon the leaders were hearing that a brother or an uncle or a sister-in-law had come to faith and wanted to be visited, or discipled, or become members of the new house church. For security reasons the groups were kept quite small, and the leader would be encouraged to start a second group, rather than run the risk of having too many coming to one home.

This is how Arthur's groups have grown. Once the first church had started, they not only multiplied themselves, but also the leaders – again men and women – came from within the groups. Now there are far too many house churches for the original students to look after, so, right from the start, Arthur asked those leaders to look out for new members who could be mentored and later called into ministry. This has happened very successfully. Now most of the leaders Arthur works with have come from within the movement. They became Christians through the house churches, and they have been trained only to look after house churches. Hardly any of them would have ever stepped into a "building" church. Yet they are deacons, ministers, elders, and supervisors serving many Christians throughout Iran.

And Arthur has brought his considerable administrative experience to these new groups. As with established denominations his churches have a constitution. For security reasons this is not written down anywhere, but leaders and members are made aware of its salient points. The groups are self-governing, and they have a clear code of discipline, similar to the established churches. The norm, though, has been for members who fall into sin to then stop coming, so there is no need for any formal church discipline.[239] So while Arthur and other leaders set the general framework, at a local level the groups are self-governing. The local groups are also self-financing.

Regarding the sacraments, Arthur has been very practical. From his many years of experience of being a Christian in the Islamic Republic he knows that baptism completely changes the way a security official views a Christian from a Muslim background. Aware that these baptised new Christians always ran a higher risk of arrest and interrogation, Arthur has made the decision that it is better to put off baptism[240] until a safer time, rather than endanger not just the individual Christians who might find themselves being questioned, but others as well.

For their own reasons the authorities do not have the same sort of hostility towards Holy Communion. So, usually after about a year, when he is sure that the group is solid, Arthur gives permission for the leader to celebrate Holy Communion. The house churches share the Eucharist once a month.

Arthur's determined effort to keep his groups operating below the radar of the government's enmity to Christianity has generally been successful. Relative to the numbers of house churches, there have been few incidents. But there have been some. In one city about thirty of these house church Christians endured arbitrary arrest and interrogation. Some have had to leave Iran. Some were given prison sentences. Suffering has also been a part of the story of these new Christians.

---

239   If later they repent then, probably with consultation with other leaders, they are welcomed back.

240   Unsurprisingly, not all Iranian Christian leaders agree with this approach.

2. Daniel Alexander's – and Fatimeh's – story

Daniel Alexander is also a seasoned churchman. He too gave his heart to Christ as a boy and he too has served His Saviour faithfully and passionately for many years. He has also shared the joys of Iran's churches – and keenly felt the pain of the suffering.

In the early 2000s Daniel and his friends became convinced that the main arena for growing Christianity in Iran was no longer in church buildings, but in people's homes. In their minds not only were homes safer, but also they felt that a home church was more biblical. Jesus ministered in homes; and in Acts and in the Epistles we only come across churches in people's homes.

So, like Arthur, Daniel and his team set about training church planters who would operate completely separately from the established churches. This happened, and the church planters got to work. With a strong emphasis on evangelism, their churches grew rapidly: by 2006 they had between 600 and 700 new Christians meeting in house churches in eight different cities across Iran. Usually a group would consist of family and close friends. The meetings often had the feel of what Iranians call a *Mehmooni*, for which "supper party" is the best English equivalent. The meetings would start with worship songs, usually unaccompanied; members were encouraged to share how God had been working in their lives; and then there was a proper message, always given by someone who had received some training. Then there would be ministry, and most of the groups tended to have a charismatic flavour. This was followed by fellowship and eating. During this time a lot more ministry would happen in private conversations. Unlike Arthur's groups these fellowships would baptize new believers when possible.

To get a better picture of how these house churches grew, we look at the story of Fatimeh in detail.

Fatimeh's house churches

Fatimeh's first house church was her own family: the change that happened in her life after the visit of her Christian aunt so impressed her parents and siblings that they too became Christians. The family began meeting together to worship, and then Fatimeh engaged in studying and training with others involved with Daniel's group.

Eventually about another 100 people would come to trace their spiritual origin to this family church. Fatimeh's mother had a friend, a lively noisy and colourful character called Simin, from another city who was an opium addict. Fatimeh's mother invited her to come and stay with the family to come off the white drug. Simin came and for twenty days Fatimeh's family prayed and cared for her. Then she was freed from her addiction. Then, just like the Samaritan woman in John 4, Simin wanted to go back to her own city to share the good news about Jesus.

This she did and a few people from one large family came to faith through her witness. When Fatimeh had finished her studies with Daniel Simin called on her for help, so Fatimeh went to spend time with the believers in Simin's city. Soon the few had become many with most of the new believers coming from this one large family. By 2010 there were about 100 believers in this fellowship. Sadly this fellowship was smashed when the persecution was unleashed towards the end of that year, but now it is re-grouping and again Fatimeh is looked to as its leader.

Due to the arrests of 2011 Fatimeh is very security-conscious. The meetings are held on different days and at different times, and nobody is allowed to use their mobile as it is possible that the signal could get picked up by the police. The group will meet in someone's home and, right from the start of the service, the bread and the wine (fruit juice) is placed on a table in the centre of the living room. On the same table the church members place their written prayer requests.

Unlike other groups the service does not begin with worship, but with testimonies. Fatimeh states bluntly that a church where the members do not have a fresh story about what God is doing in their lives is a dead church. As well as testimonies, the members are asked to share a blessing they have received from their Bible reading.

This time of sharing is then followed by singing, led by someone who has been asked to prepare the songs. There is no guitar, or laptop. The members just sing. And at some point during this worship, Holy Communion is taken. This happens every week and with Daniel's blessing. After the sharing of Holy Communion there is a time of intercession – for both the requests that have been put on the table, and for wider concerns.

For the Bible teaching, Fatimeh is the preacher. Often she will use material she looked at when she was engaged in her intensive studying; she particularly likes to teach through Acts because of the references to speaking in tongues. New members will naturally ask about this, so then Fatimeh asks them to seek God for the gift that week and at the next meeting she will pray for them. Many have received the gift. Also in her teaching Fatimeh urges her members to memorize Scripture verses as these Christians could well be arrested and put in prison. If that happens Fatimeh wants them to have the encouragement of the Bible in their hearts.

In this group there is a great emphasis on personal evangelism among family and friends. Indeed Fatimeh says that according to the evangelistic paradigm set out in Acts 1:8, "… and you will be my witnesses in Jerusalem and in all Judea and Samaria, and to the end of the earth" (ESV), Jerusalem is the believer's family. This is where all the evangelistic effort should first go. And, Fatimeh stresses, it is usually the safest place.

Regarding organization the group is very collegiate, as is Fatimeh's relationship with Daniel and other leaders. Her groups discuss everything together, and if there are two views on a matter a vote is taken. For example, one of the groups discussed whether the church should reach out to strangers with street evangelism. Some were keen as this was the duty of the church; others were concerned about security and the general effectiveness of contacting strangers. The vote was taken and the majority view was not to do street evangelism, and this decision was respected. And as with the other groups, most of the funds needed for these churches come from the tithe.

Fatimeh has also known suffering. She has faced arrest, interrogation, and imprisonment. Others from Daniel's churches have also endured arbitrary arrest and been given custodial sentences. But the ministry has not withered away. Leaders like Fatimeh remain passionate about spreading the Gospel, not least because they see how open Iranians are. So, despite the cold wind of persecution, Daniel's churches continue to grow.

3. Mojtaba and Shireen's story

Unlike Arthur and Daniel, Mojtaba knew nothing about Christianity as a boy. He was from a devout Muslim family, and if someone told him that he would one day be leading a fellowship of house churches of about 600 members he would have thought them completely mad.

As a teenager Mojtaba had been an ardent supporter of Ayatollah Khomeini's revolution. He was steeped in Islam but there was emptiness in his heart. There was no sense of God. Troubled by this Mojtaba visited Qom, the intellectual heart of Iran's Shia Islam. Here he spent time talking to religious leaders, but he returned home restless.

With courage, given his work situation, he visited a church one Sunday morning in his city, a "building" church, and talked to Christians there. He was not impressed. He left the church full of frustration: it seemed God could not be found either in Islam or Christianity.

He now took his frustration directly to God: "I know you exist," he complained, "but you do not show yourself to me."

Half an hour after praying a "fire" (Mojtaba's word) started in his heart and he felt God saying, "Give your life to me; believe in me" Mojtaba was confused. He already believed in God.

Then the same voice said, "Believe in the cross." And in an instant Mojtaba understood the meaning of Christ's cross.

"I understood in that second what the Son of God meant and why He came to the cross. Because Jesus went to the cross all the brokenness and problems went to the cross too. When I looked, a joy started in my heart. When I asked what about my religion, a depression came. When I looked to Christ, joy came."

The voice had one final sentence for Mojtaba: "Believe in me, you'll see what I will do with you."

That same evening Mojtaba returned to the church and became a Christian. He knew the exact time of his conversion. "[I knew] it was six o'clock because there was an old clock on the wall of the church."

The next day Mojtaba felt he could reach out and touch God. There was a tremendous joy in his heart. His family, though, were not joyful. They declared that Mojtaba was *najes* ("unclean"). He was put in a separate room, and his mother gave him his food with specially coloured plates and cutlery, to protect the rest of the family. Every day they asked him to return to Islam.

Mojtaba remained a Christian. He learned how to pray by himself, whispering in an audible voice under his bedclothes. He bravely joined his city's Christians when they shared the Gospel. And his behaviour changed, and this won over his family. After two years his mother threw away the specially marked plates and cutlery. The domestic apartheid ended.

Mojtaba's first house church

In 1990 there were three important events in Mojtaba's life. First, he was arrested and questioned about his Christian life and activities. This was to become a common occurrence. Second, three weeks after being released, he married Shireen, a young Muslim lady who had become a Christian in a church in a nearby city. Her pastor, a friend of Mojtaba's, helped bring the two together. Third, the church in his own city closed down due to government pressure.

Although the church was closed there was a sense in Mojtaba's heart that he should do something. Others also encouraged him. He began to do what he had already learned to do – he visited old friends and shared the Gospel with them. After three weeks three of them became Christians. Around the same time Mojtaba visited three old members of the church, a couple and the wife of the couple's mother, and encouraged them through prayer.

So, Mojtaba's first house church came into being. He invited his three newly converted Muslim friends and the Christian family to his house for a meeting. They sang songs, his wife Shireen leading. Mojtaba preached for about twenty-five minutes on Jesus calming the storm and then the group of eight prayed together. At the end the group decided to meet the following week.

A house church had started.

In the autumn of 1990 Mojtaba and Shireen attended a conference for isolated Christian groups hosted by a church in Tehran. While they were there they met another group of Christians from their area, and so on their return his group was now twice as big – sixteen people – and they were able to meet in two homes. The format of the meeting stayed the same. Shireen led the group in worship; there was sharing, sometimes testimonies, and prayer.

In the spring of 1991 Mojtaba started getting help from a priest from the church in Tehran. Until then the group had not celebrated Holy Communion because Mojtaba felt unqualified to administer this sacrament. Once the priest came, the group started receiving Holy Communion. There were also baptisms. And on one visit the priest brought with him 2,000 evangelistic books and 2,000 videos of the film *Jesus*, based on the Gospel of Luke.

A lot of evangelism happened. Mojtaba's favourite method was to go to the owner of a film club with the *Jesus* film and say, "You can watch this privately, but I would not offer it to anyone else", knowing full well that the owner would then be spurred to copy and distribute the film. This is exactly what happened. The books too found their way into people's homes.

The witnessing bore fruit and after two years the group had grown from sixteen to fifty-two. A noticeable feature of these new Christians was that when one person repented, then the rest of the family would come to the meetings too, and also repent. As well as spending time visiting these new believers, Mojtaba also trained others so they could, in future, also lead worship and teach from the Bible.

This was Mojtaba's first house church. In 2001 Mojtaba and his family moved to Tehran, and for his safety Mojtaba decided to keep a distance from the area where he had once worked

Mojtaba's second house church

In Tehran Mojtaba started sharing his faith. Three people repented and he discipled them. Then one of his old members from his first church moved to Tehran, followed by the member's mother. So now there was a group of seven meeting in Mojtaba's home. Mojtaba's second house church had been born.

As with his first church, Mojtaba put a strong emphasis on evangelism. His small group of seven would work along one street in Tehran, then another, handing out the Gospel and the *Jesus* film, along with a brochure they had made. People started coming to faith and Mojtaba and Shireen would meet with them in their homes. After two years Mojtaba was looking

Map of Iran showing major cities and surrounding countries.

Christian satellite TV has a massive impact in Iran.

The New Testament is welcomed by Iranians.

A young woman is baptised in a bath.

Massive street protests against alleged rigging of presidential elections in June 2009. (Photo: Mehr News Agency/AFP/Getty Images)

Some of the hundreds of Iranian Christians arrested in 2010 and 2011.

Farshid Fathi, arrested in Tehran in December 2010 and sentenced to six years in Evin Prison for his faith. He remains there at the time of writing.

after nearly fifty new Iranian Christians who were meeting in three separate homes. Each group would meet three times a week: once for prayer, once for teaching, and once for worship. Mojtaba went to every meeting. As well as being a pastor for these new house church Christians, Mojtaba also gave a lot of time to discipling seven potential new leaders. He took this group with him for witnessing, for teaching, and visiting. This was on-the-job training.

But Mojtaba's second church came to an abrupt end[241] in the autumn of 2004, after three years.

Mojtaba's third house church

One evening Mojtaba and Shireen were returning to their home in Tehran and they found three women and one man sitting in the street outside their home. They were members from their second church. They told Mojtaba that they wanted him to be their pastor.

Mojtaba's third house church was born. It is this church that now has nearly 600 members.

The foundation for this church was laid with intercession and witnessing. For three months the small group interceded for their city and country. Then they started witnessing, mainly to family and friends. And so the groups started. Mojtaba said he would call them a church when the group reached ten members, and because people had friends and family in different cities so the churches spread to different cities. From his experience with his second group of house churches, Mojtaba would immediately start looking for someone reliable in the group to disciple to take over the leadership. He would travel with them and give them opportunities to share. He would only give them responsibility when he was sure they had been called by God to the ministry.[242]

---

241 It is not possible to say more for security reasons.
242 Throughout the author's interview with Mojtaba it was clear that quality in the lives of believers was his passion, not numbers.

The churches soon began to multiply. A particularly important year was 2005. In June Mahmoud Ahmadinejad was elected president, and afterwards the atmosphere for Christians grew distinctly colder. But for most of that year Mojtaba's group was very active. He appointed a leader for evangelism in every group and sent them out with books and copies of the *Jesus* film. Those who showed interest were first met in a park or other public place, and when there was certainty the person was genuine, they were brought into the group. This could take between one and six months. By the end of the year Mojtaba's fellowship that had started with four now had about ninety members, meeting in six different cities.

The format of the church meetings was similar to the services Mojtaba and Shireen had first hosted in their home back in 1990. The group would usually gather in the later afternoon or evening and first there would be singing and worship for about half an hour, followed by Bible teaching from the leader, and then there would be a time for questions and answers. And time for prayer. Most of the members had had a charismatic experience and spoke in tongues. There were also healings, and while there was not an obsessive interest in the dark side of things, exorcisms did happen.

Mojtaba and Shireen would try to get to many of the meetings. They would spend three days of their week attending meetings in Tehran, and then three days travelling to other cities to visit their groups. The only day without a church service for them was Saturday, but this was the day when either church members would visit Mojtaba and Shireen to ask any questions they might have about the Christian faith, or he would visit the different groups.

There were two strong emphases in the teaching that Mojtaba gave to his churches. One was for the believers to understand their new identity in Christ. The other was that every believer is a "co-worker" with Christ, thus every believer was expected to develop a ministry. Every believer had a calling on his or her life and Mojtaba wanted them to get out and test their ministries.

Mojtaba's views on the sacraments are conservative: it is not for every believer to celebrate Holy Communion, or baptize new believers. So he sought out a senior leader from another church and was prayed for with the laying on of hands. He then administered Holy Communion once a month for each church, and would baptize new believers.

Church discipline is also exercised. Mojtaba is particularly strict in two areas: sexual relations and gossip. If a member is engaged in a sexual relationship outside marriage, they are first asked to live a pure life. If they agree, then they are allowed to stay in the group. If they do not, then they are asked to leave. It is likewise with people who "gossip" or seek to disrupt the unity of the group. They are first warned, and then asked to leave if they continue to sow seeds of discord.

On finances there is a definite view that all the churches should be self-supporting, and this includes Mojtaba and Shireen's own ministry. So all the different groups are taught to tithe a tenth of their income, and these funds finance the church's activities. There is no dependency on any other Christians.

With this foundation of prayer and witnessing, and these emphases in church life, Mojtaba's fellowship continued to grow. By 2009 there were about 200; in 2011 there were 300 in nine different cities and towns. Eventually Mojtaba and Shireen had to leave Iran for the safety of their family. Mojtaba, who was arrested and beaten many times, had been willing to endure the suffering. However, when his family was threatened, he took the hard decision, and decided to go into exile.

However, because of the foundation and the effectiveness of the methods Mojtaba had established, his churches continue to grow, and now the fellowship is about 600-strong. Mojtaba and Shireen kept in touch through the internet, and the people he had trained stepped up to the new task of looking after the churches without Mojtaba and Shireen's physical presence.

Mojtaba's views on the sacraments had not changed and so for two years the groups would celebrate Holy Communion with him present on the telephone, though this obviously wasn't possible for baptisms. So he chose four of his main leaders and they were ordained and they themselves can now baptize and celebrate Holy Communion.

This is the story of Mojtaba and Shireen and their house churches – to date.

4. Fariborz's story

Fariborz is very different to Mojtaba. When Mojtaba was out in the streets shouting for Khomeini's revolution, Fariborz was not yet alive. Today, he is not yet thirty years old.

Mojtaba is a softly spoken man, easy to miss in a crowd. Fariborz is loud, full of energy, ideas, and opinions. He is not easy to miss. Mojtaba is a Persian-speaking Iranian; Fariborz also speaks fluent Persian, but his mother tongue is Azeri.[243]

Mojtaba, like most Iranians, served in the military. Their discipline left its mark on his character. Fariborz did not serve the normal two-year compulsory military service. Even though not doing this meant facing legal problems in the future, his involvement in politics and his father's business made him a reluctant recruit.

Two very different men, and the story of Fariborz's house-church fellowships is also very different. But there are some similarities.

---

243 Making up over 20% of Iran's population, the Azeris (or Azerbaijanis) are the country's largest ethnic group after the Persians. Their Turkic language is known as Azeri. As Persian is taught in Iran's schools, all Azeris are also fluent Persian speakers.

Fariborz becomes a Christian[244]

As a nineteen-year-old in 2007 Fariborz was a normal, hard-working young man wanting to make his mark on life. While his mother and sister's loyalty was with Shia Islam, his was to Azeri nationalism.[245] This is where his spare time and energy went, attending meetings, printing leaflets, and learning how to escape the eyes of the security forces. Then a close friend gave him a pocket New Testament which he started reading. In his mind he had constructed a clichéd paradigm for religion. There were many ways to God.

Then he read John 14:6: "I am the way, the truth, and the life; no one comes to the Father but by me" (RSV). The verse gripped his mind. He might think there were many ways to God, but that was not Jesus' view. The cliché about the many ways began to pale. He then read about the Holy Spirit in Acts and how God dealt directly with people. One night Fariborz uttered a simple prayer: "Jesus, if you are really the only way to God, please show me."

As soon as he prayed this prayer Fariborz's room filled with light and a strange warm strength came into his heart. Then, just as in the book of Acts, Fariborz felt a wind in his room. And he started praising God. Just like Mojtaba, Fariborz was having a supernatural encounter with God.

The next day he phoned his Christian friend and explained about what had happened. His friend was thrilled and told him to give his heart to Christ. But then Fariborz – always a more practically minded sort of person – began to doubt. About ten days later, tired of being pulled between doubt and faith, he prayed again, but this time he made a promise. He said, "Jesus, if you show yourself to me again, I will give my heart to you." Jesus did show himself again to Fariborz. Again he felt that

244 All of this section is based on an interview conducted by the author.
245 Azeri nationalism has been active in the north west of Iran, where most Azerbaijanis live, since the 1990s.

same power in his heart, and a literal heat in his hand. It was a physical experience. Fariborz phoned his friend who contacted a Christian satellite TV station. They then called Fariborz and led him to Christ.

While Fariborz received some help from his close friend, the main factor in his growth as a Christian was the internet. He was introduced to a Christian chat room and here he attended classes given by senior Iranian pastors in the West.[246] For a while Fariborz visited this chat room every day.

Fariborz starts house churches

Fariborz is a natural enthusiast. If he had become a Christian in a free country he would have been the type who would have always appeared at church services with a group of friends with him. There was no church in the town where he had become a Christian, so he witnessed to his friends – he had many – and invited them to his private office from where he ran his electrical security and website business.

For two months Fariborz met six of his friends there, all young Azeri men, which meant the meetings were not in Persian, but Azeri. Then, for business reasons, he had to shut the office. But Fariborz went on visiting his friends.

Through the internet, Fariborz found out about another young businessman, Hussein, who had become a Christian in the same town and whose family owned a private and secluded garden. So this is where Fariborz's group started meeting. Usually there were about ten of them, sometimes more.

Over the next three years Fariborz started three other churches in his area and became responsible for looking after about 150 believers. The different groups started as Fariborz visited friends or family members connected to the original group. For example, he visited Hussein's brother Hassan and

---

246 I am acquainted with the three pastors who discipled Fariborz. They are serious, dedicated men, well-versed in theology and the Bible.

his wife Fatimeh in a small town near his city and shared the Gospel with them. Hassan believed, but Fatimeh was reluctant. As mentioned above, Fariborz is an enthusiast. So he asked Fatimeh if he could just pray for her. She agreed. Fariborz prayed and when he said "Amen" Fatimeh rose from her knees, said "Jesus is Lord" and immediately picked up the phone and invited her brother, his wife, and their son to supper so they could learn about Christianity. This family came, and that evening, the wife became a Christian. This is how Fariborz's church grew.

Usually it was not necessary to say where and when the meeting was, but if there was a need for communication Fariborz stressed that the group never used mobile phones for security reasons. All necessary communication happened via the internet using protected email. Normally there would be about fifteen coming to the service, and the people would nearly always either be from the same family or be close friends. Fariborz would signal for the service to start by standing. Everyone would then stand with him, and someone would put on a worship track from a laptop and worship would begin. During this time Fariborz would encourage members to speak out in a tongue, which would then be interpreted.

After the worship there would then be a time of intercession – not for personal needs, but for the local town and area. During this time Fariborz would urge the whole group to spend time praying in tongues. If someone did not speak in tongues, it is during this time that Fariborz and another leader would pray together for that person to receive the gift. While they did not force the issue, Fariborz said that "most of his members" spoke in tongues.

Evangelism also sometimes happened during this stage of the meeting. For occasionally the other Christians would invite a close friend or family member to the meeting and they would sense the presence of God when everyone began praying in tongues. During one such time Fariborz went up to a young man, Ali, and asked him if he wanted to give his life to Christ. Ali said yes, so Fariborz started to pray for him. While praying Ali's whole demeanour changed; he was no longer his normal self, and Fariborz realized that he had a demon. Fariborz began to order the demon to leave Ali and then a particular sin came clearly to Fariborz's mind. He asked Ali if he had committed this sin, and Ali admitted he had. So Fariborz told him to confess and repent. Tormented by this demon, Ali did not need much argument or persuading. He swiftly confessed and repented. Fariborz and other brothers then prayed over Ali and the demon left him.

This time of worship lasted for at least forty minutes, sometimes an hour. Then teaching would follow. However, the teaching would not take the form of set preaching. It was always in a question and answer format, with Fariborz, or someone he appointed, leading the discussion. So, for example, Fariborz might ask the group why Christians should witness, and the group would then talk about this together, referring to the Bible, for about an hour. At the end Fariborz would sum up the discussion. Fariborz himself would receive teaching from whatever subject he wanted to deal with from pastors who discipled him through the internet.

After the teaching there was a short time of worship, and then Fariborz – with another leader – would go round and pray individually for each person attending the service. This was the time when personal needs were brought up. Marriage and money were the two subjects that were often on people's prayer lists.

Every month or two the groups celebrated Holy Communion. The members would sit on the floor, or ground if outside, and in the middle of the circle was the bread and fruit juice. Fariborz would then pray for the elements and pass them around saying, "This is the body of Christ"; "This is the blood of Christ." It was a simple ceremony.

At the end of the meeting, which always lasted more than two hours, there would be a final prayer of blessing and then the group would disperse. The only refreshments available would be tea or water as Fariborz has a very definite view that the church meeting should not become a social party.

As with Mojtaba's fellowship, Fariborz's groups were financially independent. Fariborz's own needs were met through the tithes from the different groups, as well as the business work he did with his father. Sometimes there were special needs – such as for laptops. These needs were announced to the groups, a special collection held, and the funds came in. The main help that came from the outside church was the provision of Scriptures, especially Elam's pocket-sized New Testament, which Fariborz used for both church work and evangelism.

In 2011 Fariborz was arrested for giving out these New Testaments. He spent several days in solitary confinement while he was interrogated. He was transferred to the general prison for a further three weeks. When he was released on bail, Fariborz left Iran.

Fariborz's internet church

Fariborz's father's business was in electrical communication; Fariborz himself specialized in setting up websites. It was therefore natural that as soon as he became a Christian Fariborz started looking on the internet for fellow believers. As seen, he found one brother in his hometown. In a chat room he became friends with another Christian, from Hamedan, and together they opened an evangelistic church chat room called "Beylux". Later Fariborz's partner left, but Fariborz has remained and for the last seven years has been an "internet pastor". In this work he has been helped by other Iranian believers from outside Iran.

Initially most of the work involved witnessing and arguing with unbelievers. But then two things happened. First, some of these unbelievers became Christians, and second, isolated believers made themselves known and asked for help. So over in the chat room there was Bible teaching and prayer: this was the "internet church". Then Fariborz would travel to see the isolated believers who had visited his chat room, and on these same travels he would also visit relatives of members of his house church. His travels show how people were becoming Christians throughout Iran.

Every month he would spend a week visiting Tehran, Karaj, Andisheh, Qom, Isfahan, Rasht, Babol, Astara, and Ardabil. In Qom Fariborz initially visited just one internet believer and his friend. They held a meeting and these two believers invited others and seven more became Christians. In Isfahan Fariborz encouraged a small group of Christians from the internet church, and they then gathered another thirty believers for teaching. In Babol he managed to connect an isolated member of his internet church with a Christian lady who was a dressmaker and who was a member of a fellowship of about seventy other Christians that no other group had any knowledge of.

In addition, every month Fariborz travelled to Iran's very Islamic city, Mashad. Initially he met four believers who had come to faith through the internet. But almost every time Fariborz returned, this group grew. Sadly when he was imprisoned Fariborz lost contact with these believers.

This is the story of Fariborz when he was in Iran. In the first four years of his Christian life he established a fellowship of house churches in his own area and an internet fellowship which he regularly visited. In terms of evangelism Fariborz reckons that he personally led about 200 Iranian Muslims to Christ. When he left Iran he was responsible for about 300 believers.

5. Susan and Hassan's house church

To complete the spectrum of different people engaged in the house-church movement we end with Susan and Hassan's story. Hassan is an Iranian, but Susan is not. They both were already active believers with hearts for church planting in the Persian world before they met. Susan and Hassan met and married outside of Iran, and moved into the country early in the 2000s with the aim to engage in ministry. There they were involved in business ventures and raised their family.

The couple lived near to Hassan's extended family and so were in constant contact with family members. Hassan had already shared the Gospel with some close relatives on an earlier visit before he married, so upon their arrival as a couple, there were two young believers with whom they began to meet together regularly in a very ordinary fashion. In a room in one of their homes they prayed and worshipped. Hassan would teach from the Bible, most of the time in the dialect of their people group, and Susan would occasionally teach and lead in prayer in Persian.

Some of the relatives began to notice changes in the new believers, and Hassan and his wife were intentional in sharing about their relationship with God with them as the Holy Spirit led and as the relatives asked questions. Hassan's mother eventually came to faith, as did other family members. The gathering began to grow, and because this group was within a family setting, curious relatives who were seeking God were invited to join, especially on special occasions such as Christmas celebrations. The seekers were drawn to Christ and one by one many of them came to faith. For those who were still unsure about making the decision to give their lives to Christ, it was understood that none of them would share about the meetings with anyone who may pose as a threat to their safety.

Eventually about thirty people ended up attending this meeting, most of them members of Hassan's extended family with only a few close friends joining. It was literally a family gathering. And because it was family, the group was able to celebrate baptisms and even a wedding ceremony without creating too much suspicion.

In a nearby town another family from the same people group, who became close friends of Hassan's family, heard about Christ when Hassan was invited by a mutual friend to share with them. Their lives had been scarred by drugs, but when the extended family was gathered and Hassan shared the Gospel with them, three came to faith. They invited him back after two weeks to share more, and, little by little, more of them came to faith. This became a group of about fifteen.

Hassan was referred to another family in a village where a few believers lived. They had been too scared to meet together for worship, since it is difficult to meet secretly in the close-knit village setting. Hassan and his wife visited them regularly and held meetings at their home, showing what should happen at a Christian meeting. He continually encouraged them to meet regularly. As their courage grew, they began to reach out quietly and carefully to a neighbour's family to whom they were very close. They too began to attend the meetings. They even became bold enough to carefully share with a few others in their village.

After many years of ministry, government officials learned about Hassan and Susan's Christian activity. Hassan and Susan were aware that they could be taken in at any time by the religious police, yet continued on working with the believers, in particular the leaders. From the beginning of their time in the country, they were keen to spend time with leaders who could use their gifts to lead and teach. They were eventually arrested and over many months made numerous court appearances.

Though some of the believers from the house churches fell away, many are still actively following Christ and sharing Him with others there today.

Here then are five accounts of house churches in Iran. Each story is unique, but there are similarities. By considering these similarities it is likely we can get at least an impressionistic picture of what the house-church movement looks like, and why it has been much more successful in attracting Iranian Muslims to Christ than the traditional structures that focused on buildings.

That is the subject of the next chapter.

CHAPTER 7

HOUSE CHURCHES: WHY THEY GROW

Characteristics

From the five accounts of Iran's new Christians outlined in the previous chapter it is possible to draw some conclusions about the characteristics of these churches. It is possible they apply to all the other fellowships, known and unknown. It is worth considering them – and then seeing why house churches have been so much more successful at winning Iranian Muslims to Christ than the traditional structures.

One conclusion is that the house churches are like a mosaic. To the observer there is one general picture, but as you look closer each tile has its own shape and colour.

The groups are very different: some are large, like Arthur's; others, like Susan and Hassan's, are small. The social character of the groups enhances this sense of a mosaic. The main players in Fariborz's group were, initially, single young men; Susan and Hassan's group is almost exclusively made up of families from a people group.

The life expectancy of these groups also adds to this sense of a mosaic. A line in the pattern begins to grow, and then suddenly stops. Fatimeh's group before 2010 had about 100 members. Then the persecution came and for a while this house church ceased to exist; now it is re-grouping. Another part of the mosaic is how the groups operate. Some seem to have a fairly hierarchic feel to them; others have a more collegiate and fluid feel to them. Likewise some would hesitate to appoint a woman in a public position of leadership; many would not.

Though each church fellowship has its own unique story and character, there are also important similarities that link them all together. These similarities are worth noting, not least because these five fellowships were not even aware of each other's existence, thus making it more likely they represent features of the other house churches.

The first similarity echoes John 1:6 (TNIV): "There was a man (woman) sent from God whose name was..." Arthur, Daniel, Mojtaba, Fariborz, Fatimeh, Susan, Hassan. All of these churches started with a man or woman taking a lead to bring Christians together because they had a sense of a calling from God. Technology is playing an important role in the story of Iran's new Christians, but these accounts underline that each house church started with a courageous man or woman who in different ways had had some sort of encounter with God and then felt they were "sent" for this purpose.

The second very important similarity is that all the groups have connections with the worldwide church. Yes, there is newness about these groups – they are pioneering in every sense of the word – but at the same time they are wholly orthodox. So while all the local activity is driven by the new Christians, nevertheless there is a sense of accountability. In these five examples, every leader had some sort of connection or link to another senior leader. Strictly speaking church growth in Iran over the last seven years is not so much the "story of Iran's new Christians", but the "story of Iran's new Christians *in partnership* with Iran's older Christians".

And in the last ten years a crucial part of this partnership has been satellite TV and the internet. Both platforms have allowed the Iranian church in the diaspora to engage directly in evangelism and teaching in people's homes. However, the Satellite and internet ministries know that there is no substitute for face-to-face fellowship, and so these broadcasting agencies work hard to try and connect people who come to faith through their programmes or websites with Christians inside the country.

Though Iran's internet can be challenging, web-based phone systems like Skype and instant messaging are also playing an important role in this partnership. They allow Iranian Christians in the diaspora to get involved in a lot of one-to-one ministry; and, crucially, leaders in exile can still give some direction to their churches.

Two other obvious areas of partnership between the house fellowships and the wider church are those of resources and training. By and large these house groups are financially independent. This is not that much of a challenge because expenses are minimal as there is no church building to look after. Funds are only needed for inexpensive things like the tea after the meeting, or the photocopying for the songs. Extra funds can then be used for making visits.

However, when it comes to Bibles, books, and evangelistic material, these house churches need help. It is illegal to produce any Christian content in the Persian language in Iran. Thankfully the international church has seen this need and has worked to get Persian language resources into the country, which people like Mojtaba and Fariborz have been able to use.[247]

Likewise training is challenging. Mojtaba made a determined effort to mentor reliable Christians to be future leaders, and this has been a wise investment. However, even with the amount of time he gave to the men he chose to mentor, Mojtaba still understood they needed more teaching and grounding. He needed help. This would be the same story in

---

247 In the early 1990s when the Bible Society had been closed it was clear there was going to be a Scripture famine. In response a few mission agencies focused on trying to make the Bible available for Christians. One of the most active agencies in this regard has been Elam Ministries. See here https://www.elam.com/page/bibles-and-resources

other fellowships. Thankfully, again the international church has stepped up to the mark and provided different ways of giving training.

Due to this partnership with the historic church the format of the house church meetings is easily recognisable as Christian. Church happens in these groups, either as the leader saw church happen, or, as in the case of Fariborz, as they were taught about church by other pastors. So, as has been happening all over the world since Pentecost, there is worship, teaching from the Bible, intercession, fellowship, and, with variations regarding its regularity and timing, baptism and Holy Communion.[248] Satellite TV again plays a role here. The broadcasters have teaching programmes specifically designed for house groups, and even whole programmes of church services in which the viewers can join.

Not only are the meetings recognisably Christian, but so, crucially, is the teaching: it is mainline; it is orthodox. In a situation like Iran heresy could easily flourish. There are thousands of new believers, many from a background where superstitious practices are rife,[249] and the culture tends to look to the dominant male leader who could then easily take others with him. Generally though, there has been little heresy plaguing Iran's new Christians. Christian sects such as the Jehovah's Witnesses are certainly trying to win Iranian converts and they have had some success in the diaspora,[250] but not in Iran. There are also reports that the "Jesus Only" group, which denies the Trinity, are active in Iran, especially in Rasht and

248   Fatimeh's group celebrates Holy Communion every week, Fariborz's every month, and Mojtaba's every month, as long as an ordained minister is present. Arthur's fellowship tends to delay baptism; others baptize when possible.

249   For example, the widespread belief in the "evil eye" to deliver a curse, or picking a verse from Hafiz, using tarot cards, reading the bottom of a coffee cup to find out one's future, and more. Academic Shmuel Bar writes: "Alongside official orthodox Shiite Islam, popular heterodox beliefs and superstitions enjoy wide currency in Iran"; see http://www.herzliyaconference.org/_uploads/2614iranianself.pdf Accessed 6 June 2014.

250   Mainly in England, Germany, and Australia.

Shiraz, and it is clear that supporters of William Branham, who taught that God appears in three forms, rather than being three personalities, are reaching into Iran.[251] Some say their numbers are less than 200;[252] others more.

A key reason why Iran's new Christians are orthodox in their teaching is because, as stated, they are working in partnership with Iran's old Christians. As seen in the previous chapter, the five house churches looked at were all given pastoral oversight by older Christians, some in Iran, some in the diaspora. Furthermore all of the satellite Christian TV channels are orthodox in their basic teaching. So, along with the witness in their spirits (1 John 2:26–27), the new believers have a standard to look to, because of the commitment and involvement of the wider church to provide Scriptures and teaching – whether individually or via books,[253] TV programmes, or websites.

Another similarity in terms of what happens in the meetings is the expectation for God to work supernaturally, and especially for members to be given the gift of speaking in tongues. Sometimes this expectation has come from the historic churches, and sometimes, as with Fariborz, there is a direct experience. The leaders and others then find the gift so enriching and empowering that they want their members to also have a similar experience. The interesting point here that is worthy of note is that without any human plan, the evidence here points to the house churches of Iran tending to be charismatic.

251   http://presenttruthmn.com/blog/missions-updates/work-among-persian-speakers/ accessed 6 June 2014.

252   http://mohabatnews.com/index.php?option=com_content&view=article&id=3467:is-nadarkhani-an-evangelical-chrsitian-special-report-on-non-trinitatian-cult-inside-iran-&catid=36:iranian-christians&Itemid=279 Accessed 6 June 2014.

253   One of the major agencies providing doctrinal books is Elam Ministries. One key title for Iran, especially in the light of the activity of the presence of the "Jesus Only" group, is a book on the The Trinity by Dr Mehrdad Fatehi. It lucidly explains the orthodox teaching of the church on the Trinity: that God is one in three separate personalities. The book is available in Persian from Elam Ministries, www.elam.com.

Another similarity is this: in every account family has played a part. So even though Fariborz naturally first shared the Gospel with his friends – other young single men like him – soon family became involved. Fatimeh's emphasis about Acts 1:8 is being followed: Jerusalem for Iran's house church Christians is the family.

And finally – and sadly – there is the similarity that in all of the groups there has been persecution. All have known some suffering. This is a subject to which we shall return in the next chapter.

Why house churches grow

One of the most important conclusions regarding how the churches are growing focuses on the openness of Iranians. One man closely involved with house churches made this striking comment: "The people are so open that you can get away with anything in evangelism if you go about it in the right way."[254] In other words people want to hear about Jesus, and if approached in the appropriate way they will make a commitment.

While this is an extraordinary statement given the perceived image of Iran as a hard-line Muslim nation it is not so surprising in the light of what the earlier chapters of this book discussed: that bitterly disillusioned with Shia Islam, the most natural religious leader for Iranians to first turn to is Jesus Christ.

Iranians are open to Jesus Christ, and Jesus Christ demonstrably shows Iranians who turn to Him that He is open to them. Nearly every story of an Iranian Muslim becoming a Christian has a supernatural element to it. There is very definitely a conversion experience. There are direct answers to prayer, dreams and visions, healings, deliverance, a miracle that

254 In a private conversation with the author.

convinces the Iranian who is turning to Christ that God is real and means serious business.[255]

These five accounts of house churches show that Iranians are open; indeed the level of hostility to Christianity at a street level in these stories is surprisingly mild.[256] And they also show that reaching out to Iranians with the Gospel through house churches is most definitely an appropriate method. This is where all the action has been for the last five years or so and the spreading of these house churches has had a tremendous impact on the advance of Christianity in Iran.

So when it comes to looking at church growth in Iran in the early twenty-first century the story is not just about Iranians being open, nor is it just about Christianity being the most normal faith for Iranians to explore first – it is also, and very crucially, about the church holding meetings that ordinary Iranians feel comfortable about joining. These might well have developed of their own accord, but credit needs to be given to the church leaders in Iran who saw that the future of Christianity in their country did not rest in church buildings, but in house churches, and invested accordingly. It is a repeat of a familiar theme in history: the plan of a government to weaken the church results in the church being strengthened. There is no question that the pressure of persecution was a catalyst for Christian leaders to switch their focus to house churches.[257]

The worsening security situation made church leaders

---

255 See Pauline Selby, *Persian Springs* for the detailed stories of four Iranians who have come to Christ. See also ministries engaged with Iran for testimonies – e.g. Elam Ministries' *Iran Magazine* nearly always contains testimonies with a supernatural element. Or see Iran Alive Ministries http://www.iranaliveministries.org/page. aspx?n=17&p=Our%20Stories

256 For a year of so Mojtaba was made to eat from special coloured plates. This is the worst opposition from family and friends in these accounts.

257 For example, Pastor Eric Leon of the Assemblies of God churches: "When they put further pressure and limits on the church, more concentration went into cell groups and home churches and eventually they were hidden from the eyes of the Government to be safer." See *Christians in Parliament All Party Parliamentary Group Report*, p. 13.

focus on the question of whether church buildings were viable. But there were other factors at play too. One was history. There was a lot of respect among these leaders for the work of the missionaries who had established the three main Protestant denominations[258] that were still active in Iran after the Revolution: the Presbyterians; the Anglicans; and the Assemblies of God churches. However there was also an awareness that in terms of bringing Iranian Muslims to faith in Jesus Christ the approach of these churches had not been overwhelmingly successful.

By 1979, when Ayatollah Khomeini effectively brought traditional missionary work to an end, the Anglicans and Presbyterians had been sending money and missionaries to Iran for over 100 years. Both denominations had built impressive churches, hospitals, and schools in most of Iran's major cities: Tehran, Mashad, Isfahan, Tabriz, Shiraz, Ahvaz, and Kerman.[259] However, a generous estimate of the number of Muslims who were Christians in these churches in 1979 is 500. The Assyrian International News Agency put the figure at 200–300.[260]

---

258   As well as the three main Protestant denominations (Anglican, Presbyterian, and Assemblies of God churches) there are also of course the Orthodox churches of the Assyrians and the Armenians, and the Roman Catholics. The Assyrians have had a presence in Iran since the second century. The Armenians came to Iran first in the sixteenth century, and then as refugees after the genocide in 1915. These churches hold services in their ethnic languages and apart from bearing witness in terms of their lifestyle – they generally have a reputation for being honest citizens – they do not actively reach out to the Muslim majority. Since the revolution there has been an exodus of Assyrian and Armenian Christians from Iran; see Chapter 8. The Roman Catholics, for political reasons, have never had a strong presence in Iran.

259   The other two major cities in Iran with a population of over a million are Karaj and Qom. When there was more freedom for Christian activity no church building was erected in Karaj due to its proximity to Tehran. Religious sensitivity ruled out a church being built in Qom. Though neither city have church buildings, both have house churches.

260   See "Iran: Christians and Converts", Landinfo, July 2011, p. 10. http://www.landinfo.no/asset/1772/1/1772_1.pdf Accessed 22 May 2014.

For a detailed account of Iran's churches before 1979 see Chapter 8 of the author's *Iran and Christianity*.

Established in the 1960s the Assemblies of God churches also saw very few Muslim converts prior to 1979. As disillusionment with the revolution spread, so too more Muslims came to these churches, especially the Assemblies of God church in Tehran. Indeed, in this church the whole make-up of the congregation changed from being mainly ethnic Armenians, to mainly ethnic Iranians. But this was only in Tehran. It was not the same across the country, even though it was obvious to church leaders that interest among Muslims in Christianity was dramatically increasing.

With the benefit of hindsight it would seem there was a problem with the traditional approach to mission that expected people who were interested in Christianity to come to a public church building. One obvious reason was the risks curious Iranian Muslims faced. Outside the church building plain-clothed officials checked on who went to the service, sometimes stopping people and questioning them. If the visitors said they were Muslims, they were given a warning.[261] Officials also attended the services;[262] and at all times the government kept a close eye on the pastors. Their phones were tapped, their movements monitored, and they had to regularly report to MOIS who especially wanted to know which Iranian Muslims were coming to their services. So when an Iranian Muslim visited a church building they were risking having their name being put a list of people who, in the government's eyes, were suspect in terms of their religion and their politics.

Regarding religion their visit to the church freely tells the authorities that either they are already apostates from Islam (a crime that carries the death penalty for men and life

261 The official position of the Iranian government is that there is religious freedom in Iran for Christians, and by this they mean that the Christian ethnic minorities, e.g. the Assyrians and the Armenians, are at liberty to practise their faith.

262 Often these officials make no attempt to disguise their identity. In one service in an Anglican church the official on duty talked quite loudly on his mobile phone, disturbing the service. Outside the gate there were others in his team checking who was entering the compound.

imprisonment for women according to the Sharia law, though this is not inscribed in Iran's law books), or they are thinking of becoming apostates. Regarding politics the main building churches in Iran have been closely linked to foreign powers. The Assemblies of God and the Presbyterians have connections with the USA, the Anglicans with the UK, the two imperialist powers that were loathed by Ayatollah Khomeini and his successors for humiliating and exploiting Iran.[263] So a visit by an Iranian Muslim to such a church immediately puts a question mark over his or her patriotism in the minds of government officials.

The risk for an Iranian Muslim is not only related to the hostility of the government. There is always the danger of the visitor facing problems from their family, or friends, or employer if those people are either devout Muslims, or just tribal – "Shia Islam is Iran's religion". Even one visit to a church could cause the visitor to be ostracized from their family or thrown out of their work.

Even if the visitor has the courage to take the risk of going to a church building, once inside he or she faces another challenge: the church is culturally alien. When people enter a new group they instinctively look for people, especially among the leaders, who are like them. It has proved virtually impossible for the building churches to appoint an ex-Muslim in any position of leadership because this has attracted such murderous hostility.[264] So the newcomer will see an ethnic Armenian or Assyrian leading the service, and in the congregation there

263   In the political story presented by Ayatollah Khomeini and his successors it is the plots of the imperialists, or the "arrogant powers" (Britain and the USA) that are to blame for most of the evils in Iran. Christian missionaries – who built the modern churches – are seen as being agents in these plots. See Chapter 8, p.166–67.

264   Ex-Muslim leaders of churches who have been killed are: Revd Arastoo Sayyah, an Anglican priest in Shiraz who was murdered in February 1979; Revd Hussein Soodmand of the Assemblies of God church in Mashad who was hanged in that city in December 1990; Mohammad Yusefti, pastor of the churches in Sari who was assassinated in September 1996; Ghorban Tourani, a pastor from Golestan, who was stabbed to death in November 2005.

will be others from these minorities. There might also be other Iranian Muslims who are perhaps like the seeker, but there are also bound to be others there who are from a very different class, and ethnic background. This is not speculation. Before the 1979 revolution, the congregations in the Protestant churches were not homogeneous: they were made up of Assyrians, Armenians, Jews, Westerners, and a sprinkling of ex-Iranian Muslims.

This feeling of not being among one's own would then be underlined by the interior of the building. Physically the Iranian Muslim is entering another religious world. This sense of unfamiliarity would then intensify when the service began, not least because much of the liturgy and format of the service has originated outside Iran, often in America or Britain. None of this unfamiliarity is wrong: indeed diversity in the congregation, church buildings, and a liturgy are all the hallmarks of orthodox Christianity. The point is that, combined with the danger of a Muslim coming to a church, these factors underlined that essentially Christianity was a foreign religion. So for an Iranian Muslim to become a Christian they did not just have to change their theology – they had to jump over a wide cultural chasm. It is likely this cultural chasm was too vast before the Islamic Revolution, which is why there were then so few Iranian Christians from a Muslim background in the established churches.

As well as causing problems for the would-be Muslim visitor, church buildings also present Christian leaders with challenges. Funding is one, but by no means the most important. Dealing with the security officials is another, but again not the most important. The real danger according to one of Iran's most senior church leaders is that the church building limits vision. For when the building is full people think the church is doing well, that people are being reached. This is completely false. If all the Protestant churches in Tehran were filled, then the total number of Christians, in a city of nearly 8 million, would barely be 1,000. And since the building churches are only in the big cities, this means that all of the Iranians living in the thousands of towns and small villages remain untouched.

House churches answer all the problems created by the church buildings' approach to mission that saw so little fruit. The house churches minimize the security issue (both from the government and the family), the cultural chasm can be jumped over, and by definition there is no limit on growth – the house church goes everywhere.

By meeting in homes the house churches are making involvement much safer. First of all it is not at all easy for the security officials to even know where the meeting is being held. In the big cities there is one church building but there are millions of private homes. And of course there is no law in Iran that says family members and close friends cannot meet together. It is very normal. The danger of course is if someone poses as a Christian and then infiltrates a group. However, most groups will meet with a seeker for several months in a park or public place before allowing them into the fellowship, so this risk is reduced. Sadly house churches have not proved to be completely safe, as we will see in the next chapter; however, as is clear from the accounts above, some have managed to grow without attracting the unwelcome attention from the authorities. If we put ourselves into the shoes of an Iranian Shia Muslim who wants to find out more about Christianity it is easy to see that from a security point of view a visit to a house church is a much better option than going to a church building.

House churches, by and large, melt the cultural chasm that can be there when Iranian Muslims visit building churches. Not only are people from the same religious background (all former Muslims), not only are they from the same sort of cultural and social background (so initially single young men from a major linguistic group, as in Fariborz's group), but very often the people are all from the same family (as with Susan and Hassan's first church). Whereas in a church building, amid strangers, Iranian Muslims would initially feel vulnerable and ill at ease, in the house church some of them feel, literally, at home. Fellowship is easy, and so – apart from the issue of sinful habits – there are no cultural barriers to them also accepting Christ. In his pivotal work *Understanding Church Growth* Dr Donald McGavran[265] exposed why some mission is successful and some not, and his solid research underlined this simple point: People "like to become Christians without crossing racial, linguistic, or class barriers". This is the great strength of the house churches. They let Iranians become Christians without having to cross any of those barriers.

In the approach to mission that focuses on buildings, the spread of Christianity is equated with the putting up of more churches. This was always limiting in Iran, but after Ayatollah Khomeini's revolution, it became impossible. Indeed for the last thirty years it has been a fight to keep the church buildings open and services functioning normally.

And for many that fight has now been lost. Determined to show that Christianity is solely a religion for the ethnic Armenians and Assyrians in Iran, the government has forced the closure of services in Persian in most of the Protestant church buildings, including the central Assemblies of God Church and Emmanuel Presbyterian Church in Tehran.[266] This means that

265 First published in 1970, the title has been revised and edited by C. Peter Wagner. *Understanding Church Growth*, Wm B. Eerdmans, third edition, 1990.
266 The central Assemblies of God [AoG] church in Tehran was closed in May 2013 following the arrest of Revd Robert Assyrian. Previously, in 2009, it had been pressured into ceasing its Friday Persian language services. In February 2012 Emmanuel Presbyterian Church in Tehran was ordered to cease all activities (including its Friday Persian services) except its Sunday services. St Peter's Evangelical Church in Tehran was ordered to discontinue its Friday Persian-language services in the same month. In August 2013 a Catholic church (Latin rite) in Tehran was forced to ban Persian speakers from attending. On 8 December 2013, under pressure from the government, the pastor of St Peter's Church in Tehran, Sargis Benyamin, told his congregation that Persian-speaking attendees would not be allowed in the church anymore. One week later, church members prevented a few of the Persian-speaking members from entering the church building, including Sunday school

the number of functioning public services in Persian can now be counted on one hand. The church buildings have proved limiting, but with the present levels of hostility emanating from the Islamic Republic, they have proved unsustainable.

In contrast the spread of house churches has already proved to be limitless, and eminently sustainable. As seen from the five accounts above a house church grows in a very natural way. A small group of Christians start meeting in someone's home, and then usually other family members or close friends show interest and become Christians. When the fellowship starts to get too big the group splits and there are two meetings in two homes. So the process goes on. There is literally no limit. And they are sustainable. The hostility towards them from the government is just as intense as it is for the churches based in visible buildings, if not worse, but, as seen, house churches are much more difficult for the security forces to target.

Furthermore, even when house churches have been targeted by the security forces, they have proved they can re-group. And, as seen with Fatimeh's experience, the Christians learn lessons on how to operate beneath the radar of the government's opposition. One senior church leader with years of experience sums up the situation in this blunt way: "The authorities cannot smash the house churches. They cannot win."[267]

There are two others factors that fuel the growth and sustainability of the house churches. One is the emphasis on sharing testimonies, both on how someone came to faith,

teachers, elders, and other leaders of the church. The Ahvaz AoG church closed at Christmas 2011, after the arrest of four leaders at a Christmas meeting. The Tehran Assyrian Pentecostal Church (Shahre Ara – Passport Church) was closed in March 2009. The Urumieh/Urmia Assyrian Pentecostal Church was closed in July 2009. The Kermanshah Assyrian Pentecostal Church was ordered to close on 31 December 2009 following accusations of spreading Christianity among Muslims. The Anglican church in Kerman was closed down in the 1980s and then in 2011 it was bulldozed. Other churches linked to the Assemblies of God churches that were closed down in the 1980s and 1990s were: Mashaad (1988), Sari (1988), Kerman (1992), Shiraz (1992), Gorgon (1993), and Kermanshah.

267   Mentioned in an interview with the author.

and also on how God is continuing to work in someone's life. The impact of this sharing is to encourage other Christians in their faith, and to create an expectation that God will work. Underneath a picture of a group of people getting baptized, Elam Ministries' *Iran Magazine* poses this question: "Why so many?" And the answer in the first line of the article is: "Iranians love to tell their stories. Ideologies can be debated, but a personal witness points to the living God."[268]

Another factor is the sense of shared ownership. They are small groups. Their size, and the security situation where one wrong move can lead to prison, naturally draws them together to take joint responsibility for the group's activities. This means that each group makes its own plans, looking to God, not a single leader. This sense of shared responsibility then makes the group more evangelistic. As Sam Yeghnazar, the director of Elam Ministries, says, "in the house churches every individual Christian has a sense of responsibility to preach the Gospel, so the churches are spreading like wildfire".[269]

This is very much in contrast to the position that a Christian with a Muslim background would be in a building church. These churches all tend to operate with a top-heavy hierarchical manner, nearly always with an Assyrian or Armenian man as the leader. With this type of system, and the ethnic element, it was inevitable there could be something of an "us" and "them" feeling in the church. Certainly there was no immediate sense of shared ownership.[270]

If the Iranian from a Muslim background were a woman in the building church, then this sense of being kept out of

268 *Iran Magazine*, Issue 8, Spring/Summer 2014, published by Elam Ministries, p. 6.
269 In private conversation with the author.
270 This feeling was accentuated when a building church had got used to being supported largely by foreign money. Outside a major city in Iran there is a Christian graveyard owned by the Anglican Church. In the 1990s this graveyard was not well kept and during a visit by an Englishman one of the church members told the foreigner that something should be done about the graveyard. In the Iranian's mind, responsibility for the graveyard rested with the Englishman, because the graveyard was originally owned by the English.

the decision-making would be even stronger. A quick glance at all the leaders of the official Iranian church shows it is a male church. There is no place for a woman at the director's table. This is not the case with the house churches. Yes, there are some churches that prefer to appoint men to positions of responsibility, but that is by no means the norm. Indeed one well-known Christian leader has stated publicly that 70 per cent of the leaders in the house-church movement are women; while Sam Yeghnazar has written, "I praise God for the ministry of women. Without them the church in Iran would not be growing as fast as it is. Women have shared the Gospel with hundreds of thousands of people, discipled new believers, and helped establish house churches."[271] So, ironically in Iran's sexist Islamic Republic, women are not only fully a part of the decision-making in the story of the new Christians, but are often out there in front. They are leaders. This obviously helps in terms of growth and sustainability, especially in the context of house churches. For while men are greatly honoured in public in Iran, an Iranian woman generally has authority in her own home. So in the home the women can be fully engaged in building up the church and spreading the Gospel. The women are playing a key role in growing the home fellowships, and this greatly improves their sustainability.

The story of Iran's new Christians is, then, very much a story about the house churches. This is where all the growth is happening; indeed without the house churches, it is hard to see that there would be a story to write.

The characteristics of these house churches are that they begin with a man or woman "sent by God"; they then grow in partnership with the wider church, and are especially helped by satellite TV, the internet, the provision of Scriptures, and training (thus encouraging orthodoxy); there is an expectation that God will work supernaturally (generally Iran's new Christians

271   *Iran Magazine*, Issue 8, Spring/Summer 2014, published by Elam Ministries, p. 1.

speak in tongues); there is a tendency for the churches to be among family and close friends; there is an emphasis on sharing testimonies; and finally there is a shared sense of ownership that increases the group's evangelistic zeal.

Yes there is great openness amongst Iranians to the Gospel of Jesus Christ, and the reason why this openness is being translated into a story of new Christians is because of the emergence of house churches.

Maryam's house church

We end this chapter with another brief story of a house church that brings together the main characteristics of house churches, and which especially underlines the role of women.

A few years ago, in a small town in Iran where there was no church or Christian witness, Maryam found that her marriage was drying up. Her story brings together all the reasons why house churches have been so successful.

Highly educated, hard-working and married to a university lecturer, Maryam until a few years ago looked the picture of success. But inside she was holding back rivers of hurt and anger and regret. Her marriage was dead. Her husband had betrayed her and told her he would only stay with her until the children grew up. Even though she lived in a very religious Islamic city, she was able to hear the Gospel by watching Christian programmes on satellite TV. Her broken spirit was attracted to Jesus. Slowly His love and acceptance won her heart. On the day she gave her life to Christ in front of the TV set she danced like a drunk for joy.

Before becoming a Christian there was only one word that came to Maryam's mind when she thought about her husband: divorce. But the Jesus she had met talked of loving your enemies. The Holy Spirit convicted Maryam's heart and she decided to forgive and love. Her new joy and the love she showed her husband worked its way into his guilty heart. He began to show warmth to the wife he had betrayed, and he then too gave his heart to Christ.

Reconciled they began to build their marriage on Christian principles, and then they joined forces to witness to their families. Maryam was a very active evangelist. In the beginning they faced a lot of coldness and ridicule, but slowly different people responded, until there was a group of seventeen believers. This became a house church.

And the Bible teacher and pastor of this new fellowship is Maryam. She is recognized as the spiritual mother of the church, and when other churches relate to this group, it is Maryam that they contact. Without Maryam this church would not have come into being.

Maryam is the woman "sent by God", but, as with all the other house churches we have looked at, she – and her church – was also helped by the wider body of Christ. Maryam became a Christian through watching satellite TV, and as initially she had no Bible, this is where she received all her spiritual nourishment.[272] She grew as a Christian because of teaching from the wider church.

Maryam did not know any Christians in her town from whom she could get a Bible, but she refused to give up. She decided to ask a bookseller discreetly if he could obtain a Bible for her. He obliged, for a fee. So after six months Maryam owned her own Bible, published by Elam Ministries, and was more able to grow in her own faith, and later teach those who became believers through her ministry.

Maryam was able to buy that Bible because of the wider church. If it had been twenty years earlier it is unlikely she would have been able to do so, as the hostility of the Islamic Republic to the Christian Scriptures had created a severe Bible

272   The author has heard of another believer who copied down every verse that she heard on the TV and this became her Bible.

famine in Iran. In the 1980s and 1990s if a traveller brought in a few copies of the Scriptures, pastors referred to them as "gold dust". So severe was the famine that Rashin Soodmand, the teenaged daughter of the martyred priest Hussein Soodmand, copied out all of the Gospel of John by hand so she could use it for evangelism.[273]

While demand far outstrips supply, Maryam's success in being able to obtain an Elam Bible from a bookseller in a city where there is no visible Christian presence shows there has been something of an improvement. And this is because of the work of the wider church to get Scriptures into Iran.

It is interesting that Maryam was able to get her Bible from a commercial bookseller. This shows that almost certainly those engaged in sending Scriptures to Iran are in a win–win situation. For sometimes shipments of Scriptures are discovered by customs officials and confiscated. One group of smugglers was told: "You can bring in alcohol, you can bring in drugs, but never bring in these [New Testaments]."[274] It is known that once the customs officials burned the Bibles they had confiscated. But this would not seem to be the norm. This then leaves the question of what happens to the Bibles and New Testaments that are confiscated. It is unlikely that underground Christians would risk supplying commercial booksellers who could then inform on them, so there is a strong likelihood that Maryam, and many others, were able to buy their Bibles from a shop because customs officials have sold on the confiscated Scriptures. Maryam has now made contact with other Christians and is able to provide her church with other Scriptures and books. She has also received some training with an agency and is now much better equipped to serve her congregation.

---

273   A short film about Rashin Soodmand's determination to have Scriptures for evangelism can be seen here: http://www.elam.com/article/video-resources Accessed 7 March 2014. For comments on the Scripture famine, please see footnote 247 above.
274   In a private film seen by the author.

The story of Maryam and her new Christians is again unique, but it shares those same connections with the other accounts. The church starts with someone who has had a supernatural encounter with God. The wider church is involved – this time very much through satellite TV, and later with the provision of Scriptures and training. There is an expectancy for members to have a charismatic experience. The whole church is based on the family. In this account, as in some of the others, Maryam's gender is of absolutely no importance. She is recognized as the group's leader.

Thankfully there is – as yet – no suffering in Maryam's story. Sadly, though, this is often a part of the story. It was for Mojtaba, Fariborz, and Fatimeh. All endured arrest, imprisonment, and interrogation. Mojtaba was continually beaten, and was once put through a mock execution.

The purpose of the persecution is to weaken the church and so to let Christianity "wither" away once the misguided have been separated from their foreign sponsors. But, as this book has shown, the opposite has happened. The church has been growing and growing, and ironically suffering has played a part in making this come about.

This is the final part of the story of Iran's new Christians, to which we now turn.

CHAPTER 8

PERSECUTION: THE STRANGE EQUATION

Church history throws up a strange equation: when the church is persecuted, the church grows. In a recent interview the veteran evangelist David Hathaway was asked about Iran. Now in his eighties he has preached to thousands of people in difficult countries like Siberia. Hathaway does not hesitate to underline this strange equation: "Whenever you see Christians being persecuted, you see the church growing. Look at China; look at Iran. The reason these churches are growing is because they are being persecuted."[275]

The suffering in Iran has thankfully never reached the intensity of what Christians are enduring in countries like Egypt, Syria, Iraq, Nigeria, Sudan, Pakistan, Vietnam, and, most barbaric of all, North Korea where an estimated 50,000–70,000 believers are incarcerated in murderous prison camps.[276]

Nevertheless, ever since the Islamic Republic came to power, the church in Iran has faced different levels of persecution. The nationalistic narrative of the Islamic Republic makes antagonism and aggression towards Persian-speaking Christians inevitable. Ayatollah Khomeini was swept into power with the belief that he and his colleagues were best

---

275   This interview was made with the author. David Hathaway, whose father was closely involved in the early days of the Elim Pentecostal Church, preached his first sermon aged thirteen. He has had a long career as an evangelist. His ministry has tended to be towards Eastern Europe where he still holds large evangelistic crusades.
276   See http://www.worldwatchlist.us/ for a swift overview of persecution against Christians around the world. Also see Rupert Shortt's *Christianophobia* for detailed accounts of the worst countries.

able to protect Iran's Shia identity from the colonizing and corrupting influences of both "East and West" (the then Soviet Union and the USA). As seen, especially in the drama of the 2009 presidential elections, his successors have constantly beaten this same drum.

Discrimination

In this narrative no Christian can be trusted as a loyalist, hence all Christians must be kept out of any area of influence. This, of course, means official discrimination. And in this narrative the guardians of Islamic Republic have a responsibility to root out any threat to Iran's Shia identity. So, any Christian who is actively seeking to convert Shia Muslims must be dealt with. This means active persecution.

The discrimination is demeaning and debilitating. In education, in the military, in the police, in the legal system, and in the job market – all of which are dominated by the Islamic state – all Christians (Armenian, Assyrian, and especially those of a Muslim background) meet outright prejudice,[277] as do other religious minorities such as Zoroastrians, Sunnis, and especially Baha'is.[278] However brilliant they are, would-be students can be barred from going to university if their religious credentials are suspect; in the army no Christian can be an officer;[279] in the legal system there are different rules for Muslims and non-

277 "Non-Muslims cannot work in the legal system, the security services, or hold the position of headmaster in the public school system." See "Iran: Christians and Converts", Landinfo, July 2011, http://www.landinfo.no/asset/1772/1/1772_1.pdf, p. 6, Accessed 22 May 2014.
278 "There is little doubt that non-Muslim minorities in general are vulnerable groups in the Islamic Republic." Ibid., accessed 22 May 2014.
279 The case of the army officer Hamid Pourmand is dealt with below. It is relevant here to point out that the charge against him that stuck was that he had allegedly not told his seniors that he was a Christian, because if he had done so he would have been barred. This point illustrates the reality of discrimination for Iran's Christians in the military.

Muslims;[280] and with the government owning about 80 per cent of the economy and with an overcrowded employment market, jobs for Christians are not easy to find.

This discrimination creates a feeling of insecurity for all Christians, and while many of the older generation would instinctively prefer to stay in their own country and remain loyal to their own pressurized church, the moral case for emigration becomes strong as circumstances force them to conclude that their children will not have a future in the Islamic Republic. So the result of discrimination has been the ordeal and upheaval of Christians, from every denomination, leaving Iran for a new country.

This exodus has been happening since the early 1980s. Well over 100,000 Armenian Christians have left Iran. In the early 2000s the United Nations Special Envoy to Iran estimated that 15,000–20,000 Armenians were leaving every month. The exodus of the Assyrians is just as dramatic. From about 100,000 in 1979 there are now only about 15,000 Assyrians left in Iran – perhaps even less. Likewise many Christians from the Presbyterian, Anglican, and the Assemblies of God Churches have also left. Iran's new Christians have also been a part of this exodus.[281]

Though undramatic compared to arrests and torture, it is important to underline that this exodus does represent suffering. There is the packing of a home and a life into a few suitcases,

280   For example, Article 881 of Iran's penal code states that a non-Muslim cannot inherit property from a Muslim. Article 88 states that a Muslim who commits adultery with a Muslim should get 100 lashes; a Christian could face the death penalty. For murder the blood money for a Muslim in a murder case is twice that of a Christian's. Article 1059 of the civil code prohibits the marriage of a Muslim woman and a non-Muslim man, though it allows the marriage of a non-Muslim woman to a Muslim man. Under Article 1192, a Muslim child guardian (father/grandfather) cannot appoint a non-Muslim to take over guardianship upon their death.
281   Some of these new Christians left because of this general intimidation and discrimination; many others have left because of the ferocious persecution the government unleashed against the house churches in 2010, as detailed later in this chapter.

the goodbye to all that was familiar, and then the journey into the unknown. For many it is a very long one. A few, usually using expensive and not always reliable smugglers, manage to get directly to Europe or America where they then face a long process to getting a legal status. In the UK some have waited for over ten years. Most make their way to a second country – usually Turkey,[282] but also Armenia, Georgia, and Pakistan – and there ask UNHCR to accept them as asylum seekers. In Turkey it can take up to two years just to be interviewed. If accepted, then it can take another two years to be re-settled in the West, usually in the USA, Canada, or Australia. When an Iranian Christian decides to emigrate this usually means they are going to face about five years of uncertainty, and, for many, severe economic pressure. In Turkey the UNHCR offers no financial support for refugees, so, unless there is support from home, the only option is to work long hours for low wages in the "black" economy.

The policy for Christians who do not actively threaten the status quo of the Shia state is discrimination, which often leads to the ordeal of emigration. This still includes apostates, i.e. anyone who has abandoned Islam. It is true that many hard-line Muslims in Iran interpret the Sharia law as demanding death for male apostates and life imprisonment for females. Hence, in more colourful publications, the impression can be given that a Muslim in Iran who becomes a Christian spends every waking moment in fear of being murdered or dragged off to a kangaroo court to be sentenced to death. However, even Iranian officials can be uncomfortable with this image[283] and there is no record

282 "UNHCR estimated that [in Eastern Turkey] about 20–25% of the [Iranian] asylum seekers [about 6,000] reported that they were converts." See "Iran: Christians and Converts", Landinfo, July 2011, p. 7. http://www.landinfo.no/asset/1772/1/1772_1. pdf Accessed 22 May 2014.
283 The author was once on an internal flight in Iran and was seated near to a group of Revolutionary Guards. When he asked for a comment from the leader of the group about Islam's demands for apostates to be dealt with harshly, the leader's associate started shaking his head and saying that there was no death penalty for the

of any Christian facing that sort of treatment in Iran – as long as they are quietist and not active at all.[284] Certainly prejudice for the Muslim is potentially sharper – such as immediate dismissal from work – than that faced by an ethnic Christian. However, unless they are active, the main problem the Muslim convert must deal with is discrimination.

The issue is that many Christians are not quietist. They are active and are not prepared to hide their faith in the public sphere. And so from 1979 onwards, along with this constant discrimination, Christians have been targeted by the government.

Persecuting the Christian activists[285]

Iran's recent history of persecuting Christian activists has happened in three phases. First there was a ferocious attack on the country's Anglicans. Then there was a long drawn-out confrontation with the other Protestant churches, especially the Assemblies of God; and finally, since especially 2008, there has been a concerted effort by the authorities to crush the house-church movement.

Attacking the Anglicans

The first phase was against the Anglican Church, very much in the public square with its church buildings and hospitals, its services in Persian, and scores of Muslim background converts. For the Khomeinist the Anglican church with its open connections with England, the mother of modern imperialism,

apostate in Islam. His leader quoted something in Arabic, presumably a verse from the Koran, which contradicted his associate. The story shows that even members of the Revolutionary Guard are not keen on apostate males being executed.

284   In a statement to Elam Ministries one Christian prisoner said she was told by her interrogator "that I can be a Christian, but I am not to do anything as a Christian". Statement seen by the author on 4 June 2014.

285   To read in more detail about the first two phases of this persecution, against the Anglicans and the Assemblies of God, see Chapter 9 of the author's *Iran and Christianity*.

was exactly the sort of threat to Iran's Islamic identity that needed to be rooted out. Indeed in one publication Ayatollah Khomeini had openly called for foreign churches to be destroyed:

> The missionaries, those other agents of imperialism, are also busy throughout the Muslim world in perverting our youth, not by converting them to their own religion, but by corrupting them. And that is the very thing imperialists are after. In Teheran itself, propaganda centers for Christianity, Zionism, and Bahaism, have been set up for the sole purpose of luring the faithful away from the commandments of Islam. *Is it not our duty to destroy all these hotbeds of danger to Islam?*[286]

Ayatollah Khomeini's words bore bitter fruit for the Anglican Church. Their hospitals and schools were taken over,[287] their clergy attacked. Revd Sayyah Arastoo had his throat cut in February 1979; Bishop Dehqani and his wife Margaret were shot at in their bed in October 1979 (miraculously they survived); the bishop's secretary, Jean Waddell, was beaten up and shot in May 1980 (she too miraculously survived); the bishop's son, Bahram Dehqani, was abducted and shot in May 1980. He did not survive. In August 1980 two other clergy, a missionary couple, and three church members[288] were imprisoned for six months on false charges of spying: an easy accusation given Ayatollah Khomeini's verdict on the churches.

After this baptism of fire into the Islamic Republic, the Anglican Church has still managed to remain in the public sphere and the doors of three of its churches (Tehran, Isfahan, and Shiraz) are open for its Persian-speaking services. However congregations have dwindled, and, closely monitored by MOIS,

---

286 From Ayatollah Khomeini's "The Little Green Book", http://islammonitor.org/uploads/docs/greenbook.pdf, p. 6, Accessed 23 May 2014. Author's italics.

287 In Shiraz, Isfahan, and Yazd.

288 Revd Iraj Mottahedeh (who later became bishop), Revd Nosatullah Sharifian, Revd Coleman, Audrey Coleman, Jean Waddall, Dimitri Bellos, and one other.

it is clear that the powers that be had decided these churches did not pose a threat to the Islamic Republic. Indeed, their presence helped the government with its disingenuous claim that there was religious freedom in Iran.

Against the Assemblies of God churches, the Presbyterians, and Roman Catholics

The second phase of persecution against activist Christians was mainly directed against the Assemblies of God Churches, with the Presbyterians and then later the small Roman Catholic Church.

Established in the 1960s the Assemblies of God Church was mainly made up of ethnic Armenians and some Assyrians who had had a charismatic experience. At the time of the revolution there were hardly any ex-Muslims in their congregations. Then in the very early years of the new regime members of this church with a passion for evangelism realized there was not only interest in Christianity, but also a certain amount of freedom. The new government had a lot of other concerns: establishing the Islamic Republic; dealing with the monarchists; conducting a civil war with the Mojahadin;[289] and then, from September 1980, defending Iran against the Iraqis. Keeping an eye on a few Armenian Christian enthusiasts was not an immediate priority.

And so a lot of evangelism happened, not just in Tehran, but in other large cities and towns: the leader of an important ministry states that in the first five years after the revolution his teams gave out about a million pieces of Scripture and evangelistic tracts.[290]

There was a response from Muslims, an indication that for some the bruising of their relationship with their national religion began to happen early on under the Islamic Republic. In Tehran the central church grew to having about 250 members, many of them from a Muslim background, and across Iran

289　See footnote 43.
290　As detailed in a private conversation with Luke Yeghnazar who began a literature ministry in Tehran in the late 1970s.

nine new fellowships were planted, all with some ex-Muslims included.

There was also a response from the government. In 1985 a letter arrived at the office of the central Assemblies of God church in Tehran demanding that all attempts to convert Muslims cease. The message was clear. Quiet Christianity will be tolerated in the Islamic Republic; enthusiastic Christianity will be opposed. The then leader of the denomination, Revd Haik Hovsepian Mehr, a passionate evangelist who longed to see Muslims turn to Christ, ignored the request. Again, probably because of the war and the worsening economic situation, church life continued.

In 1988 the government campaign to control the Assemblies of God Church and its outreach to Muslims began in earnest. First Haik Hovsepian Mehr and his brother Edward were summoned to the offices of MOIS and ordered to stop preaching to Muslims. The Hovsepians again ignored the request. In reply their brother, Rubik, leading a church in Ahvaz, was arrested and incarcerated in solitary confinement for a month.

Also in 1988, the Assemblies of God pastor in Mashad, Revd Hussein Soodmand, a Muslim convert,[291] was facing constant intimidation from the authorities. His church was closed, but as Revd Soodmand continued to gather the small number of Muslim converts there for prayer and Bible study, he was routinely arrested and questioned. The issue for the authorities was activist Christianity led by an apostate in Mashad, where the shrine of the eighth Imam Reza attracted over a million Shia pilgrims a year. In early 1990 Revd Soodmand was again arrested, and this time put into solitary confinement. The Assemblies of God leadership negotiated his release and urged him to leave Mashad. But he stayed.

291   Revd Soodmand's life story can be read in "Iran: Christian news and insight from Elam Ministries" issue 4, April 2011. Also see Chapter 9 of the author's *Iran and Christianity*.

In November he was arrested again. On 3 December he was hanged in Mashad prison. Activist Christianity would not be tolerated in the Islamic Republic.

When Hussein Soodmand first turned to Christ, he was discipled faithfully by a very devout ex-Muslim Christian. Mehdi Dibaj had become a Christian in 1953 when he was fourteen years old, and by the 1980s was connected to the Assemblies of God Church. Living in Conservative Babol in the north of Iran, Mehdi Dibaj's fervent evangelism had already caused ripples, but then in 1983 unknown enemies accused this apostate from Islam of slandering Iran's Supreme Leader. Hence the initial imprisonment Mehdi Dibaj endured in 1983 was not so much a part of the government's general campaign against the Assemblies of God Church, but more related to this particular issue of demeaning Ayatollah Khomeini. Mehdi Dibaj was cleared of this slander, but in 1984 was again imprisoned for apostasy. However, since in most of Iran's major cities there were ex-Muslim Christians living relatively normal lives, it is safe to assume that the real reason for this imprisonment was Mehdi Dibaj's insistence on evangelizing. He was an incurable activist. And perhaps there were local and even personal reasons involved.[292]

For the first two years or so Mehdi Dibaj was treated viciously in prison. He was kept in solitary confinement in a small unlit three-yard cell for two years; and endured physical beatings and mock executions. Again, this points to the authorities in Sari having a particular hatred for Mehdi Dibaj and his Christian faith.

292 Local reasons: The northern towns of Iran have a reputation for being more conservative in their religion and some have a special loathing for middle-class Iranians who live in Tehran and come to the north flaunting their wealth and Western fashions. Mehdi Dibaj was not wealthy. He gave 50 per cent of his English teacher's salary away. But his Christianity associated him with the West. Personal reasons: As often happens in situations where a minority faces legal intimidation, personal enemies can use the situation for their own advantage. There is no certain evidence this happened in Mehdi Dibaj's case, but it still stands that keeping someone in prison for apostasy was not the norm then; nor is it now.

In 1986 Mehdi Dibaj was found guilty of apostasy by the Sari Revolutionary Islamic Court, a crime that carries the death sentence for men in the Sharia law (but not in Iran's national codified law).[293] Mehdi Dibaj appealed against his conviction on the grounds that the Koran does not stipulate this harsh treatment of apostates.[294] After making the appeal, Mehdi Dibaj sat in prison and waited.

In the early 1990s Iranian Muslims continued to come to the Assemblies of God church in Tehran. The congregation grew to about 350, and a senior leader at that time estimates that about 80 per cent were from a Muslim background.[295] The government became more determined to root out this activism. In the spring of 1993 the Assemblies of God Church superintendent, Haik Hovsepian Mehr, was summoned again to the MOIS offices and ordered to close down the Friday services in Persian (popular for Iranian Muslims), hand over a list with the details of all their present members, and refuse to accept any more Iranian Muslims into the congregation. The activism was to stop. Again Revd Hovsepian Mehr and his brother Edward refused to comply – even when a contingent of police arrived at a service intent on closing it down. As it was, the police lost their nerve because of the large numbers in the church and left. In the provinces the government campaign against the Assemblies of God churches continued successfully.

293 In 2008 there was a proposal in Iran's parliament to make the death sentence mandatory for Iranian citizens who leave Islam, so incorporating the "apostasy law" into Iran's codified law. This proposal was not successful. However, in Iran's codified law there is a provision that the national law can always be superseded by the Sharia law, which has the death sentence for male apostates. There is only one case of an Iranian court using this provision and that is the court of Sari in 1993 when dealing with the Christian Mehdi Dibaj.

294 Mehdi Dibaj had a case, for while across the Muslim world most accept that Islam teaches that the apostate male should be killed, nevertheless there is an important minority that disputes this. One was the late Ayatollah Montazeri, formerly designated Ayatollah Khomeini's successor. He argued that Mohammad never meant that people should be killed for renouncing Islam, but only if they were deemed a political threat. He advocated that people be free to choose their religion.

295 In private conversation with the author.

Their church in Sari was closed down in 1988; in Kerman and Shiraz in 1992; and in Gorgon in 1993.

Now Mehdi Dibaj's case moved centre stage in this battle between the Assemblies of God Church and the authorities. In December the court in Sari made a decision on Mehdi Dibaj's appeal. In his final appearance in the court he gave a powerful testimony. This was later publicized around the world.[296] Despite his testimony, the appeal was rejected, and Mehdi Dibaj was sentenced to death.

Unwisely the court gave the sentenced man a copy of the verdict. This was given to an Armenian Christian working in the Sari prison due to go to Tehran for his Christmas break, and so the document first came to Haik Hovsepian Mehr, and then by fax to his friend Sam Yeghnazar in the UK. Soon the whole world knew that Iran was about to execute a Christian because of apostasy from Islam.

As a result of the international outcry, the Vatican, which has an embassy in Tehran, sought an appointment with the Supreme Leader. Ayatollah Khamenei, who presumably had not been properly briefed by his aides about the Mehdi Dibaj case, denied that Iran executed apostates. He was then shown the official verdict by the Vatican ambassadors. It must have been an embarrassing moment for the Supreme Leader. Back-pedalling, the Vatican officials were now assured that the judge in Sari had made a mistake and the situation would be rectified.

It was a mistake – but it was not rectified.

Mehdi Dibaj was released – but the churches were to face a bitter revenge. Hardliners were determined that the last word would be murder for Christian activists, not sweet smiles to the Vatican. Mehdi Dibaj was freed on 16 January 1994; on 19 January Haik Hovsepian Mehr was abducted. Ten days later his eldest son Joseph identified his mutilated body. The superintendent of the Assemblies of God Church had been

296   See Appendix 3 for the full transcript.

stabbed twenty-seven times.[297] Five months later, on 24 June Mehdi Dibaj went missing. His body was identified on 5 July. He too had been stabbed.

In this attack the Presbyterian Church was not spared. The logic of rooting out all threats to the identity of Iran's Islamic state was at work. The senior pastor of the Presbyterian Church was the ethnic Armenian Revd Tateos Michaelian, a brilliant scholar and a fearless critic of the government's unjust treatment of Christians. Asked by a journalist at the funeral of his friend Haik Hovsepian Mehr about who was to blame for the murder of the Assemblies of God superintendent, Revd Michaelian did not hesitate to accuse the government. Furthermore, while his own church, St John's Presbyterian Church in Tehran, did not attract as many Muslims as the central Assemblies of God church, services were held in Persian, and there were ex-Muslims in the congregation. And like the Hovsepian Mehr brothers, Revd Michaelian had refused to make any promises to officials that he would cease preaching the Gospel to Muslims. He was also a prolific translator of Christian books into Persian, and the main man behind the Good News version of the New Testament in Persian. Revd Michaelian was very actively spreading the Gospel to Muslims. And the Islamic Republic will not tolerate activists. On 29 June 1994 Revd Michaelian went missing; on 2 July his family were asked to identify his body.

For the next two years the government periodically put pressure on the Assemblies of God Church, now led by Edward Hovsepian Mehr, to stop evangelizing Muslims. The authorities specifically wanted the pastor to close down the service held on Fridays at the central church in Tehran whose now 300-strong congregation was mainly made up of Muslims. Revd Hovsepian Mehr resisted these calls, knowing full well the price he might have to pay. To an inquiry held in London into the persecution

297   The story of Haik Hovsepian Mehr's martyrdom is movingly told in a documentary film *A Cry From Iran* made by his sons Joseph and Andreh. The film was released in 2007 and won several awards.

of Christians in Iran, Revd Hovsepian Mehr described the sort of pressure he constantly faced:

> They always threatened me as somebody responsible for the church and there were three areas that they would threaten. First, that they would close our churches if we didn't listen to them and obey. Second that they would imprison us, and the third threat was that they could kill us. And they would say, we will kill you in such a way that no one would know that it was our work.[298]

Revd Hovsepian Mehr was thankfully spared the assassin's dagger. His colleague in the northern province of Mazandaran, Mohammad Bagher Yusefi, known as "Ravanbaksh" (soul-giver) was not. The body of this apostate from Islam and Christian evangelist and pastor was found hanging from a tree in a wood near his home in Sari on 28 September 1996. The authorities asked Revd Hovsepian Mehr to confirm their claim that this was a case of suicide. With a letter from Ravanbaksh outlining all his plans for Christian work on his desk, Revd Hovsepian Mehr refused to offer this confirmation, despite very intense pressure from government officials.[299]

The government had again made their position crystal clear. Christian activism, whether practised by ethnic Christians or Muslim converts, would not be tolerated in the Islamic Republic. Normal church life as set up by the missionaries with congregations based in buildings reaching out to Muslims via the means of preaching and good works was not possible.

---

298 *Christians in Parliament All Party Parliamentary Group Report*, p. 19.
299 In a statement to the Westminster Hearings, 30 April 2012, Revd Edward Hovsepian Mehr said: "They (the authorities) called and told me that 'if you don't declare to the whole world that this man has committed suicide we will put more pressure on you'. Of course I didn't give them the letter that they wanted, I told them, 'I am very sure that you have killed him because a week before his death he had written a plan that he had for the whole year for his Christian activity.'" Ibid., p. 14.

As the house churches began to develop, so the government pressure against the formal structure of the Assemblies of God Church continued. In September 2004 security officials interrupted a church council meeting and arrested all eighty Christians who were present. One report talks of the police "swarming" into the meeting which was being held in a prayer garden on the outskirts of Tehran and "blindfolding all the men and women present and taking them off to be fingerprinted and interrogated".[300]

Ten of the eighty, who were leaders, were then imprisoned. Revd Edward Hovsepian Mehr made this statement concerning their confinement.

> In 2004 they suddenly came in the meeting of 10 Assemblies of God churches and took them to prison. For four nights they kept them in solitary confinement and released them only with this condition: you have no right to evangelise or accept new members, you have no right to baptise anyone. You have to submit to us the full list of all the church members. You have no right to conduct any conferences outside the church building. Inside the church also if you want to have a conference we should be informed and we should know about the subject of the conference. You have to report all the journeys you are making and you have to submit to regular reports to us.[301]

This tight control of the Assembly of God Church continued for the rest of the decade. The pastors had to submit reports of all their activities; cameras were in place outside the church monitoring who was going in;[302] staff had to get government

300   https://www.worldwatchmonitor.org/2004/09-September/newsarticle_3399.html/ Accessed 27 May 2014.
301   *Christians in Parliament All Party Parliamentary Group Report*, p.18.
302   "The Government has put CCTV across the street to take the picture of everyone who going inside the church." Revd Sam Yeghnazar to Westminster Hearings. *Christians in Parliament All Party Parliamentary Group Report*, p. 19.

permission for any international travelling; and the baptisms of ex-Muslims ceased.[303]

This control was also punctuated with arrests and imprisonments. From that group of ten arrested in September 2004, the authorities sentenced Hamid Pourmand to three years' imprisonment because he had served as an officer in the Iranian Army and allegedly had not informed his superiors he was a Christian. He was released before completing his sentence in July 2006. In 2005 a married couple with links to the Assembly of God Church were arrested in Mashad; and in 2006 a Muslim convert connected to the Assemblies of God church in Gorgon before it was closed was kept behind bars for six weeks.

While there were other arrests of Christians with earlier links to the Assemblies of God, after 2006, the next formal attack on an Assemblies of God church came just before Christmas 2011 in the southern city of Ahvaz. The security forces arrested the entire congregation of about fifty-five – men, women, and children – and took them off in two buses to a detention centre. All were released that same day, except four of the leaders who were later sentenced to one year's imprisonment.[304]

A year later, again around Christmas time (27 December), the authorities arrested the much-loved singer and ordained Assemblies of God pastor, Vruir Avanessian. The 61-year-old, suffering from a weak heart, diabetes, and kidney failure, was an irrepressible activist. And activists are not tolerated. The pastor was released on bail after fifteen days, and in September 2013 was sentenced to three and a half years in prison.

In May 2013 the officials campaigning against Protestant Christianity scored their greatest success: the central Assemblies of God church in Tehran, which in recent years had been perhaps the only "building" church to attract hundreds of Muslims to

303 Information given by Christian Human Rights activist Mansour Borji, founder of Article 18, in private conversation 27 May 2014.
304 *Arrests and Incidents 2013*, unpublished report from Anna Enayat, St Antony's College, Oxford University.

its services, was closed down. One of the senior leaders of the church, Revd Soorik Sarkisian, was given an ultimatum: cancel the Friday Persian-speaking service, or the whole church will be shut down. In the background to this ultimatum were shadowy threats that officials would not be able to protect the church from the actions of radicals who might resort to violence, even blowing up the church.[305]

After discussion the church leaders informed the church on 19 May about this ultimatum, and said they would let them know of their final decision shortly.[306] Two days after this announcement, another of the church's senior leaders, Revd Robert Asserian, was arrested and taken to Evin prison. It is not public knowledge whether there was then more communication from officials or not with Revd Sarkisian, but on 26 May he hung a notice on the door of the church saying it was closed for repairs. The church has remained shut. Robert Asserian was released on 2 July. He has not spoken about his imprisonment.

At the time of writing (May 2014) there is only one small Persian-speaking congregation in Rasht connected to the Assemblies of God denomination. They are allowed to function, and according to one commentator it would seem that this group have come to an understanding with the local authorities. Apart from this small group, after fifty years of reaching out to Muslim Iranians, the Assemblies of God Church has no witness in the public space. The government campaign seemed to have won.

The Presbyterians have not fared any better. Their active churches in Tehran, Tabriz, and Hammedan have been closely monitored. In September 2008 the pastor for the Persian-speaking congregation for St Peter's Church in Tehran, Revd Ramtin Soodmand, son of Revd Hussein Soodmand, was arrested and kept in prison for over two months. On his release

305   Information given by Mansour Borji in private conversation, 27 May 2014.
306   https://www.persecution.com/public/newsroom.aspx?story_ID=NTgx Accessed 27 May 2014.

such was the pressure on the other church officials that Ramtin Soodmand was not able to continue his ministry with St Peter's. The Presbyterian church in Mashad was closed down in the late 1980s; however, a retired banker Ibrahim Montazami remained connected with the denomination. For this Ibrahim Montazami was regularly called in by the MOIS for questioning.

After Ramtin Soodmand's arrest in 2008 the authorities then demanded to see the identity cards of all who attended the Persian-speaking services in Tehran. Not surprisingly, this deterred Muslims from coming. Then in 2010 the Presbyterian Church was ordered to close down all their Persian-speaking services. After 180 years of ministering directly to Iranian Muslims, the Presbyterians now have no Christian services left in Persian.

The Roman Catholic presence in Iran, for political reasons,[307] had never been as strong as that of the Anglicans and Presbyterians. And their main ministry has been among the Armenians and Assyrians, posing no threat to Iran's Islamic identity. Furthermore the Islamic Republic understands the influence the Pope holds over the world's 1.2 billion Roman Catholics and so has always hosted a Vatican Embassy in Tehran and employs over eighty full-time diplomats in Rome.[308] Active only among ethnic Christians and representing a major diplomatic influence the Roman Catholics have not attracted the hostile attention of the officials mandated with protecting Iran's Persian Muslim identity – until recently.

307 The first Roman Catholic missionaries in the sixteenth century were supported by the Portuguese who became the enemy of the then king, Shah Abbas. In the seventeenth century, as Europe ripped itself apart with its Christian civil war, there was little support for mission and so the Roman Catholic attempts were underfunded. By the eighteenth century Iran was under the shadow of Russia and the UK, neither power friendly towards Roman Catholic mission. See Chapter 8 of the author's *Iran and Christianity* for more details.

308 http://www.embassypages.com/missions/embassy20786/ Accessed 28 May 2014. It would seem the Islamic Republic's investment has paid off. For after more than thirty years of intimidating other Christians, still the Holy See has never launched a public verbal attack against Tehran.

Father Pierre Humblot is a Frenchman with an Iranian passport who has spent most of his life in Iran serving Roman Catholics. As well as ministering in the Roman Catholic Cathedral of the Consolata in Tehran,[309] Father Humblot also set up St John's Institute (a theological centre) in 1973, providing teaching, orally and in print, about Christian doctrine in Persian.

In 2010 the Institute was closed down, Persian speakers wanting to attend the Roman Catholic cathedral were barred, and Father Humblot was expelled from Iran.[310] Though Father Humblot's work was very low-key, nevertheless it was clear he was actively trying to teach Iranian Muslims about Christ, and so, even though he was a representative of the most famous Christian in the world, he was ejected from a country where he had lived for over fifty years.

The treatment of Father Humblot, and the recent closure of all the Persian-speaking services, raises a question. The MOIS has been formally asking the churches to stop working with Muslims since the mid-1980s. Why did it take until 2013 for nearly all the public church services conducted in Persian to be closed down?

One of the answers to this question is that in 2009 the church portfolio moved from the MOIS, a government agency, to the Revolutionary Guards, a military agency.[311] Both of course are wholly hostile to activist Christianity, and, as seen, the MOIS has certainly been responsible for harassing Christians – and worse. However, perhaps for internal reasons, this agency did not ruthlessly push through what they claimed they wanted – the closing down of Persian-speaking Christian services in the public sphere. The Revolutionary Guards, on the other hand, have.

---

309   The cathedral follows the Latin rite. Most of the other Roman Catholic churches follow the Chaldean.

310   See http://www.franceculture.fr/emission-foi-et-tradition-noel-en-iran-2012-12-25 Accessed 28 May 2014.

311   Confirmed by Mansour Borji. For those being arrested they were often dealing with agents from the MOIS; however, Mansour Borji says that after 2009, the campaign against the churches was masterminded by the Revolutionary Guards.

Part of the reason for the Guards' success in this matter is their being an effective military organization. But it is also important to underline that in 2009 there was a sharp political edge to their activities.

In 2007 Ayatollah Khamenei relieved the then commander of the Revolutionary Guards, General Safari, and appointed General Mohammad Jafari to the post. In a narrative where Iran was constantly threatened by her enemies engineering regime change, General Jafari had at least three qualities that suited him for his new role. He had a reputation for being tough – indeed some sources linked him to the murder of the Kurdish leader, Dr Abdulrahman Ghassemlou, and his aides in 1989. He was also an expert on "soft revolutions", having studied the "coloured" uprisings in the former countries of the Soviet Union and its sphere of influence.[312] Finally he had a very clear strategy on how to meet Iran's foreign enemies, whether they attacked externally or internally: asymmetrical warfare.[313] This is the use of unconventional military means to deal with a larger enemy. Within Iran itself, asymmetrical warfare means ensuring each region has the power to act independently. So once in office General Jafari decentralized the command structure of the Revolutionary Guards into thirty-one command centres in twenty-nine cities and two in Tehran.[314]

When Tehran and other cities erupted after the 2009 presidential elections there was no doubt in Mohammad Jafari's mind as to what the protests were all about. The demonstrators had all adopted the colour green; certain brands (Nokia and Siemens) were boycotted; on some of the marches protestors

---

312　Czechoslovakia's Velvet Revolution of 1989, Georgia's Rose Revolution of 2003, Ukraine's Orange Revolution of 2004, and Krygyzstan's Tulip Revolution of 2005.
313　For a helpful article on Mohammad Jafari see http://www.pbs.org/wgbh/pages/frontline/tehranbureau/2010/01/a-hardliners-hardliner.html Accessed 28 May 2014.
314　http://www.pbs.org/wgbh/pages/frontline/tehranbureau/2010/01/a-hardliners-hardliner.html Accessed 28 May 2014.

were silent; on others slogans were chanted.[315] These were all the hallmarks of a soft revolution as taught by the Harvard professor Gene Sharp, the godfather of non-violent revolution. His booklet *From Dictatorship to Democracy* was available in Persian on the internet and was being downloaded by thousands of Iranians. The protests, or "sedition" as General Jafari called them, were a brazen attempt by Iran's enemy, the US, to create another colour revolution and to overthrow the regime.

It is not difficult to see where churches like the Assemblies of God and the Presbyterians would fit into Mohammad Jafari's scheme of things. Though seemingly small and insignificant to the layman, experts like him could see how these sorts of churches were fifth columns, which, with sudden expansion, would represent a threat to Iran's internal security. For the Revolutionary Guards under Jafari, getting the churches to stop holding Persian-speaking services was not an aim, as it was under the MOIS, but an immediate military necessity. And so it happened, even if it meant risking Iran's relationship with the Vatican.

The irony is that as the Revolutionary Guards were closing down the churches in the public sphere, Christianity in people's homes was already spreading all over Iran. The closure of the Persian services confirmed not the success of the Revolutionary Guards control of Christians, but the success of those Christians who several years earlier had decided to concentrate on developing house churches.

Of course some of these house churches had already been picked up by the Revolutionary Guards' radar; and in Mohammad Jafari's mind, steeped in asymmetrical warfare that depended on hidden cells, they were even more dangerous than the official churches.

315   Gene Sharp lists 198 strategies for non-violent protest. From this list here are the ones used by the protesters in Iran: 7. Slogans; 18. Symbolic colours (green); 26. Paint as protest; 28. Symbolic sounds; 38. Marches; 52. Silence; 71. Consumer boycott (Nokia, Siemens); 135. Popular non-obedience; 194. Disclosing identities of secret agents. See http://www.csmonitor.com/World/Middle-East/2009/1229/Iran-protesters-the-Harvard-professor-behind-their-tactics Accessed 28 May 2014.

Against the house churches

Born out of persecution, the story of Iran's new Christians in the house-church movement has been constantly marked by suffering. A few who have been persecuted are well known to the wider Christian public. Maryam Rostampour and Marzieyeh Amirizadeh were arrested in 2009 and attracted international headlines during their nine-month ordeal in Evin prison, Tehran. They have since written a book, *Captive in Iran*[316] about their experiences. The case of Youcef Naderkhani, a Christian[317] house-church leader, also attracted a lot of media attention. This is because he was sentenced to death for apostasy in 2010, a decision upheld by the Supreme Court in Tehran in 2011.[318] As well as human rights groups and churches, political leaders such as US President Obama and the former UK Foreign Secretary William Hague spoke out. Youcef Naderkhani was released in January 2013. President Obama and the world-famous evangelist Billy Graham have also campaigned for the release of the American Iranian pastor, Saeed Abedeni, who, on a visit to Iran in July 2010, was arrested and then sentenced to eight years' imprisonment in 2013.

Another name that briefly appeared in the international press was that of Ghorban Tourani, Iran's first house-church martyr.[319] Ghorban's conversion to Christ was dramatic. As a

316   Maryam Rostampour and Marzieh Amirizadeh, *Captive in Iran*.

317   There has been some discussion as to whether Youcef Naderkhani's Christian faith is orthodox. The Mohabat News agency has alleged that the pastor belongs to the non-Trinitarian sect "Jesus Only", which has links to the teaching of the American preacher William Branham who did not accept the church's traditional understanding of the Trinity. See http://mohabatnews.com/index.php?option=com_content&view=article&id=3467:is-nadarkhani-an-evangelical-chrsitian-special-report-on-non-trinitatian-cult-inside-iran-&catid=36:iranian-christians&Itemid=279 Accessed 6 June 2014. In an interview, Youcef Naderkhani has rejected these accusations. During his imprisonment most Christians took the view that he and his family deserved all the support possible as he and his family were suffering unjustly. The issue of false Christian teaching is addressed in Chapter 7.

318   An outline of Youcef Naderkhani's ordeal can be read here: https://www.worldwatchmonitor.org/2012/09-September/1792744/ Accessed 6 June 2014.

319   It is true "Ravanbaksh" was leading house groups, but he was operating under the auspices of the Assemblies of God Church. Ghorban Tourani was the first house-

teenager he was a devout Muslim, but, failing to find God in Islam, this Turkman from the north of Iran became a dedicated atheist. Work took him to then Soviet-controlled Turkmenistan in the early 1980s and here he ended up in prison for fifteen years on a charge of manslaughter. In prison he heard the Gospel from a cellmate and after reading the New Testament he became a Christian. On his release in 1998 he returned home to his family and after two years he had led twelve of his family and friends to Christ. This was his house church. Again – as with all the other house churches we looked at in Chapter 6, Ghorban Tourani received mentoring from established church leaders, but this was a group of Iran's new Christians.

On 22 November 2005 government officials arrested Ghorban Tourani at his home in Gonbad-e-Kavus in the north-east of Iran. A few hours later, his corpse, covered in blood from stab wounds, was left in front of his house. Government officials returned to search through Ghorban Tourani's house. They told his widow, Offool Eachicke, that her husband had been killed by fanatical Muslims, angered over his apostasy. There seems to have been no search for those murderers.[320]

As well as these few people who have quite rightly won international media attention, hundreds of other new Christians have suffered. Thankfully the brutality meted out to Ghorban Tourani has not been the norm for Iran's new Christians. Nevertheless as news of his bloodied corpse being dumped outside his family home broke across Iran it was a chilling reminder of what can happen to a Christian in the Islamic Republic. Though uncommon, the event etched violent murder onto the background of the story of Iran's new Christians.

church leader, with no connections to an established denomination, to be killed. Thankfully, so far, he has been the last.

320   Commentators have noted that the security forces in the north of Iran tend to have a more aggressive approach to Christianity: "In recent years, authorities in Iran's northern provinces along the Caspian Sea coast have been particularly harsh toward the growing number of house churches cropping up in the region, arresting lay pastors and individual members known to be involved." See https://www.worldwatchmonitor. org/2006/06-June/newsarticle_4413.html/ Accessed 29 May 2014.

Murder, though, has not been the norm; more typical has been this sort of ordeal: house raids; arbitrary arrest; the confiscation of personal items; detention, often in solitary confinement; long hours of interrogation, always with psychological torture, sometimes physical; imprisonment; release for a very large bail which forces families to hand over property deeds; eventually a court case and a prison sentence – not for a religious felony, but crimes against Iran's national security.

Every house church looked at in Chapter 6 has endured this sort of persecution. At least thirty from Arthur John's church have known prison. Fatimeh, and many others from Daniel Alexander's group, spent weeks behind bars. Fariborz was arrested and held for sixteen days in solitary confinement, and then twenty-two days in prison; Hassan and Susan were also arrested and imprisoned.

From these five groups the man who suffered most was Mojtaba. He was imprisoned many times before he eventually left Iran in the early 2000s. Sometimes Mojtaba was held for two weeks, sometimes a month, sometimes three months. Every time he was taken he was beaten. The authorities wanted to know the names of other Christians he was connected to, and Mojtaba would not say. Sometimes the guards would tie one of his hands to his waist, and then tie the other to one of his feet. Mojtaba would be beaten until he became unconscious, but he would never agree to give names to his captives.

The last time Mojtaba was taken he was told he would he executed. He was blindfolded, taken to a platform, and he felt a noose going round his neck. He was then pushed off the platform. He fully expected to die. Instead he landed on a padded floor unharmed. The guards had put stretchable elastic around his neck. It was a mock execution.

Mojtaba was then released, with this threat ringing in his ears. If he did not stop evangelizing to Muslims his children would die. This threat sent him and his family out of Iran.[321]

As the 2000s continued many other house-church Christians would be forced to endure arbitrary arrest, imprisonment, interrogation, excessive bail, and court sentences.

In 2006 there were reports of arrests in Tehran, Karaj, Rasht, and Bandar-i Anzali.[322] While for each Christian arrested the ordeal was terrifying, the number of reported arrests of house-church Christians was small – less than ten.[323] Then in 2008 the numbers begin to climb, sharply. According to the cautious and meticulous researcher Dr Anna Enayat[324] (Senior Associate Member of St Antony's College, Oxford) at least 576 house-church Christians experienced arbitrary arrest in towns and cities across Iran from March 2008 to May 2014.[325] The sharp rise began in 2008 when by October there were at least fifty-three cases of arbitrary arrest reported.[326] This continued into 2009 and 2010 when the total rose to over 300. In the summer of 2010 it seemed all the government machinery for hounding Christians went up a gear.

321   The author was given this information in a private interview.

322   https://www.worldwatchmonitor.org/2006/12-December/newsarticle_4685.html/ Accessed 29 May 2014.

323   Issa Motamedi Mojdehi from Rasht (August 2006); Behnam Irani and Peyman Salarvand, from Karaj; Behrouz Sadegh-Khandjani, Shirin Sadegh-Khandjani, and Hamid Reza Toluinia, from Tehran; and Yousef Nadarkhani, Parviz Khalaj, and Muhammad Reza-Taghizadeh, from Rasht (December 2014). Source: www.worldwatchmonitor.org

324   For background on Dr Enayat see footnote 34 in Chapter 1.

325   "Arrests and other incidents relating to converts to Christianity reported from the beginning of the Iranian year 1387 (21 March 2008) to the end of 1389 (20 March 2011)", extract from unpublished report by Anna Enayat, St Antony's College, Oxford, analysing the position of converts to Christianity in Iran. The figures from this report (489 arrests) are here added to the number of Dr Enayat's report for 2013, seen by the author (71 arrests). The figures for 2014 (Jan–May) are also included. The 2014 figures are from the Elam Ministries advocacy officer. Other sources: World Watch Monitor: www.worldwatchmonitor.org; Elam Ministries www.elam.com; and *Christians in Parliament All Party Parliamentary Group Report.*

326   Elam Ministries, "Iranian Christians Under Attack – Call For Prayer", October 2008.

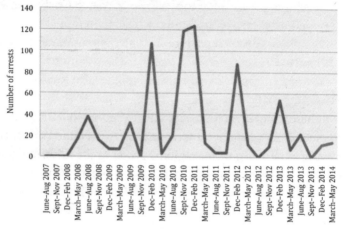

**The arrests of Christians in Iran
June 2007–May 2014**

In October 2010 the Supreme Leader of Iran, Ayatollah Ali Khamenei, made a public speech about influences that he believed were causing young Muslims to fall away from the "pure" Islamic faith, including Salman Rushdie, Hollywood films, and philosophies or religions such as Sufi Islam, nihilism, and the Baha'i faith. Khamenei also warned about the deception of the "enemy" through the expanding "network of house churches".

Christmas can be a generous time in Iran. Christians tend to gather in larger groups to celebrate which makes arresting them easier for the authorities. The yearly crackdown has become ironically known as "the Christmas gift".

In September 2013, the newly elected President Rouhani went to New York to attend a meeting of the UN General Assembly. It was in Iran's interests to present a good image at the UNGA. This may explain why there were no arrests in the September to November period, and why a couple of Christian prisoners were also released in this window of time.

Just from June until September over 100 Christians endured arbitrary arrest.[327] And then over Christmas and the New Year the machinery went into top gear: eighty-five Christians in twelve cities were arrested, and officials attempted to seize another fifteen, but they were not in their homes.[328] From 2011 to 2013 there have been at least seventy more arrests.[329] At the time of writing at least sixty known Christians are in prison.[330]

These figures are a part of the story of Iran's new Christians. As a whole they represent a determined effort by the government of a major regional power to use its formidable security apparatus to eliminate house-church Christianity. There was nothing sporadic about the arrests over the Christmas of 2010. They were coordinated and planned. Officials have held meetings, looked at maps, agreed on timings, and assigned personnel all with one aim: to crush Christianity.

Each raid and arrest also has its own story. For many it was the awfulness of arrest and being taken, usually blindfolded, to a police station for questioning, or being held in a home while the police, with threats, urge them to sign a form promising not to spread the Gospel of Jesus Christ among Muslims. When the police detain a large group they usually release most of the members after questioning, but the leaders are detained. This is what happened in Tehran on 29 August 2013. There was a raid on a house group with fifteen members:

> **The agents video-taped us all, then divided us into three groups and held us in separate rooms. They then placed prepared interrogation forms in front of us and, without allowing us to read them, ordered us to sign the blank**

---

327   Elam Ministries briefing document: "Severe intensification of arrests and imprisonment of Christians in Iran", 25 January 2011.

328   Ibid.

329   Dr Anna Enayat's 2013 report, seen by the author.

330   http://www.elam.com/page/persecuted-not-forsaken Accessed 29 May 2014

papers... and then sign the back. The agents' behaviour was
very threatening and insulting.[331]

The group members were allowed to then leave. The leaders of
the group, Amir Ebrahami and Kamiyar Barzegar and his wife,
were not. They were arrested.

For Iranians who are used to a reasonably comfortable
lifestyle and being treated decently, prison is a grim shock.[332]
An atmosphere of fear is created on arrival. One Christian
was brought blindfolded to the prison and then entered with
another man who had also been arrested. As the two came
into the building one of the guards shouted out, "What's
happening?" and then another shouted back, "Oh nothing, just
two prisoners, one for prison, the other for execution."[333] This
was a deliberate practice to inject fear into people's hearts, not
least because every Iranian knows from the most casual reading
of recent history that executions without due legal process have
happened in Iran's prisons.

After the arrival there is the strip search. This is degrading.
Humiliation is the word used by Maryam Rostampour when
this happened to her.

> We were escorted into a room where two sleepy, grumpy
> female guards waited for us. "Hand over all your
> belongings," one of them ordered. We gave them our
> wristwatches and everything we had. "Now take off all your
> clothes. Underwear, too." We were then subjected to the
> humiliation of a full body search.[334]

331   Dr Anna Enayat's 2013 report, seen by the author. Dr Enayat's source is FCNN
(Persian), 5 October 2013.
332   For a detailed account of what prison is like for Iranian Christians see Maryam
Rostampour and Marzieh Amirizadeh's *Captive in Iran*. *Then They Came for Me* by
Maziar Bahari gives a vivid description of life for political prisoners inside Iran's
prisons.
333   Testimony from an Anglican Christian serving in church in Isfahan, heard by
the author.
334   Maryam Rostampour and Marzieh Amirizadeh, p. 20.

One middle-aged lady was arrested and taken to prison. After having her photo taken she was led blindfolded to a small dirty room and told to take her clothes off. She said, "All right, but give me the clothes I am to wear." The guard said, "No – first take your clothes off." The lady had to obey. Now free, the memory has scarred her.[335]

After the humiliation of the strip search, there is the shock of the living conditions. This is Maryam Rostampour's memory of her first night in detention.

> … the place was filthy beyond imagining… the stench of sweat, vomit, and backed up toilets was overpowering. It took all our self-control to keep us from retching… the floor of the toilet area was awash in muck from two overflowing commodes; the trash bin was piled high with used sanitary pads… [The blankets] were loathsome – stiff with dirt and smelling strongly of urine, some them still wet.[336]

After arriving in the prison system, the Christian prisoners might spend a few nights in a general detention centre and that might be the end of their ordeal. Others, though, are sent to solitary confinement. This was the experience of Arash Basirat and Mahmoud Azad, arrested in Shiraz in 2008. These house-church Christians spent two months in isolation. This was also the experience of Ali Golcin, arrested in Veramin in May 2010. He spent eighty-seven days in solitary confinement. This too was the experience of the Iranian-American pastor, Said Abedini. He spent four weeks alone. And this too was the experience of Farshid Fathi, arrested in Tehran in December 2010. He spent 100 days in solitary confinement. There are many others.[337]

335 Testimony heard by the author.
336 Maryam Rostampour and Marzieh Amirizadeh, p. 20.
337 For example: Mahmoud Azadeh arrested in Neyshapour in 2009, held in solitary confinement for five days; Behman Irani arrested in Karaj in April 2010, held for seventy-six days in solitary confinement; Neshan Saeedi arrested in Ahvaz in July 2010, kept in solitary confinement for seventy days. Source: "Arrests and

While some of the isolation cells are small and cramped, reports of prisoners who are later released say that it is clear that the main pressure is the silence, the total separation from other humans, and especially the disruption of normal sleeping patterns.

Masoumeh was held in solitary confinement for over two weeks. Her cell was small, but the pain of the ordeal was the complete severance from human contact. The only people she saw were the guards who brought her food, and they were cold and rude to her.

Another Christian prisoner, Nader, testified to how the system deliberately disoriented the prisoner's sleeping patterns.

> My cell was 2m by 1.5m and the loo was in the cell too.
> There was a bare, bright lamp that was on 24 hours a day,
> so I could neither sleep nor have any privacy. I had maybe
> one hour of sleep per day towards the end. I begged them to
> turn the light off but they wouldn't. The door of the cell was
> steel with a little hatch; in the middle of the night they could
> come and bang it just to disturb and scare us.[338]

Though completely alone in many isolation cells there are cameras whirring all the time. The inmate knows that everything they are doing is being watched. This is unnerving, and of course embarrassing as the toilet is also in the cell being watched.

Some of the isolation cells did not even have their own toilets. The prisoner had to get the attention of a guard who could therefore humiliate a prisoner by not responding.

This is what happened to Reza, a Christian prisoner, arrested in the north-west of Iran in 2011.

other incidents relating to converts to Christianity reported from the beginning of the Iranian year 1387 (21 March 2008) to the end of 1389 (20 March 2011)", Anna Enayat. Information from Elam Ministries indicates that many of the house-church Christians arrested over the Christmas of 2010 endured solitary confinement – e.g. Sara Akhavan; Mehdi Forootan; Khalil-Ali; and Mostafa Shokrollahi.

338 *Christians in Parliament All Party Parliamentary Group Report*, p. 17.

> For fifteen days I was held in the Ministry of Intelligence
> detention centre and kept in a small cell alone. There was
> no toilet in the room and sometimes they refused to let me
> out to go and use the bathroom, so I was forced to go in the
> cell.[339]

It seemed that using the toilet was deliberately made into a
tormenting experience in some prisons. One Christian prisoner
explained how the toilet area was not just kept in darkness, but
the lavatories were on a different level, so the prisoners had to
climb up into the dark in order to relieve themselves.[340]

One Christian's cell was next to the prison's torture room, a
grim warning of what could await the obstinate.

> I was put into solitary confinement. I soon discovered my
> cell was located next to a torture chamber because every
> night I would hear the sounds of people screaming and
> crying.[341]

The Christian prisoners kept in solitary confinement also
endured long hours of questioning, at all times of day – and
night.

> Very late at night whilst making a lot of noise to instil fear,
> they used to open cell's metallic door, put the blindfold on
> my eyes and lead me to the interrogation room. In the room
> they would lead me to a chair directly facing the wall, and
> would ask me to move the blindfold up, just enough to see
> the paper they were providing on which I was to answer the
> interrogator's questions.[342]

339   Witness statement made to Elam Ministries Advocacy Officer. Seen by the
author, 30 May 2014.
340   Information given to the author in a private conversation.
341   Statement of Khalil Yar-Ali, *Christians in Parliament All Party Parliamentary
Group Report*, p. 16.
342   Witness statement made to Elam Ministries Advocacy Officer. Seen by the
author, 30 May 2014. Though this description relates back to an arrest that occurred

These interrogations can be truly traumatic experiences for people who just a few days earlier were living normal lives, simply trying to be faithful Christians.

Sometimes the officials will be abusive and violent, as they were toward Mostafa Shokrollahi, arrested in 2011:

> When we arrived they took me for interrogation... Four people stood there and took it in turns to shout and scream at me or beat me and slap me in the face... They regularly beat me on the head and even when the lunchtime call to prayer went out, they would not stop. To this day I still get pain in my head from those beatings.[343]

Nearly all those who have spoken about their ordeals in the interrogation room talk about the threats and deceit the officials use to break the prisoner's spirit. The poison of these words can continue to disturb a prisoner long after they have been released. Christian prisoner Khahlil, arrested in 2011, was threatened with electric torture:

> They took me to the torture chamber and strapped me on a torture bed. The interrogator said, "I am not a child to be messed with. Tell me everything or we will torture you. The torturer rested a belt studded with metal pieces on my back and threatened to beat me with it...[344]

Christian prisoner Soraya, arrested in both 2008 and 2009, was threatened with rape:

> I felt someone caress my head and pull my head covering up. He said, "What a nice neck you have. It is good for the priests. You are available to them, but not for us? You

in 1995, these methods are still used today.
343   Witness statement made to Elam Ministries Advocacy Officer. Seen by the author, 30 May 2014.
344   Ibid.

are the group that has to be sodomized until you die!" He kissed the back of my neck and I pushed him away. He slapped me so hard that I screamed and fell to the ground.

Then my interrogator called his colleague. When they were both inside the room he said, "… We can do you right here. We can do you right in front of the eyes of your husband and brother." I didn't understand what they were saying. Then the other one said, "No Haji! They are the whores of the church and they would enjoy such a thing. We have to use a glass bottle."

I felt so terrible that I threw up blood.[345]

Christian prisoner Mostafa Shokrollahi was also threatened with rape. When the officials asked him for his email password, he replied that his password was personal.

Then they replied, "We will show you what is personal" and they made me stand up and they stripped off my shorts. They threatened to rape me. So I gave them my password and they lay me down and whipped me. They would regularly threaten me with execution during my interrogations.[346]

Prisoners are also told horrible lies about their loved ones. This was the experience of Christian prisoner Khalil, arrested in 2011.

They tortured me psychologically… they spoke against my fiancée, and said she was sleeping around with various men. They even told me that the principal of her university had confirmed this to them. They said they had pictures of my fiancée with no clothes on as more proof.[347]

345   Ibid.
346   Ibid.
347   Witness statement made to Elam Ministries Advocacy Officer. Seen by the author, 30 May 2014.

It was also the experience of Christian prisoner Matthew, arrested in 2010:

> Worse than the physical mistreatment was the psychological pressure: they told me my wife was sick and dying. They also said, "Your mum is now in the hospital dying from worry; what have you done for her?"

This sort of psychological torture tore a wide wound in the heart of Fatimeh. She and her sister Fara were both arrested in December 2010. A few weeks later Fara was called out of the prison cell and was then released. However Fatimeh did not know this, so when Fara did not return she asked the guard where her sister was. The guard replied that Fara had been sent for execution. Fatimeh collapsed in grief, completely distraught. Two days later she was able to talk to her family who had arranged the bail for her release. Even when they told her Fara was alive and well, she remained inconsolable until she actually saw her sister again.

After solitary confinement and interrogation the Christian prisoners are then sent to the general ward, which has its own challenges of overcrowding, sickness, and danger from other prisoners.

This was made clear in Vahik Abrahamian's testimony in the Westminster Hearings:

> In a room where 22 people can hardly stay, 45 people were there. In a hall that 120 can stay, 325 were there… Most of the time we were sick. We couldn't get well… My wife [also imprisoned] was very unwell… she would say, "I cannot drink the water because it is contaminated." She said, "I cannot eat because if I eat I cannot retain the food."[348]

348 Statement of Vahik Abrahamian, *Christians in Parliament All Party Parliamentary Group Report*, p. 15.

The overcrowding meant using the toilet became a major trial, as Khalil Yar-Ali, arrested in 2012, explained in the Westminster Hearings:

> There were three bathrooms and three toilets for about three hundred people in that section of the toilet.[349]

In these over-crowded wards Christians were not always given a warm welcome by the other prisoners, many of whom were drug addicts, or even convicted murderers. Thankfully there are no reports to date of Christians being beaten up or raped by other prisoners, but from what was told to Matthew, arrested in 2010, it is clear there could be tension:

> I was asked why I was there by my cellmates, so I told them that I am a Christian. One of them contradicted me and said I must have done something wrong. I said, "No, I had just converted." He said, "Return to Islam then." I refused: "No, I have found something wonderful I don't want to give up." He said, "If I were a judge I would have you killed." He was about forty years old.[350]

Of the hundreds of house-church Christians detained since 2008, sixty are still behind bars. Many therefore have been arrested, imprisoned, and then released – but on bail. And that is another part of the suffering they have endured. In research that looks at over 100 cases of Christians being arrested in 2010 it is not difficult to conclude that many families had to pay an exorbitant amount of money to provide bail for their loved ones.

One lady, arrested in July 2010, was released on a bail of $250,000. The average salary in Iran is $500 a month. So the bail

---

349   Statement of Khalil Yar-Ali, *Christians in Parliament All Party Parliamentary Group Report*, p. 16.
350   Witness statement made to Elam Ministries Advocacy Officer. Seen by the author, 30 May 2014.

figure represents over forty years' work. More usual amounts were between $50,000 to $80,000; that is eight years and thirteen years' worth of the average salary respectively. These are crippling figures. At least seven families in 2010 had to hand over the title deeds of their properties to secure the freedom of their relatives.

This then immediately causes a dilemma. When they are out on bail the Christian can then either wait for the court case, where it is likely they will be sentenced to several years in prison for actions against "national security", or they can go into exile. But then their family faces the risk of losing their property. In some cases of Christians going abroad, this risk is seemingly becoming a reality.

Once released on bail some Christians decide to leave Iran. They then join the long waiting list of Iranians waiting first for acceptance by the UNHCR (UN High Commissioner for Refugees) as bona fide refugees, and then another long wait for re-settlement. Effectively their punishment is exile.

Others choose to stay and wait for the court hearing knowing full well that they are likely to get a custodial sentence for several years, usually for the crime of "endangering Iran's national security".

There is much irony when it comes to considering the government's motives for unleashing this persecution against Iran's house Christians. First there is the irony that the arrest of Christians *seems* to be about religion, but in fact these recent arrests are really to do with politics. Iran is ruled according to a political narrative that presents those in authority as being the guardians of the country's identity. The basis of their authoritarian power is that they are serving the greater good of protecting Iran from her devious and determined enemies whose hearts are set on overthrowing the Islamic Republic and making Iran their puppet.

In the aftermath of the presidential elections of 2009 this

narrative went into top gear. The need for evidence for these nefarious foreign conspiracies became an urgent political necessity, especially for the Supreme Leader whose credibility had been severely shaken by the protests and the ruthless way in which they were suppressed.

There were murmurs even in the religious heartland of Qom. So in the autumn of 2010 the Supreme Leader made a much-publicized visit to what is in effect Iran's religious capital to renew his relationship with the religious establishment.[351] In this most important speech Ayatollah Khamenei reiterated the old script: it was impossible to understand the 2009 protests without including foreign involvement. And then – completely in tune with the views of Mohammad Jafari, the leader of the Revolutionary Guards – the Supreme Leader emphasized how Iran's enemies were seeking to destabilize the country from within:

> [Iran's enemies] want to diminish the people's faith in Islam and Islam's sanctities. Inside the country, using various means they [want to] shake the foundation of the faith of the people, especially the young generation. From the spread of loose and shameless lifestyles, to the promotion of false mysticism – the fake variety of real [Islamic] mysticism – to the spread [of] Baha'ism, to the spread of a network of house churches; these are the actions that are being undertaken today – with tact and calculation and careful study – by enemies of Islam. And their goal is to weaken the religion within the society.[352]

This speech by Iran's head of state clearly condemned house-church Christians as the enemies of Iran who are controlled

351   For a full explanation of why Ayatollah Khamenei needed to make this visit see http://www.pbs.org/wgbh/pages/frontline/tehranbureau/2010/11/khamenei-coerces-qom-into-submission.html
352   http://www.iranhumanrights.org/wp-content/uploads/Christians_report_Final_for-web.pdf Accessed 3 June 2014.

by foreigners. They were a fifth column. And now the security forces needed to prove they existed and show their constituents that the government was well able to deal with this threat. Arrests were needed. And as we have seen, there was a sharp increase in the number of Christians being arrested from the autumn of 2009 onwards.

When in one day (26 December 2010) over twenty house-church leaders were arrested in Tehran, the governor of the city, Morteza Tamaddon, made a statement that in every detail underlined the familiar political narrative that was the foundation of the government's authority:

> Just like the Taliban… who have inserted themselves into Islam like a parasite, they have crafted a movement with *Britain's backing* in the name of Christianity… But their conspiracy was unveiled quickly and the first blows were delivered to them… Various kinds of fake, deviated and corrupt cults have sharpened their teeth for our beliefs and one can see their activities among the youth. [Author's italics.][353]

The governor first emphasizes that the Christians are an "enemy within", then he insists they are supported by a name that is synonymous for most Iranians with duplicity and malign meddling – Britain;[354] and finally there is the reassurance that the regime is protecting the Islamic Republic – "their conspiracy was unveiled quickly".

The government itself had broadcast the theme music for their harassment of the house-church Christians. The music is essentially political. And this has later been confirmed by the charges of which the Christians are found guilty. They are usually from a section within Iran's Islamic penal code entitled

353 http://www.alarabiya.net/articles/2011/01/04/132214.html
354 So the popularity of the book *My Uncle Napoleon* by Iraj Pezeshkzad that satirizes the belief that the British lie behind all Iran's woes.

"Offenses against the National and International Security of the State".[355]

Whether the government actually believes that these Christians pose a serious threat to Iran's national security is an interesting question. What is fairly certain is that these arrests bolster the whole political narrative that the government is the trusted guardian of Iran's Shia national identity. This, as well as possibly a genuine concern for people's spiritual welfare, also explains why many Christian prisoners have faced a lot of pressure to return to the faith of their birth.

So one Christian prisoner said during his interrogation:

> They would send people to try and make me pray Islamic prayers. They said if I complied just once then I would be released.[356]

Another, Khalil, was offered bribes to return to Islam:

> They tried to make me reconvert to Islam during interrogations. They also told me they would get a good job for me if I returned to Islam. They offered me a good financial position... these things were being offered to me repeatedly.[357]

There are other accounts of the prison guards putting on Islamic prayers very loudly near to the cells of Christians, or of Christian prisoners being put in a room with an Islamic

---

355 Articles 498 and 499 of Iran's Islamic penal code describe a category of prohibited behaviour that is wide and vague and can be easily used against Christians. The provisions state that whoever forms or joins a group or association either inside or outside Iran, which seeks to "disturb the security of the country", will be sentenced to between two and ten years of imprisonment. Likewise Article 500 can be used against Christians. It states, "Anyone who undertakes any form of propaganda against the Islamic Republic of Iran Regime, or in favor of opposition groups and organizations, shall be sentenced to three months to one year in prison."
356 Statement to Elam Ministries Advocacy Officer, seen by the author.
357 Ibid.

expert – obviously hoping there would be a conversion back to Islam.

There is a final irony at the heart of all this persecution, well known by all students of church history. It is this: while the government persecutes for political reasons, the impact on the Christians is entirely spiritual. And that spiritual impact brings about church growth.

Those who have survived Iran's prisons testify to the way their suffering strengthens their spiritual life. The account of Mojtaba, the church leader who was arrested many times, testifies that the purpose of his suffering was to mould his character. One can see how prison achieved this from his account here:

> Your greatest enemy in prison is time. How to control time?
> One routine is to exercise. Do so much so you cannot stand.
> Then lie down and start thinking. God created you, and
> then go through the whole Bible. This helps your mind.
> This means your thinking is kept fresh. And then preach
> to yourself: about the return of Christ; the glory of the
> believer. Find sermons and preach to yourself. With this you
> have used up four to five hours. Then talk to someone in
> your family. Then walk in your cell.[358]

Fatimeh, the church leader from Tehran, makes the same point about how her suffering in prison impacted her character.

> I had been a Christian eleven years. I learned more during
> my days in prison than I had during the eleven years… I
> matured. I learned how to trust God. My vision became
> bigger. A few weeks before being taken into prison it was laid
> on my heart to share messages based on Romans 5:3–5 about
> suffering producing hope. My first week [in prison] was very
> hard, and then God spoke. "What was that message you were
> preaching? You must walk according to what you preached.
> Get up and stand on this. *I am building your character.*" So I

358   Private interview with the author.

got up and first of all I repented for not trusting God. And I started proclaiming that God was in control.

Like Mojtaba, Fatimeh experienced God's presence:

> Before prison we read a lot about the Holy Spirit giving us the right words; in prison I experienced it. Sometimes I would return from a period of interrogation with tears of gratefulness in my eyes because things had come to my mind that I had no idea of.

Fatimeh came to value the power of prayer:

> I was very aware of people praying for me. Sometimes a spirit of laughter would fill me. This was because of intercession.

Also like Mojtaba, Fatimeh deeply appreciated the Bible:

> Also in prison remembering verses became very important to me. I spent a lot of time doing this.

Fatimeh's conclusion of the experience is this:

> Overall the prison experience has increased my anointing and authority. Telling people to trust that God can find a way out is not a theory for me. I have seen this happen. I know he can be trusted.

And Mojtaba says:

> Persecution and church growth are connected… if we stay in our faith while being persecuted, we will definitely see miracles and growth.[359]

359   In private interview with the author.

Perhaps a few of Iran's new Christians have faltered in the fires of persecution, but most of them have let that fire do its divine work and they have come out of prison, as Fatimeh testifies, with more anointing and more authority.

And Christians have also come out of prison with more wisdom. For the experience of prison has trained Iran's new Christians to be extremely cautious as they share the Gospel.

And yet the Christians who have suffered have more zeal for the Gospel. Indeed, even in prison, their zeal increased. There are numerous stories from Christian prisoners of how they used their time in prison to share Christ. Christian prisoners Maryam Rostampour and Marzieh Amirizadeh Esmaeilabad witnessed to many other prisoners. Marzieh makes this clear as she describes their departure from Vozara detention centre.

> The people who arrested us thought we were suffering in misery. In fact, we had shared the Gospel more openly behind bars than we had ever been able to do on the outside… As we entered each cell, we prayed for all the people who had been locked up there… There were damp places on the walls, where little chunks of plaster had fallen off. Using these pieces of plaster as chalk, we wrote Bible verses and Christian messages all over the walls, and on the ceilings where prisoners could read them as they fell asleep. We prayed aloud and sang songs until late in the night. All alone in an underground prison cell, we shared a joyous celebration of faith.[360]

A middle-aged Christian lady who shared her faith with many while in prison said, on her release, that she wanted to go back "to finish the job".

Christian prisoner Mani was chained to another prisoner, both waiting to go into the court. When the other prisoner found out Mani was a Christian he became very happy and

360   Maryam Rostampour and Marziyeh Amirizadeh, p. 71.

asked about Jesus. Mani whispered the Gospel into his ear. And then, surrounded by the guards of the Islamic Republic, this prisoner gave his life to Jesus Christ.[361]

Iran's new Christians have suffered – and continue to suffer. Those who inflict persecution on the Christians want their spirits to break, and their numbers to diminish.

But that is not how the story ends.

Despite the constant threat of arrest, interrogation, and imprisonment, the spirit of Iran's new Christians is absolutely not broken, and, as seen in our first chapter, their numbers are most definitely rising – indeed Iran's church is reckoned to be the fastest-growing in the world.

This is the double irony at the heart of the story of Iran's new Christians. Wanting to eliminate Persian-speaking Christianity from Iran, the government from the mid-1980s put more and more pressure on the official churches to exclude Iranians from a Muslim background. Their campaign has been largely successful. There are very few public Christian meetings in Iran in Persian. But this success is a Pyrrhic victory. For out of this persecution against the official churches, the house churches have been born. There is a clear link, almost like an umbilical cord, between the harsh hostility of the Islamic Republic towards Christianity, and the emergence of the house churches.

And the irony has continued. Since 2009, as this chapter has recorded, there has been a determined effort to crush the house churches. Many have suffered. But the result is that now there are more purified Christians in Iran who are passionate to spread the Gospel of Jesus.

---

361   Elam Ministries, *Iran Magazine*, Issue 7, Summer 2013, pp. 5–6.

CONCLUSION

GOD'S BEAUTIFUL SOVEREIGNTY

The story of Iran's new Christians is full of heroes and heroines. They are mainly unknown, but they are beautiful.

There are those brave church leaders who, though immersed in the rhythm of work in a building church, were ready to break away from those familiar routines and launch house-church churches.

There are the hundreds of men and women who have stepped forward to be trained as church planters and then started fellowships in their own homes, fully aware of the risks they were taking.

There are the thousands of house-church Christians who have witnessed to their family and close friends, won them to Christ, and so caused the church to grow.

These are the main players on the pitch. They are actively supported by two other groups.

First, there is the church of Iran in the diaspora – in Australia, Europe, America. These Christians are hosting satellite TV programmes that are having a massive impact throughout Iran: they are sending in Scriptures; translating Christian books; and now with Skype they are constantly behind the computer counselling and teaching Iran's new Christians. These Christians are not on the sidelines; they are virtually on the pitch as well.

Then there is the support of the international church. The list of nationalities actively involved in some way is too long to list here, but it includes the Chinese, Koreans, Vietnamese,

Japanese, Malaysians, Indians, South Africans, Americans, the French, Germans, the Dutch, Swedes, British, Rumanians, Canadians, Bolivians, Argentinians, and many others. Some are travelling to the Iran region, many are giving – and many are praying. Some of these Christians, like the Vietnamese, the Rumanians, the Koreans, and the Chinese, know the pain of persecution, and intercede with passionate empathy and intensity for their brothers and sisters in Iran.

So the story is not just about groups in Iran. It is a wider story, working on a richer tapestry. The Iranians in Iran, both from the established churches, including the churches of the ethnic Christians, and the new house-church Christians, the Iranians outside the country, and the wider church – all are involved; all are playing a role.

And those involved in any of these groups have no doubt about how events are being orchestrated. There is a divine conductor. The whole story belongs under the majestic title, "The Beautiful Sovereignty of God".

There are numerous examples in the ministry of those engaged in mission to Iran when, gently, they have been reminded that if they remain faithful to whatever work to which they have been called, the other parts of the story will fall into place, however impossible the scenario might seem.

As a child Maryam was orphaned and sensing she might find comfort in Christianity she would go with her Armenian friend to their Orthodox Church. She did not understand the language but she just did whatever the other worshippers did. At home she would pray her Muslim prayers, but then also prayed to Jesus. She was seeking God.

In her early twenties Maryam married and was often in the home of her in-laws. One day she spotted a New Testament. Her husband's family were devout Muslims, so she was surprised. Nobody seemed to know how this New Testament had found its way into the home. Later she found out it belonged to her brother-in-law who, it turned out, was a Christian.

Whenever she was with her in-laws she would sit alone and read about Jesus. At the end of this particular New Testament the reader is invited to ask Jesus Christ into their hearts as Lord and Saviour. Maryam happily prayed this prayer.

When her mother-in-law found out that Maryam had become a Christian she gave her a stark choice: Christ or her husband. Distraught Maryam cried out to her new Lord. She wanted both Christ and her husband.

Though for a while her husband seemed very hostile, he too gave his heart to Christ. Her brother-in-law knew about a house church, and the couple were introduced and brought into the fellowship. The couple began to grow, but Maryam felt she needed something more intense to really root her in her faith.

Thousands of miles away from Iran, Azin, a mature, middle-aged Iranian Christian, was longing to bring her wealth of experience and her gift of Bible teaching to other Iranian women: women just like Maryam. By faith Azin began to arrange a small conference for women.

Back in Iran Maryam was watching a lot of Christian TV. One day after the programme finished she started praying and saying to God: "I want to spend time with Bible teachers. I want to learn more; please open the way for me." As Maryam said "Amen" her phone rang. It was her brother-in-law: "Would you like to attend a small Bible-teaching conference just for women?"

It is not difficult to see the divine conductor at work in this story, using different instruments to reach into Maryam's wounded but open heart. There were the strange but still eerily beautiful services of the Armenian Orthodox Church (God using the witness of Iran's ethnic Christians); the New Testament in the home of Maryam's in-laws (God using the work of international Christians who send Scriptures to Iran); the brother-in-law (God using his courage to be a Christian in a very religious home); the satellite TV (God using Iranians in the diaspora to teach new believers in Iran); and finally there was Azin (God providing a guiding hand so that she can encourage women like Maryam).

Ethnic Christians in established churches, house-church Christians, Christians in the diaspora, and international Christians – all play their part faithfully. The divine Author writes the story, making the seemingly impossible – Azin teaching Maryam face to face – possible. It is God's beautiful sovereignty. If all the stories were told that illustrate this, another book would be easily filled.

It is fitting to end with a final group who are at the heart of this story: those who have paid a price for being new Christians. As seen in Chapter 8, hundreds have been arrested and interrogated; sixty are still in prison. They are beautiful heroes and heroines, who are willing to suffer rather than to deny their faith in Jesus.

And we have to accept that their suffering is also a part of God's beautiful sovereignty. Ultimately there will be deliverance; ultimately there will be justice for every human being who sides with evil and torments God's children. But, as in so many stories in the Bible, there is a waiting time when it seems the enemies of the church are victorious.

There is a time of suffering, but it is woven into beauty. On its own there is nothing beautiful about the horror of the knock on the door, the strip search, the foul conditions in prison, the cruel threats of the interrogator, the injustice of the judges, the prison sentences.

This is a truly traumatic ordeal. But these ordeals are not the only picture; they are a part of a wider canvas. And the title of that wider picture is not Iran's suffering church. The title is, "Iran's suffering *but* growing church."

The beauty of God's sovereignty is in the "but". Just as Joseph turned to his brothers and said, "You intended to harm me, *but*

God intended it for good to accomplish what is now being done, the saving of many lives" (Genesis 50:20, TNIV, author's italics), so too Iranian Christians turn to their tormentors and know in their hearts that what they intend for evil, God is working out for good. This is a beautiful "but".

Some Christians who have suffered have already experienced this "but". Masoumeh was a house-church Christian, as was her mother and her brother. Masoumeh's cousin and fiancé were not Christians, indeed they were cold towards her faith. Masoumeh was rounded up during the Christmas 2010 crackdown on the house churches. She spent twenty-five days in solitary confinement; thirty-three days in prison. She found the solitary confinement unbearable. When she came out Masoumeh was shown a glimpse of the answer to the mystery of why God had allowed her to suffer. While in prison her cousin and husband had given their hearts to Jesus Christ.

Another Christian prisoner, Farshid Fathi, sentenced to six years in prison for his involvement in house churches, also seems to have caught a glimpse of this same mystery. Farshid recently wrote a poem from his prison cell. He acknowledges his wilderness. It is painful. But there is a "but": his wilderness is also lovely.

God is weaving beauty into his suffering.

This book is dedicated to the hundreds of others who have suffered in the story of Iran's new Christians.

So it is fitting that we end with Farshid Fathi's poem.

My wilderness[362]

> *My wilderness is painful, but lovely.*
> *Some parts of my wilderness are covered with thorns and*
> *hurt my feet,*
> *But I love it, and that's why I call it "lovely pain".*
> *My wilderness is so hot that my tears disappear before*
> *falling on the ground,*
> *But it is cool under Your shadows.*
> *My wilderness is like an endless road,*
> *but short compared to eternity.*
> *My wilderness is dry,*
> *but an oasis with the Holy Spirit's rain.*
> *My wilderness seems to be a lonely trip,*
> *but I am not alone – My beloved is on me.*
> *Not only Him, but my faithful brothers and sisters,*
> *I carry them all in my heart.*
> *My wilderness is dangerous,*
> *but safe, because I dwell between his shoulders.* *
> *So I love my wilderness,*
> *because it takes me to the deeper part of You, Lord,*
> *and no-one can separate me from your arms for ever.*

Farshid Fathi

* Deuteronomy 33:12

362   First published in *Iran Magazine*, Issue 8, Spring/Summer 2014, published by
Elam Ministries, p. 4.

APPENDIX 1

HISTORY OF CHRISTIANITY IN IRAN BEFORE 1979[363]

Introduction

This book is about the story of Iran's new Christians. It is a very modern story, starting at the end of the 1990s. However, Christianity in Iran is not modern at all. There has been a Christian presence in the country since the second century, probably since apostolic times.

Most Iranians are aware of Christianity's long presence in their country and generally there is a positive attitude, even pride, that Christians have been a part of their national history.

The historical presence of the church confirms both Iran's tradition of tolerance, and the Iranian understanding that their country's identity is broader than just one division of one religion.

As today's Iranians consider becoming Christian, this long history of the church in their country plays a role. They know they are not joining a new religious sect, but rather a faith with deep and respected roots in their own country and across the whole world.

The long history also serves as an encouragement to those who are already Christians. Though at times the Christian faith

---

363   For an account of Christianity in Iran before 1979 also see Chapter 8 of the author's *Iran and Christianity*. This appendix is based on that chapter, together with Samuel Moffett's masterly *History of Christianity in Asia*, vol. 1.

seemed to be only a trickling stream, sometimes even a bloodied one, the waters have never stopped flowing. Iranians who have become Christians have joined a church which, though battle-scarred, has never surrendered.

And more than that, they have joined a church that exercised great influence, not just in the Iranian plateau, but right across Asia into China and India.

The overall picture of Christianity's story in Iran initially seems simple. There is tremendous growth until the seventh century and then a decline, so that by 1500 Christianity is just the faith of two vulnerable ethnic minorities in a Shia sea.

It is easy to assume that the root cause of Christianity's dramatic demise was the arrival of Islam, brought in with the Arab invaders in the mid-seventh century.

This is not true.

Certainly the arrival of Islam weakened Christianity, but there was no death blow. The church more than survived. So much so that when the Mongol Holagu Khan together with his Christian wife swept into Iran in the early thirteenth century there was excitement that this was the church's hour. It was not to be. And then, in the next century the death blow came. The sword of another Mongol drenched Iran's soil with rivers of blood.

This was Tamerlane.

It was he, not the early Arab invaders, who decimated Iran's church. And since his bloody work, Christianity has largely been about two vulnerable ethnic groups: the Assyrians, who survived the massacres, and the Armenians who came to Iran in the seventeenth century. Until Western missionaries began to arrive in the nineteenth century, they kept a witness to Christ alive.

For this brief overview of Iran's Christianity from the first to twentieth century the story divides chronologically into seven overlapping sections.

1. 2nd–7th century: Major presence

Christianity became a major religious presence in Zoroastrian Iran, despite vicious opposition.

2. 7th–13th century: Successfully surviving

With some success the church learned how to survive under the Arab Muslims who had invaded Iran in 637.

3. 13th century: Destined for triumph

For most of the thirteenth century the church enjoyed some prominence under the rule of the Mongols, who were not initially Muslim.

4. 14th century: The dark decimation

Tamerlane's sword turned the Iranian plateau red with the blood of his victims – Christian and Muslim.

5. 15th–19th century: The Assyrians and Armenians

After Tamerlane's massacres Christianity was almost exclusively the story of two ethnic minorities: the Assyrians and the Armenians.

6. 19th and 20th centuries: The missionaries

Numerically the Assyrians and Armenians continued to dominate Christianity in Iran right up to the 1979 revolution. However, from the late nineteenth century onwards they were joined by energetic and enthusiastic Protestant missionaries, mainly from the USA and the UK, who won some converts from Islam.

7. 1950s–1979: The Pentecostals

After the 1979 revolution the Assemblies of God denomination became the largest in Iran. These mainly Armenian Christians can trace their roots back to the 1950s.

Today we are in the eighth period of Iran's church history, the period of the house-church movement.

1. 2nd–7th century: Major presence[364]

All the evidence from archaeology and the surviving manuscripts points to the rapid spread of Christianity across the Iranian plateau from the faith's earlier days. The Chronicle of Arbela (modern-day Erbil in Kurdistan) traces its first bishop back to AD 104.[365] An inscription on a monument dating from the mid-second century, found near Hierapolis in Turkey, informs us of Bishop Abercius' travels. Writing about his travels east of the Euphrates the bishop says, "everywhere I had brethren", which probably means that wherever he went he came across Christians. From the pen of a Gnostic in Edessa, Bardaisan, we learn that in the early 200s there were Christians in Pars, Media, Kishin, and Parthia. And archaeologists have discovered sixty Christian tombs on Kharg Island in the Persian Gulf. Professor Richard Foltz records that "by the year 225 twenty bishoprics had been established throughout the Parthian-held lands"[366] (i.e. from central eastern Turkey to eastern Iran).

Apart from the authority of the Gospel of Jesus Christ there are at least three other reasons why Christianity spread so swiftly in the Iran region in these early centuries. One was political: while the churches in the Roman empire endured seasons of persecution until the early fourth century, the Parthians, ruling

---

364 Samuel Moffett's *History of Christianity in Asia*, vol. 1, gives a comprehensive treatment to this period of Christianity in Iran.
365 http://bmcr.brynmawr.edu/2003/2003-11-01.html Accessed 12 June 2014.
366 *Religions of Iran: From Prehistory to the Present*, p. 107.

Iran, tended not to interfere in religious matters. Christians were free. Furthermore Christian refugees from the Roman empire tended to flee eastwards and so strengthened the growing church in Iran. Another reason is geographical: the Silk Road ran through the northern part of Iran,[367] so giving missionaries a well-established road to use. The third reason is cultural and linguistic. Tatian the Assyrian had great influence over the early church in Iran. He was a radical church leader, the author of the *Diatessaron*, a harmony of the four Gospels, and was "emphatically and unashamedly Asian".[368] He zealously promoted the *lingua franca* of the Iran region, Syriac, and this became the language of the Eastern Church, allowing the faith to spread to towns and villages.

As politics has cast its shadow over Iran's new Christians today, so it cast an even darker shadow over those early believers. In 313 Emperor Constantine issued his edict of toleration and soon Christianity became the official religion of the Roman empire. In 337 the Parthian Emperor Shahpur II began hostilities with Rome. The Iranian Christians now shared a religious faith with their country's enemies, as was bluntly stated by Shahpur: "These Nazarenes inhabit our country and share the sentiments of our enemy Caesar."

Persecution began. Shahpur ordered the Christians to pay double in tax, then the destruction of churches, and then on Good Friday 355, five bishops and 100 clergy were beheaded. As today, the extent of the persecution is a part of the evidence that Christianity was a significant presence in Iran in the fourth century. Over the next forty years between 35,000 and 190,000 Christians lost their lives.[369]

There was a short lull in the early 400s, but then at the

---

367   See Map D here: http://www.chinainstitute.cieducationportal.org/cimain/wp-content/themes/chinainstitute/pdfs/education/fromsilktooil_pdf2.pdf Accessed 12 June 2014.

368   Samuel Moffett, *History of Christianity in Asia*, vol. 1, p. 74.

369   Historian Christopher Buck cites 35,000; Samuel Moffett 190,000.

instigation of the Zoroastrians, threatened by the success of the growing church, another vicious bout of persecution broke out in 420. One account records that, at Kirkuk, 153,000 Christians were cut down. The soldier in charge of the slaughter became so revolted that he himself became a Christian and was martyred.[370]

The lesson Iran's new Christians can take from the murderous onslaught unleashed on their forebears is this: persecution failed. Despite the shedding of so much Christian blood, the church was not destroyed, emerging from the fires of persecution more dynamic and more zealous with regard to spreading the name of Jesus Christ throughout Iran.

The next 200 years saw Christianity become an acknowledged part of Iran's establishment.

By the mid-fifth century Christians were an organized presence in at least eighteen of the Sassanid empire's twenty-five provinces, overseen by thirty-eight bishops and five archbishops that looked to a Patriarch in Seleucia-Ctesiphon. By 650 the number of bishops had risen to 106.

Also the end of the fifth century Iran's Christians separated from the Western Church when Iranians followed Nestorius, the former bishop of Constantinople, who had refused to call Mary the "mother of God"[371] and emphasized the division between Christ's divine and human nature. Politically this separation dulled the accusation that Christians were allied to foreigners and so strengthened the church's standing. From now on Iran's Christians would often be known as Nestorians.[372]

370 Samuel Moffett, *History of Christianity in Asia*, vol. 1, pp. 160–61.
371 A very clear outline of this christological controversy can be found here: http://www.nestorian.org/the_christological_controversi.html Accessed 12 June 2014.
372 The Nestorians were a strong presence in Iran and Mesopotamia. There were two other major Christian denominations in the Iran region in these early centuries. There were the Monophysite Jacobites who were mainly in Syria. They believed in the unity of Christ's nature, following the sixth-century bishop Jacob Baradaeus. And there were the Chalcedonian orthodox, also known as Melkites due to their support for the emperor, the Melek, in Constantinople. This group were strong in all the former Byzantium regions.

The strength and vibrancy of Iran's church was such that by the sixth century Christians were not just spread throughout the country, they were also familiar faces in the corridors of power. Shah Khosrow I's favourite wife, his physician, and a number of his courtiers were all Christian.

The Zoroastrians clearly felt their position as Iran's official priests was threatened. For many years they tried to conspire against the then Patriarch, Mar Aba. They failed. Once they tried Mar Aba for apostasy and evangelism. He pleaded guilty and was condemned to death, but the Shah intervened and sent the bishop into exile into Azerbaijan. Claiming his enemies were trying to assassinate him in exile, Mar Aba returned. He should have faced execution. But instead the Shah first imprisoned him and then Mar Aba was released. It was clear Christianity enjoyed royal favour.

This was made official by a later Shah, Hormizd IV (579–90) who issued this order to the Zoroastrian priests:

> Even as our royal throne cannot stand upon its two front legs without the back ones, so also our government cannot stand and be secure if we incense the Christians and the adherents of other religions, who are not of our faith. Cease therefore to harass the Christians.[373]

Within this order to stop harassing the Christians is the acknowledgment that the Christians were like the back legs of Iran's state. They were a part of the establishment.

A part of the establishment at home, and abroad Iran's Christians were taking the Gospel eastwards. From manuscripts and inscriptions in Pahlavi (Middle Persian) it is clear that the Iranian Christians were exercising some sort of supervision over Christian communities in Socotra off the coast of Yemen, southern India, and Ceylon. And it was Iran's missionaries

373 Richard Foltz, *Religions of Iran: From prehistory to the present*, Oneworld Publications, 2013, p. 110.

who first brought the Christian Gospel to Central Asia and, as attested by the famous Sian Fu stone, China. There is even a legend that an Iranian missionary went to England in the seventh century. His name was Ives, hence the seaside town in south-west England called Saint Ives.

Away from the Iranian plateau this missionary work continued into the seventh and eighth centuries; back home a shadow was falling over Iran's great Nestorian Church.

2. 7th–13th century: Successfully surviving

The fall of Zoroastrian Iran to the Muslim Arabs was an earthquake; its tremors reaching into every town and village, shaking Zoroastrians and Christians alike.

There is, then, a fanciful picture of the barbaric Arabs brandishing their swords and slicing up any Christian who did not become Muslim. This is not what happened. Indeed Christians were accorded respect – for two reasons. First of all, along with Jews, Christians were known to Muslims as "people of the Book".[374] From the time of Mohammad, there are records of victorious Arab Muslims allowing Christians to maintain their faith. This policy was continued by Mohammad's successors. The treaty Umar I arranged after the conquest of Jerusalem in 638 gives the flavour of this approach:

> **He gave them security for their lives, property, churches, crosses, their sick and healthy, and the rest of their religion. Their churches shall not be used as dwellings nor destroyed... They shall not be persecuted for religion's sake.[375]**

---

374 While Muslims assert that Mohammad is God's final prophet, they also believe that both the Jewish prophets and Jesus were sent from God, as recorded in the Jewish and Christian Scriptures, the Book.
375 Moffett, p. 336.

And then, second, the new Arab rulers needed all the administrative help they could get from the Iranians to settle their vast new empire, so they worked to attract expert Iranians into the bureaucracy. This included Christians, who were especially well known for their medical expertise.

So rather than a cruel crushing of the church, there is instead calculated collaboration. The deal was that the Christians would be segregated, forced to pay more tax and kept out of politics and the military. In return, as seen, the Christians were to be given security and the right to practise their faith within the confines of their own community. A Christian was to be a *Dhimmi*,[376] a protected people, in the Muslim state.

In outline this arrangement was not that different from the situation of Christians living under the Zoroastrians. Indeed some believed it would be better, so a Christian chronicler writing about the Christian reaction to the arrival of Muslims reports:

> The Arabs treated them with generosity and by the grace of God (may He be exalted) prosperity reigned and the hearts of Christians rejoiced at the ascendancy of the Arabs.[377]

In its broad outlines the *Dhimmi* deal seemed reasonable, especially as the Christians had no fire power. And if our chronicler knew how murderous the Zoroastrians had been, perhaps it is no surprise that he welcomed the new Arab rulers and their approach to Christians.

However, with hindsight, it is easy to see that there was little that was generous about the *Dhimmi* deal for Iran's Christians. Many did not feel they were in a safety net, but a pressure cooker; for them the segregation proved so burdensome and humiliating that that over the next several centuries they

376   For a comprehensive description and discussion of the concept of "Dhimmitude" see Bat Ye'or's *The Decline of Eastern Christianity Under Islam*.
377   Moffett, p. 325.

preferred apostasy to Islam rather than having to endure their lowly status.

Obviously there was much regional variation regarding the sharpness of the discrimination endured by Christians, but if applied to the letter of the law, the impact was financially draining and demeaning. The main extra taxes Christians had to pay were a land tax and a military tax.[378] Another financial issue was that being barred from government or military service meant that Christians were never eligible for any pension. It is easy to see the financial pressure pushing Christians into the Muslim fold. Sometimes a zealous ruler would then use the system to encourage conversions to Islam. So Umar II (717 –20) hiked up the taxes on Christians and offered rewards to new converts to Islam. As a result, many abandoned the church.

There was also social and legal pressure. Christians had to wear distinctive clothing so they could not be mistaken for Arabs (yellow patches on their fronts and backs); for the same reason they had to have special hair cuts (short in the front). They had to ride their horses or donkeys side-saddle, as a mark of their lowly status. And they were never allowed to ride in the middle of the road. This had to be kept clear in case a Muslim was coming round the corner.[379] Of more importance than these social humiliations was the status of Christians in the Islamic judicial system: their testimony was not valid in a Muslim court.[380]

Generally during the period of the seventh to thirteenth centuries the safety part of the net worked. The Christians and their churches were *Dhimmi* – protected. But occasionally the net tore. The same Umar II (eighth century) who hiked up the taxes also ordered newly erected churches to be razed to the ground. In the ninth century the Caliph Harun al-Rashid

---

378   Known as Jizya; the Christians were not allowed to enter the military, but were expected to help pay for it.
379   Moffett, p. 346.
380   Ibid. p. 357.

ordered the demolition of all the churches in the "border lands" with Constantinople. There is also a report that another Caliph, al-Mutawakkil, demanded that the graves of Christians be destroyed, something particularly shameful for Asians. The net occasionally tore, but there is no record that it ripped so badly that the Christians were victims of widespread and wanton state murder, as had happened under the Zoroastrians. By and large the Christians did enjoy protection.

The most debilitating part of the deal for Christians in Iran was that they were not allowed to evangelize to Muslims. This was strictly illegal. And for a church like Iran's, which was founded by travelling preachers and had gone on to spread the Gospel east to Central Asia and China and India, it was wholly unnatural. A true Christian shared the Gospel – with everyone. This uneasiness about Christians and evangelism emerged from a debate held between a Christian and a Muslim apologist before the Caliph Mamun in the ninth century. At the end of the discussion, the Christian, Abd al-Masih al-Kindi, sadly admitted, "But now the monks are no longer missionaries."[381]

If even the monks were not missionaries, and if Christians faced such humiliation in the *Dhimmi* system, one would expect there to be a sharp decline in the church's overall influence during this period. But here is something strange. There is clear evidence that as an organization the church grew in this period, and also retained its influence. Towards the end of the fifth century there were five Nestorian metropolitanates (archbishoprics); at the end of the tenth century, after 300 years of the *Dhimmi* system, it is recorded that there were fifteen such metropolitanates. The monks were no longer missionaries, and the Christians were subjected to humiliating restrictions – but eight new regions had come under the auspices of the Nestorian Patriarch, based in Baghdad.

381   Ibid. p. 361.

The Patriarch was a major figure in this period, recognized as the leader of the church by Muslims and Christians alike. As well as having the allegiance of those fifteen archbishops, a further 250 bishops looked to the Patriarch as their leader, as did numerous priests and millions of members. The historian Samuel Moffett estimates that his total flock was made up of about 12 million souls. By the early eleventh century there were roughly 50 million Christians in the world, out of a population of 250 million. So the Nestorian Patriarch was responsible for nearly a quarter of the Christians in Christendom. To say he was a major figure is perhaps an understatement.

There is also evidence that the churches still had "great wealth" and that Christians were still to be found in senior positions, especially in medicine. In 765 the second Caliph brought the Iranian Christian, Georgius ibn Buhtisu, to Baghdad to be his doctor, and for the next 250 years his successors followed suit. Christians were also recruited by Muslims to be teachers and private secretaries. These occupations – doctors, teachers, secretaries – are revealing for they all entail a personal, even intimate, working relationship signalling very possibly that Christians had a reputation for trustworthiness.

There is no doubt that a visitor to Iran in the eleventh or twelfth century would have easily been able to find a Christian. They were still very much a part of the social landscape. No longer was there talk of their being an official part of the establishment as was the case towards the end of the Zoroastrian period. But neither was there any talk of the church withering away. Christianity had very successfully survived.

Given that today's house-church Christians are living under those same shadows cast by the *Dhimmi* system initially set up in the seventh century, it is worth (very briefly) considering the reasons for this successful survival. One is certainly numerical. By the seventh century there were millions of Christians, and they were allowed to go on living as Christians. So despite the occasions of mass conversions to Islam, and the inability of Christians to win converts from the Muslims, still, biologically, they managed to maintain their numbers. In short – by the seventh century there were simply too many Christians for them not to remain a presence. Another is the organization and traditions that had been established by the time the seventh century came round. The churches had an accepted way of doing things and a clear command structure that was able to maintain a witness as Muslim rule enveloped them. Then there is language. The official language of the Nestorian church was Syriac; however, there is much evidence that Persian, the language of the masses, was also used in Iran.[382] This would mean that many Christians understood the faith in their own language, and this would explain, despite all the pressure, their reluctance to renounce Christ.

Another reason for the church's successful survival would have been the nuanced and diplomatic approach the Nestorian church leaders took towards Muslims. Generally it was not at all confrontational. The leaders seem determined to respect the religion of their rulers, without being dishonest. Their skill at this is well illustrated during a debate organized by the third Caliph, Mahdi, between the Nestorian Patriarch, Timothy I (779–823) and Muslim teachers. On the second day the Patriarch was asked a tricky question: "What do you say about Mohammad?" Timothy replied that, "Mohammad is worthy of all praise, by all reasonable people, O my sovereign", because like the prophets of the Bible he taught the unity of God. No doubt other Christians might object to this reply, but nevertheless there is no outright deceit in the Patriarch's response. And, more practically, Timothy went on to give his church many years of wise leadership that might not have been the case if he had abused the name of Mohammad in front of the Caliph.

382   See the author's *Iran and Christianity*, p. 141.

The final reason is sensible speculation. The Nestorian church that spread through Iran and beyond in the early centuries of the first millennium was radical, ascetic, and thoroughly evangelistic. They preached Jesus and pioneered mission to Central Asia and China, because this is how they were taught to be Christians. As the great scholar of mission the late David Bosch wrote – the Iranian church was wholly "missionary minded". It is therefore sensible to speculate that unbeknown to the chroniclers of the time, and so to us, the children of these missionary-minded Christians kept on sharing Jesus to whomever they met. There is no record of a Muslim ever becoming a Christian in this period, but given the character of Iran's church, to assume it did not happen is unwise. And even if no Muslim did embrace Christ, the likelihood that the Nestorian church remained evangelistic in outlook would further contribute to the fact that these Christians successfully survived.

3. 13th century: Destined for triumph

In the thirteenth century the Iranian plateau was again invaded, this time by the ruthless Mongols. Their general, Genghis Khan, was on a mission. This is what he told the petrified citizens of Bukhara before ordering the city's destruction: "(I am) the scourge of God sent to men as a punishment for their sins."[383] After Bukhara his armies went on to destroy most of the major cities in the north of Iran. Only Tabriz was spared, after paying the invaders off.

This is how one chronicler described a city after a visit by the Mongols:

> The people of infidelity and impiety roamed through those abodes... so that those places were effaced from of the earth

383　Eileen Humphreys, *The Royal Road*, 1991, p. 174.

as lines of writing are effaces from paper, and those abodes
became a dwelling for the owl and the raven; in those places
the screech-owls answer each other's cries, and in those
halls the winds moan responsive to the simoom.[384]

It seemed a dark cloud was overshadowing Asia, but not for
the Christians. They welcomed the invasions – for the Mongols
were not Muslims. They tended to be Buddhist or Shamanist
– and Christian. In the tenth century the Keraits, one of the
large Mongol tribes, had responded to the message of the
missionaries from Iran's Nestorian church and, following their
prince, about 200,000 Mongols had been baptized.

When in the late twelfth century Genghis Khan organized
the Mongol tribes into a united fighting group, the Christian
Keraits were to continue to have influence. It is thought
Christian teaching impacted Genghis Khan's written law, which
includes the command: "All men are to believe in one God,
Creator of Heaven and earth." There was another command
against adultery. And the clergy – Christian, Buddhist, or
Shamanist – were exempted from taxation.

And three Christian women from the Kerait tribe found
themselves in the heart of Genghis Khan's family. These were
the daughters of the Kerait leader. The eldest, Ibaka-beki,
became Genghis Khan's wife; the second, Bektutmish, became
the senior wife of Jochi, Genghis Khan's eldest son; and the
youngest, Sorghaghtani, became the wife of Tolui, the Khan's
fourth son. Sorghaghtani then became the mother of three
emperors – of the Mongols, of China, and, most relevant to our
story, of Iran.

Genghis Khan shook Iran; but he did not conquer the
country. This was the work of his grandson, Hulagu, the son
of the Christian Sorghaghtani, whose queen, Dokuz, was also a
Christian. In 1258 Hulagu's armies surrounded the then Muslim

384   Ibid., p. 175. Eileen Humphreys' source is the British E.G. Browne, who was
quoting from Yaqut-al-Hamawi, a famous twelfth-century Greek Islamic writer.

capital Baghdad and put the city to the sword. Respecting a tradition that royal blood should not be spilt the Caliph was not cut down, but Hulagu's soldiers rolled him in a rug and "trampled him under their horses' feet".[385]

In the midst of all this destruction there is one small detail that is very relevant to the church's stance on the invaders: in this massacre only the Christians were spared.

The outlook for Christians with the new regime was decidedly good. For a start their despised *Dhimmi* status would be swept away and tolerance for all religions, the usual policy of the Mongols, would be established. The Christians could look forward to being treated as equals with Muslims. But there was more: an expectancy that the church was going to be given preferential treatment. Already during the collapse of Baghdad the Christians had been spared, and, as Hulagu began his rule, it was noted that he had given a former palace of the Caliph to the Nestorian Patriarch. It would be hard to think of a stronger public message of support for the Christians than setting up their leader in what was effectively a state palace. Hulagu also supported the building of many churches. One chronicler wrote:

> Hulagu heaped favours upon (the Christians) and gave
> them every token of his regard so that new churches were
> continually being built... [386]

There were even rumours that Hulagu – with his Christian mother, and Christian wife – was going to get baptized. The Armenian chronicler, Vartan, wrote excitedly that Hulagu had told the Crusader Prince of Antioch that "he felt much attached to the Christians". It seemed a new triumphant day was coming for the church, filled with the tantalizing hope that the Mongol empire, in Iran at least, would be a Christian state.

385   Moffett, p. 423.
386   Moffett, p. 426, quoting the Muslim historian Rashin al-Din.

Hulagu continued to protect Christians, but he never got baptized. In 1265 Hulagu and his Christian queen both died. Hulagu was succeeded by his son Abaka, and he continued his parents' policy of guarding the interests of the Christians. Then in 1282 a cloud appeared in the sky of the church's new day. The next ruler, or ilkhan, Ahmad Teguder, was an apostate – from Christianity, to Islam. And he immediately showed his hostility to his old faith by locking up the Patriarch. Fortunately for the Christians this cloud soon blew away. Other Mongols were not happy about being ruled by a Muslim, there was a rebellion, and Arghun, a son of Abaka, became the ilkhan. The Patriarch was released from prison, and again the Christians were protected.

Again during Arghun's reign, it seemed Iran was edging nearer to becoming a semi-official Christian state. Three times (1287, 1289, and 1290) Arghun sent envoys to Europe to explore the possibility of an alliance between the Christian West and Mongol Iran against the Muslim Middle East. On at least one occasion the diplomats were accompanied by a Christian priest. It seems the Iranians were politely turned down. No treaty was signed; effectively the diplomats returned empty-handed.

This would have repercussions for Iran's Christians. Since the arrival of the Muslims the Nestorians had enjoyed prominence and protection in Iran. Free from the shackles of *Dhimmi* status the church had again celebrated her faith in the public sphere and continued to support mission in the East. The historian Samuel Moffett concludes that:

> The thirteenth century can with some justification therefore be called the years when Christians spread the faith more widely in Asia than at any time in the first millennium and a half of church history.[387]

Sometimes it seems that it was going to be in this century that the church was destined for triumph. But it was not to be. The

387   Moffett, p. 435.

refusal of Christian Europe to enter into an alliance with Iran focused political minds. The Mongol elite were surrounded by Muslims and their fanaticism could be easily roused, especially if provoked by the Christians. So when the Patriarch Denha I attempted to baptize a Muslim convert in Baghdad, he found himself fleeing from an angry and violent crowd. For a while Denha had to leave Baghdad.

With no support forthcoming from Europe and the Crusaders now a spent force in Palestine, the writing was on the wall. Political survival meant the rulers needed to identify with the majority, the Muslims. And so it happened that in 1295 Ghazen, the seventh ilkhan after Hulagu, proclaimed himself a Muslim.

Immediately the skies darkened; but nobody could have foreseen how bloodied they would become in the next hundred years. From being seemingly destined for triumph, the church now seemed destined for desecration and destruction.

4. 14th century: The dark decimation

After Ghazen's proclamation of his conversion to Islam the ilkhan ordered the destruction of all the churches throughout the land, and at street level his announcement was a signal to start a general persecution against Christians. One chronicler records: "Those who were recognised as Christians were disgraced, and slapped, and beaten, and mocked."[388]

It was worse for the Patriarch. He was stripped naked, tied up, beaten, and his mouth was stuffed full of ash. Ghazen intervened to stop the violence, and to save the Patriarch. It seems later Ghazen might have had regrets about allowing the Patriarch to endure such humiliation. In his later years he allowed a large new monastery to be built in Baghdad, and showered gifts on the churchman. Nevertheless every Christian knew there had

388   Bar Hebraeus, *The Chronography of Bar Hebraeus*, trans. E. A. Wallis Budge, Gorgias Press, 2003, p. 507.

been a major change in how they were to be treated. The hope of the early days of Mongol rule had evaporated.

Under Ghazen (1295–1304) there was intermittent persecution. Under his successor, Oljeitu (1304–16), it worsened. Oljeitu demanded that the Patriarch surrender his new monastery in Baghdad; the people of Georgia were ordered to renounce Christ and turn to Islam (an order that was ignored and not enforced); and worst of all the Christians in Arbela were massacred by Kurds and Arabs in 1310. Despite the Christians again being a *Dhimmi*, "protected", people with curtailed rights, there was no protection forthcoming from Oljeitu.

It would seem the church's future would again be about adjusting to life in the Islamic net: always restricted, usually protected, but sometimes vulnerable to violence. In fact the immediate future was going to be much worse.

After Oljeitu the line of Hulagu faltered and then died out. The Mongol empire in Iran broke up into fiefdoms ruled by warlords. And then in 1381 there was a second Mongol invasion led by Tamerlane who was even more ferocious and ruthless than his ancestor Genghis Khan from whom he claimed descent. Though a Muslim, Tamerlane seemed to be an enemy of humanity, slaughtering Christians, Muslims, and Jews alike as he spread his destruction throughout all Iran. He delighted in cruelty: prisoners were buried alive, thrown off cliffs, and after sacking some cities his soldiers left a parting present: pyramids of skulls. At Isfahan they managed to build 120 pillars with 70,000 skulls. In Baghdad Tamerlane ordered every soldier to bring to him one or two human heads. There 90,000 people perished; it is not known if their skulls were made into pyramids. Hundreds of thousands of Iranians, if not millions, died as his bloody sword swept through Iran. One historian has estimated that it took until the middle of the twentieth century for Iran's population to recover the numbers it had had before Tamerlane's invasion.

As a Muslim Tamerlane did not seem that concerned with the delicacies of the *Dhimmi* status of Christians. As his troops marched forward, so churches came crashing down and Christians were massacred "with cold-blooded, calculated ferocity".[389] Tamerlane campaigned ceaselessly to crush Christianity in Georgia. He razed 700 villages to the ground, murdered the inhabitants, and reduced the churches to rubble. As soon as his hordes left, the Georgians, including the king, returned to their faith in Christ. At Smyrna Tamerlane personally directed the slaughter of the Christians, collecting their skulls as souvenirs.

Tamerlane died in 1405 and his empire soon collapsed after him. He had only destroyed; he had not managed to build. However, the impact of the destruction he unleashed on Iran was to last for centuries, especially for the church.

Before Tamerlane, as seen, the Nestorian Church was still a power with which to be reckoned. Living in Baghdad, known to kings and khans its Patriarch was the shepherd for millions of souls and easily the most important Christian leader in the world after the Pope in Rome; certainly the most important in the East. At least 200 bishops and perhaps thousands of priests looked to him as their leader. Furthermore, despite all the difficulties of *Dhimmi* and the unpredictability of the Mongols, the missionary endeavours of the Nestorians had never ceased. In short, for over 1,000 years, the Nestorian Church had borne witness to Jesus Christ throughout the Iran region and beyond.

Tamerlane destroyed this great church.

Fleeing the destruction, the Christians eventually found refuge in the north west of Iran, in the inaccessible highlands between Lake Van and Lake Urmia, and in the plains of Salmas among the not-so-friendly Kurds. Here they settled and began to eke out a living as farmers and shepherds.

389 Moffett, p. 485.

Organizationally this once national and international church was now crippled, proved by the large gaps in the lists of the Patriarchs. The fragility and weakness of the Nestorians is also seen in the way they changed how the Patriarch was chosen. Traditionally it had been through a council of bishops, proof of the organization's vitality. However, in the fifteenth century the hereditary system (uncle to nephew) was adopted as it was simpler and less noticeable.

The collapse of the Nestorian Church was a great tragedy, not just for Iran, but for all of Asia. But in the ashes of this catastrophe there is one glimmer of hope that can encourage today's house churches.

Their witness to Christ in Iran never died out completely.

5. 15th–19th century: The Assyrians and Armenians

For the next 400 years Christianity was almost exclusively the story of two minorities: the Nestorian Christian survivors of Tamerlane's massacres, who became known as Assyrians; and the Armenians, who were forced to migrate to Iran in large numbers in the early seventeenth century. Both groups of Christians were a very small smudge on a vast canvas, which in the sixteenth century turned wholly nationalistic and Shia – and has largely remained so ever since.

Tamerlane's brutality painted a simple lesson in blood: Iran needed its own strong nationalistic religion and political system. The Arabs had incorporated Iran into a wide Muslim Caliphate, which ultimately failed to defend the people from the Mongols; once in power the Mongols had failed to defend the country from Tamerlane.

The man who gave Iran her own religion and political system was Ismail, the charismatic founder of the Safavid dynasty. Claiming that Mohammad's son-in-law, Ali, had married the daughter of the last Sassanian (pre-Islamic) king, Ismail brilliantly fused Iranian nationalism with the Shia branch of Islam. Then he capped this by declaring that he was a descendant of Ali, as well as being an incarnation of God. For good measure he added that he knew that Mahdi, the Imam who had disappeared in the ninth century, was coming soon. Well-funded and armed from a rich landed party and boasting this wonderful exotic mix of religious and nationalistic credentials, Ismail became the undisputed master of Iran in 1510.

Once in power, Ismail then set about enforcing religious unity. Everyone had to become a Shia. Though of course this branch of Islam had been around since the faith's earliest days, Ismail was determined that the Shia faith was to become Iran's religion. And that is what happened. The Sunnis either converted or were marginalized, and most Iranians became Shia and moulded the heroes of the Shia story, Ali and Hussein, into quasi-Iranians.[390]

Politically Ismail wholly rejected the concept of the Sunni Caliphate as this swung the spotlight away from Iran to an external body. Instead he returned politics to their pre-Islamic model whereby the military chief in Iran was the king in a covenant with his subjects. The king had the right to rule them, arbitrarily, but he had to provide them with protection and provisions.

These were the religious and political foundations of Safavid Iran, and they are still largely in place. To be in the centre of things an Iranian has to be both a Shia and loyal to the ruler of the day. This is as true today as it was back in the sixteenth century.

The Assyrians

A small and traumatized minority, the Nestorians were only onlookers as Ismail created his new nationalistic and Shia Iran.

390   For more on why the Shia faith suited Iran and her history see Chapter 1 of the author's *Iran and Christianity.*

But of course his shaping of the country would inevitably have an impact on the survivors of Tamerlane's massacres.

As the Nestorians slowly re-grouped in the north-west of Iran it became clear that the script Ismail had written had radically changed their identity. While it is well known that the official language of the church was Syriac, it is clear that Christians also spoke Persian, and indeed there is evidence that even some of the church's liturgy was in Persian.[391] This would explain why there is no record of the Nestorians, who as seen at times were very prominent on the national stage, ever being dismissed as being non-Iranians. Until the fifteenth century, Nestorian Christians were wholly Iranian.

However, in Ismail's scheme of things an Iranian was a Shia Muslim. This meant the Nestorian remnant were foreigners. Ismail's image of Iran was helped by the fact that Iran's Christians also spoke Syriac. So from being fully fledged Iranians, now Christians became an "ethnic minority". As such, according to the general rules of *Dhimmi*, also adopted by the Shias, these Christians were to be tolerated and protected – but they were always to stay on the margins.

Small now in numbers, the Assyrians were indeed very much on the margins of Iran's national life. While under the Safavids, and especially Shah Abbas (1571–1629), Iran became a regional power, and the Christians remained a forgotten and impoverished minority, barely a footnote in the history books.

However, these Christians kept on worshipping and trying to maintain some semblance of being an organization. Evidence for this is that in the mid-sixteenth century there was a dispute over the succession to the Patriarchy. The result was an unsightly split, but this is at least proof that there were still enough Christians around to ensure there was a Patriarch

391   For a detailed discussion regarding Nestorian Christians and language see Christopher Buck, "The Universality of the Church of the East: How Persian was Persian Christianity?", in *Journal of Assyrian Academic Studies* 10, no. 1, 1996.

– and with enough energy to argue. Though a dispute is not edifying, it shows there was still Christian life flickering in the hills between Lake Urmia and Lake Van.

And when news of this flickering flame reached the churches of the West newly revived by the likes of John Wesley, George Whitfield, Jonathan Edwards, and Charles Finney, the missionary-minded became very interested in these Assyrian Christians, as we shall see.

The Armenians

The Armenians were also meant to stay on the margins of the new Iran Shia story; but from their earliest days in their adopted homeland their presence was somehow more noticeable and energetic than the Assyrians.

As well as being the world's oldest Christian nation,[392] Armenia has long been a buffer state between Iran, Russia, and Turkey, whose armies have at various times held sway in this small but beautiful land.

In the early seventeenth century it was the turn of Iran under Shah Abbas to be the dominant power. To secure his own borders the Shah deported 300,000 Armenians and settled them in Iran. The Armenians were happy to leave the increasing oppression of the Ottoman system. The wealthier ones were from a trading town called Julfa. Shah Abbas settled them on the outskirts of his own capital, Isfahan, in a town called New Julfa. Here these Armenians prospered.

They were truly a *Dhimmi*, allowed to build their own cathedral and churches – the cathedral, and thirteen of the churches survive today – and to practise their Christian faith. It seems Shah Abbas liked his new Armenian subjects. He awarded them a very lucrative monopoly on the silk trade and soon they were growing fabulously wealthy. When the Shah came to visit

392 Armenia's king, followed by his subjects, became Christian in 301 after a member of the royal family experienced a divine healing.

the Armenians they would serve him dinners from gold plates. The Armenians in Iran's other cities also enjoyed the Shah's protection, and they too prospered. Seeing the generally decent lifestyle their countrymen enjoyed over the next two centuries, thousands of Armenians made their way to Iran to settle.

By the end of the nineteenth century there were at least 100,000 Armenians settled in about twelve of Iran's major cities. They were accepted as a part of the country's social landscape and more. They were also respected as the minority who helped bring Western technology to Iran. So it was an Armenian priest who operated the first printing press in Iran. The first book off its press in 1638 was the Armenian translation of the Book of Psalms.

The Armenians belong to the Orthodox branch of Christianity that operates more under the missionary paradigm of "come and see" rather than "go and preach".[393] So there is no record of these Armenian Christians risking all to evangelize to their Muslim neighbours. And under the banner of Shia nationalism created by Ismail, this would have been a risk.

However, because of their presence and active churches, Iranians could "come and see". Again there is no record of Muslims secretly converting, but given the general regard Iranians had for Armenians – and still do – as trustworthy people, it is reasonable to conclude that the Armenians of that period did leave a witness for Jesus Christ.

6. 19th and 20th centuries: The missionaries

Roman Catholic missionaries had had brief contact with Iran first in the thirteenth century,[394] and then with more energy in

---

393   See David Bosch, *Transforming Mission: Paradigm Shifts in Theology of Mission*, Chapter 6 for a detailed discussion of the Eastern Church's view of mission.
394   Innocent IV (1243–54) was keen to establish contact with the Mongols who had devastated Russia and were threatening Europe. Hence between 1245 and 1342 ten missionary teams were sent to Mongolia. It is very likely that these Roman Catholic missionaries would have had contact with Iranians.

the sixteenth and seventeeth centuries. However, probably for political reasons, they had little success. Until the Industrial Revolution got under way the Muslim world generally did not believe it had much to learn from the West. And certainly no Iranian ruler wanted to undermine the Shia identity of Iran painstakingly established by the Safavids. And then Roman Catholicism was very much a part of Europe's political furniture. There was nothing to gain by hosting her missionaries – and plenty to lose. So it is no surprise to read that in the 1620s Shah Abbas expelled some Portuguese missionaries and ordered the execution of five of their Iranian converts.

By the nineteenth century politics had changed. Iran and the rest of the Muslim world were shocked to find they had been swept aside by the technological advances of the West. Economically and militarily they were in no position to compete with the other major powers, especially Britain, Russia, and the USA. To survive, Iran now had to look to these countries for loans. This meant Iran's rulers could not treat Christian missionaries in the same way Shah Abbas had done. The door to Christian work began to open – and the missionaries came.

The first Protestant missionaries, two German Moravians, arrived in Iran in the mid-eighteenth century. They were not very successful. Twice they were robbed of all they had, and that ended their mission to Iran. The Englishman Henry Martyn had much more impact. Arriving in Iran in 1811 he went to Shiraz to check a translation of the New Testament that he had worked on in India. He also disputed with local Muslim teachers. Martyn finished the New Testament in 1812 and, failing to present a copy personally to the Shah, he instead left it with the British ambassador, Sir Gore Ouseley, who did give the book to the king. Sir Ouseley also gave Martyn's translation to the Russian Bible Society, who printed the New Testament and sent copies to Iran. As for Henry Martyn, he died of fever on his way back to England in Tokat, Turkey, near the Iran border in

September 1812. He was just thirty-one years old. Dr William Glenn from Scotland, determined to complete Martyn's work, arrived in Iran in 1817 and in 1846 he oversaw the printing of the whole Bible in Persian.

While Glenn was working on the Bible, other Western missionary-minded Christians were getting excited over the reports of the Nestorian remnant in the north-west of Iran. In 1834 the American Justin Perkins and his wife made their way to these previously isolated Christians, convinced they were the "Protestants of the East", and once revived, they would be the bridge head that would bring about the conversion of Iran. They were later joined by another American, Dr Grant, who – along with many others – was convinced that these Nestorians were one of the lost tribes of Israel. As well as preaching, Justin Perkins started schools, and Dr Grant did medical work. They were both heroic pioneers, but it is difficult to describe the immediate impact of their work as a success.

News of their work inspired others and by the end of the nineteenth century there were no less than nine separate missionary organizations all trying to work with these descendants of the great Nestorian church. Inevitably there was much Christian disunity, and worse. The never-too-friendly neighbours of the Nestorians, the Kurds and Turks, did not take kindly to all the attention the Christians were receiving. They feared that these immigrants with their foreign friends would displace them. So in the 1840s they attacked the Nestorians who fought back. The violence took the lives of about 10,000 Iranians.

The Kurds and the Turks were not the only people upset by the arrival of the Western missionaries. The Nestorian clergy were also displeased. This is because the missionaries, coming from the Western churches bathed in revival language, constantly spoke about the need for the Nestorians to experience the new birth. If pushed, this meant these foreign missionaries were telling these children of one of the world's oldest churches, that they were not actually Christians; that the Nestorians needed to become Christian.

This was of course the first step to Perkins' whole vision: revive the Nestorians to reach the Muslims. But the Nestorian clergy did not like being told they needed to be revived. In 1846 their bishop informed his members that they could no longer attend the mission schools that were continually preaching the need for personal renewal.

So the missionary churches separated from the Nestorians and became the Presbyterian Church, accountable to the Presbyterian Board of Mission in the USA. By the end of the nineteenth century this was a national church with about 6,000 members in twenty-five congregations. Common to most missionary endeavour of that era, the Presbyterian mission to Iran also concentrated on providing education and medical help to the people they were reaching. By the mid-1930s about 2,000 Iranians were being educated in their schools. These schools declined when Reza Shah's nationalism turned on them, but right up to 1979 and beyond, the Presbyterian Church provided a strong witness to Christ for all Iranians.

Perhaps Messrs Perkins and Grant felt a little depressed as they saw the Kurds and Turks attack the Nestorians, and then the Nestorian clergy rejecting their revivalist message. They could have concluded that while their life's work had been romantic and visionary, it was useless, even destructive. They would have been unwise: for they were the founders of a denomination that is still active and, despite the limitations of the "building" approach to mission discussed in Chapter 7, brought the blessings of Jesus Christ to hundreds of thousands of people.

The Episcopalians (Anglicans) were the other major missionary presence in Iran in the late nineteenth and twentieth centuries. Their ministry started when a Church Missionary

Society (CMS) missionary Robert Bruce found himself in Isfahan in 1870 in the midst of a grim famine. People needed feeding, and this he set out to do. Then he set up an orphanage, and in 1875 the CMS board officially acknowledged that they had started work in Iran. It almost seemed accidental. However, missionaries and funds soon started making their way to Iran. By the early twentieth century, following the "building" pattern for mission dominant in that era, the Anglicans had established hospitals, schools, and churches in Isfahan, Shiraz, and Kerman: in Yazd there was medical and educational work. CMS missionaries and their converts also carried out village evangelism, sometimes resulting in churches. It will be noted there were no Anglican churches in the north of Iran; this is because CMS came to a gentlemanly agreement with the Presbyterians that they would concentrate on the south, while the Americans focused on the north. In the 1950s, though, the Anglicans opened a church in Tehran, mainly to cater for the diplomatic and business community.

Their church congregations were not that large, and, as noted in Chapter 7, were usually made up of a mix of ethnic groups – Armenians, Assyrian, Jews, and some Muslim converts. One historian who worked with CMS estimates there were 350 in the 1930s.[395] The work of the Anglicans continued right up to 1979, and beyond, despite the grim violence they faced in the immediate aftermath of the revolution, which was outlined in Chapter 8.

While it is difficult to describe either the work of the Presbyterians or the Anglican missionaries as a major success in terms of winning Muslims to Christ it is important to underline at least three aspects of their contribution to Christianity in Iran.

The first is geographical: these missions vastly strengthened the presence of Christians throughout the country. Before their arrival Christianity was mainly limited to the Nestorian

395   See Robin Waterfield, *Christians in Persia*, p. 171.

heartlands around Lake Urmia, and the Armenian quarters of the major cities. By the mid-twentieth century when both missions were firmly established there was a definite sense of a national network of Protestant Christianity throughout Iran. Iranians were meeting many more Christians.

The second and third factors are psychological. The schools, and especially the hospitals, stamped on the minds of millions of Iranians that, in line with what they already knew about Jesus from Islam, Christians brought healing and enrichment. When an Iranian thought about Christians, unless he or she was completely sunk in the dark conspiracy theories of the Middle East, they thought of them as people who were there to help Iranians.

Finally these Christian missions were a constant and important reminder to Iranians that there was a very large world beyond their borders – and it was not Shia, or even Muslim. While Christianity was practised only by Assyrians and Armenians, it was easy for the official view of Islam to have traction: that since the arrival of Islam, Christianity as an inferior faith was withering away. With the arrival of the missionaries with all their modern equipment, this storyline collapsed. Not only were Christians manifestly enjoying a superior way of life materially, their self-sacrificial service for Iranians also pointed to spiritual strength in their religion. For some Iranians wanting to improve their lot in the world it might well have seemed that the future was Christian, not Muslim.

7. 1950s–1979: The Pentecostals

The witness of the Assyrians, the Armenians, the Presbyterians, the Anglicans, and other denominations, including the Roman Catholics who began a work in 1966, continues to this day.

Towards the end of our period (second century to 1979) these churches were joined by another branch of the Christian family, the Pentecostals. The first Pentecostal church was started in Urmia among Assyrians who later opened a congregation in Tehran. The second Pentecostal group, the Assemblies of God, can, ironically, trace its roots back to the Brethren, a denomination that has historically always been cautious about the gift of speaking in tongues.

The Brethren church in Tehran was started in the 1920s by a Kurdish Muslim convert called Dr Sayeed Kurdistani. The congregation was mainly made up of Armenians. In 1933 this church was joined by Seth Yeghnazar, who worked for Iran's Bible Society. He had a reputation as a man of prayer determined to live a holy life, separate from the world. In the 1950s Seth Yeghnazar had a dramatic experience with the Holy Spirit, and undertook a 42-day fast where he only drank water. This level of devotion caused unease in the Brethren Church and at the end of one meeting Seth Yeghnazar asked the gathering if anyone wanted him to leave. Two ladies put up their hands.

Seth Yeghnazar and his wife and five children left the Brethren Church and every night for four years (1956–60) held prayer meetings in his house. Sam Yeghnazar, Seth's eldest son, refers to these meetings in his foreword to this book. As the meetings grew, there were plans to turn this meeting into a church. However in 1959 two Pentecostal Armenian blood brothers, Haikaz and Hrand Catchatoor, arrived in Iran from England (where they had received their education) determined to spread the Gospel. As they began their preaching, so they met Seth Yeghnazar, who graciously decided to support their vision. The two brothers rented a basement in Pahlavi Street that had formerly been a chelo-kabab restaurant and so the first meetings of what was to become Iran's Assemblies of God Churches (AoG) began.

Tragically the Catchatoor brothers died in a car accident on 3 December 1961. Tateos Michaelian and Levon Hyraptetian, two men from Seth Yeghnazar's prayer fellowship, stepped into the leadership of the new church, and the work expanded. As well as the meetings in Pahlavi Street, fellowships were planted in the Armenian suburbs of Majidieh and Narmak. Then in 1963 AoG missionaries persuaded this national church to formally join the AoG denomination. They then helped the church build its own sanctuary, start a Bible school and launch correspondence courses, which attracted about 10,000 students.

There was no shortage of evangelistic passion in this new church; but nevertheless very few Muslims came to Christ through their witness. The church was almost wholly made up of Armenians. But these faithful Christians kept on praying, and as seen, their prayers were answered. After the revolution their congregation in Tehran grew to over 300, and by the 1990s about 80 per cent were ex-Muslims.

Conclusion

This brief overview underlines that there has been a continual witness to Jesus Christ in Iran for nearly 2,000 years in Iran. And for well over 1,000 years the church was a vibrant entity, very much a part of the country's national life, her leader the Patriarch honoured by all. For about two hundred years after the evil rampages of Tamerlane the Christian candle spluttered, but then with the arrival of the Armenians in the seventeenth century again the light grew. And then the witness became even more vibrant with the arrival of the missionaries, mainly in the nineteenth and twentieth centuries.

The light has never gone completely out. And that means that despite the furious and murderous opposition of the church's enemies, especially the Zoroastrians and the Mongols under Tamerlane, Christianity has always survived in Iran. Rooted into the country's soil by the zeal of the mobile and monastic missionaries of the early Assyrian church, no human government has ever been able to uproot this ancient Christian tree.

As seen in this book in recent years there has been another attempt to stamp out Christianity in Iran. This attempt too has failed. Again Christians have suffered; but again out of their suffering, the house-church movement has been born.

And this new chapter in the long story of Christianity in Iran could well prove to be its most exciting.

LIST OF AGGRESSIVE ACTS TOWARDS CHRISTIANS IN IRAN[396]

The following appendix is a catalogue of violations of the religious freedoms of Iranian Christians, as reported from January 2009 to June 2014. It is almost certain that far more incidents have occurred than are reported publicly, and than are catalogued here.

Not all the incidents listed below could be verified by more than one source, given the difficult nature of obtaining information from Iran, yet the sources used are deemed trustworthy. Those used for this report include: Christian Solidarity Worldwide (CSW), Elam Ministries, Farsi Christian News Network (FCNN), International Campaign for Human Rights in Iran, Middle East Concern (MEC), Mohabat News, Open Doors, World Watch Monitor (formerly Compass Direct). This appendix also draws on the reports of Dr Ahmed Shaheed (the UN Special Rapporteur for Human Rights in Iran), Dr Anna Enayat (St Antony's, Oxford), and the *Christians in Parliament All Party Parliamentary Group Report on the Persecution of Christians in Iran* (2012).

The violations are divided into four categories:

1. Church closures and the pressures and limitations that the regime has inflicted upon churches that meet (or met) in duly registered buildings.

396   Available on request as a separate document from Elam Ministries.

2. Corporal punishment against Christians and the brutal treatment of Christians inside prisons.

3. Arbitrary arrests and detentions of Christians or the Christians' family members.[397]

4. The judicial sentences that have been handed down to Christians in the past five years.

Incidents of social discrimination against Christians are not catalogued here, not because they are not equally as traumatic for the Christian community as other forms of maltreatment, but because it would be impossible to document all the incidents that occurred between 2009 and 2014, given that discrimination occurs every day; discrimination against Christians is woven into the legal and social fabric of Iran, as Chapter 8 describes.

1. Church closures and limitations

Prior to 2009, various churches had been closed down by the authorities; for example, the 1995 UN Report on the situation of human rights in the Islamic Republic of Iran (prepared by the Special Representative of the Human Rights Commission, Mr Reynaldo Galindo Pohl) states that churches in Gorgan, Mashad, Sari, Ahvaz, Kerman, and Kermanshah had been closed by the authorities. However, from 2009 onwards there was an intensified effort to terminate all church activities that were reaching out to the Muslim-background population (as opposed to the ethnically Christian Armenian and Assyrian populations) and to curtail all Christian services held in the nation's most widely spoken language, Persian (Farsi).

---

397 Some individuals were arrested multiple times during the given time frame. Each arrest is recorded as a separate incident, since each arrest entailed its own trauma for the individual and their family.

2009

1. On 29 January 2009 the Assyrian Assembly of God church in Shahrara, Tehran was ordered to close its weekly Persian service. The pastor, Victor Tamraz, was reportedly called in for questioning multiple times, as was his daughter.

2. In March the Assyrian Assembly of God church in Shahrara, Tehran was ordered to be closed by the Islamic Revolutionary Court. It had 700–800 members at the time. The closure order was delivered in person to the pastor; the keys were seized and the locks changed. The order stated that the reason for the closure was that the church was allowing non-Assyrian members into the church services, and that the pastors were preaching to and converting Iranian Muslims. The pastor was arrested on 18 May.

3. The Urmia[398] Assyrian Assemblies of God Church was closed on 8 July. The pastor reportedly left Iran shortly after this closure.

4. On 30 October, the Tehran Central Assemblies of God church was forced to close its Friday church services, following threats from the Revolutionary Guards that if it did not comply, the church would be closed down.

5. The Assemblies of God church in Shahin Shahr (near Isfahan) was reportedly forcefully closed in 2009. Edison Gharibian was the pastor at the time. He later took on the responsibility of leading the Assemblies of God church in Isfahan when its leader, Revd Leonard Keshishian, was arrested in late 2010.

6. The Assemblies of God church in Urmia was closed down during 2009.

---

398   Urumieh/Oroumiyeh (in north-west Iran).

2010

7. The Assyrian Pentecostal church in Kermanshah was sealed closed by authorities on 2 January 2010 (some reports state 31 December 2009) and the pastor, Revd Wilson Issavi, was ordered not to reopen it. The church continued to have meetings in private homes, and authorities charged Issavi with not cooperating with the government. Issavi was arrested in February 2010.

8. A small number of Persian-speaking believers who were attending an Assyrian church in the Urmia region were asked to leave the congregation at Christmas 2010, presumably following pressure on the church from the authorities. The church reportedly still operates, but no Persian speakers are allowed to attend.

2011

In August 2011, the building of St Andrew's Anglican church of Kerman was bulldozed. The building was not functioning as a church at the time of its destruction.

2012

9. In February 2012 Emmanuel Evangelical (Presbyterian) Church in Tehran was ordered to cease all activities (including its Friday Persian-language services) except Sunday services. An elder of the church and his wife were later arrested in May 2012, thus putting more pressure on this church to comply.

10. Also in February, St Peter's Evangelical (Presbyterian) Church in Tehran was ordered to discontinue its Friday Persian-language services.

11. In late May officials from the Revolutionary Guard intelligence organization forced the Assemblies of God church in the Jannat Abad neighbourhood of Tehran to

close its doors and discontinue services. The authorities told the church leaders that if they did not voluntarily close the church, it would be forcibly closed and confiscated. The final service was held on 28 May 2012. The church had been meeting in the building for fifteen years and had owned the building since 2007.

12. On 26 July Iranian authorities forced the Emmanuel Presbyterian Church in Tehran to close its doors and discontinue services. The Elders were informed that the church's licence had been revoked and the building was ordered to be cleared. An international outcry forced the authorities to deny the church closure, to allow it to re-open its doors, but intelligence agents were assigned to the building and a tight control is held over the affairs of the church.

2013

13. In late April, pastors of the central Tehran Assemblies of God church were ordered to provide a list of all the members of their congregation with personal details, such as their ID numbers. The pastors told the congregation that they must comply.

14. Around 19 May pastors of the central Tehran Assemblies of God church were ordered to terminate all its Persian-language services. The church refused. Two days later, a leader of the church, Revd Robert Asserian, was arrested. Following his arrest, the church was closed and a sign hung on the door stating that the church was "closed for essential repairs". The church has not reopened since that time.

15. In August the St Abraham Catholic Church (Latin rite) in Tehran was forced to ban Persian speakers from attending.

16. On 8 December, under pressure from the government, the pastor of St Peter's Evangelical (Presbyterian) Church

in Tehran, Sargis Benyamin, told his congregation that Persian-speaking attendees would not be allowed in the church any more. This church has always been a Persian-speaking church, with a congregation largely composed of second or third-generation Christians. Their exclusion means that the church has closed in all but name.

2. Arbitrary arrests and detentions

2009

1. A married couple, Jamal Galishorani and Nadereh Jamali, were arrested in Tehran on 21 January. They were converts to Christianity and members of the officially registered Assemblies of God church in Tehran. Jamal was released on bail on 8 February, while Nadareh was released a week earlier. They were informed that the case against them remained open; a clever way of exerting pressure on the couple not to engage in Christian ministry once released. It is not clear whether a case against them was pursued.

2. Also on 21 January Hamik Khackikian was arrested. Hamik was a pastor of the Assemblies of God church in Tehran, of Armenian ethnicity. He was released after one week of detention without charge. The intimidation of leaders of registered churches has been a regular occurrence for many years, and continues to be a tactic of the authorities.

3. On 30 January, Hossein Karimi, a house-church leader, was arrested in Karaj and his house raided. He was released on bail in February after twenty-seven days of detention. On 15 March he was given a suspended sentence (section 4, point 1). He had previously been arrested on 16 November 2008, held for four days, and released upon signing a

statement declaring that he would not engage in further Christian activities.

4. A blogger and evangelist identified as "Mazaher R" was arrested in Isfahan with his sister and a friend on 22 February. They reportedly were enticed to a vacant house by intelligence agents,[399] where the arrest occurred.

5. Friends and flatmates Maryam Rostampour and Marzieh Amirizadeh Esmaeilabad were arrested at their flat in Tehran on 5 March. They were held in a detention centre for many days before being sent to Evin prison. They spent a total of nine months in illegal pre-trial detention. During that period they were threatened with apostasy convictions and taken before a judge and asked to recant their Christian faith, which they refused to do. They were released on 18 November 2009 on bail. Later they were both acquitted of all charges by Iran's judicial authorities. In May 2010 they left Iran.

6. Victor Tamraz, pastor of the Assyrian Pentecostal church in Shahrara, Tehran, was arrested on 18 May, following the closure of the Shahrara church.

7. A house church in Karaj was raided on 20 May, and five Christians were arrested, including the house owner Javad Abtahi.

8. In late July a house-church meeting of twenty-four Christian converts was raided in the village of Amameh (15 miles north of Tehran). All twenty-four were taken in cars to their homes, where police took their passports, cash, CDs, computers, and mobile phones, and they were all then taken to a police station. Seventeen were released the same day, but seven were held longer, including Shahnam Behjatolla, for an unknown length of time. Shahnam has

399 "Intelligence agents" refers to agents of the Iranian Ministry of Intelligence and Security (MOIS), also referred to as "VEVAK", "VAJA" or "Ettela'at" in Iran.

a daughter who was six years old at the time. Some of the group were re-arrested on 7 August.

9. Eight Christians from were arrested in Rasht in late July. Seven were released rapidly, while one male was detained until at least November 2009, possibly far longer.

10. Youcef Nadarkhani, the pastor of the Rasht "Church of Iran" fellowship[400] was detained on 13 October 2009 and was held incommunicado in Lakan prison. He was later famously sentenced to death for apostasy[401] (4.2), which sparked a massive international outcry. He was finally acquitted and released on 8 September 2012 after nearly three years in prison.

11. On 2 December, Christian convert Hamideh Najafi was arrested in her home in Mashad. During interrogation, her husband was summoned, blindfolded, and threatened with being beaten in front of his wife if she would not sign a confession that she was "mentally and psychologically unfit and disturbed". She was therefore coerced into signing a confession. Later in December she was sentenced to three months of house arrest (4.3).

12. Seventy Christians who were celebrating Christmas together were arrested on 16 December in Karaj. They were interrogated and bail was posted for them. Two of the leaders, Kambiz Saghayee and Ali Keshvar-Doost, were detained and taken to an unknown location.

13. During a Christmas celebration in Pakdasht, twelve Christians were arrested. Nine were released on 4 January 2010. Three – Maryam Jalili, Mitra Zahmati, and Farzin Matin – were held for eighty days and released on 18 March 2010.

---

400 The "Church of Iran" is a house-church network that holds non-mainstream beliefs regarding the Trinity. Most other house-church networks have some concerns over their beliefs and practices.
401 Apostasy: abandoning Islam.

14. In late December the sister of one of the Pakdasht detainees was arrested in Isfahan. No further details are known about this incident.

15. Mostafa Bordbar, a Christian in his early twenties, was arrested in 2009 (date unknown) in his hometown of Rasht for converting to Christianity and attending a house church. He was found guilty of apostasy (abandoning Islam), but he was released after posting bail. The apostasy conviction remained on his record. He was later arrested again in December 2012 (2.91).

2010

16. Four members of the "Church of Iran" group: Amin Farzad-Manesh, Parviz Khalaj, Mehdi Forutan, and Abdolreza (Matthias) Ali Haghnejad were arrested between 7 and 9 January. Roxanna Furouyi and Mahyar Afradoust were also arrested around this time. They were released on bail pending trial: Amin was released on 22 February, Parviz on 24 February, Mehdi on 3 March, Roxanna, Mayhar, and Abdolreza on unknown dates.

17. A leader of the Church of Iran group, Behruz Sadegh-Khanjani, was invited to attend a meeting in Shiraz on 10 January, but was arrested on his arrival. He was released on a 50-million toman bail on 22 February. He was later re-arrested when he went to attend a court hearing (2.29). He had also been arrested twice in the previous four years.

18. On 11 January Davoud Nejat-Sabet was arrested in Rasht. He was later sentenced (4.4).

19. On 2 February 65-year-old Revd Wilson Issavi, leader of the Assyrian Pentecostal Church in Kermanshah, was arrested in Isfahan in the home of a friend. During his imprisonment he was tortured and sustained significant injuries to his back. His wife was told by intelligence agents

that he could face execution for his ministry work. Revd Issavi was conditionally freed from prison on 28 March 2011 after posting bail.

20. Mohammad (William) Beliad and his wife Nazli Makarian were arrested on 17 February in their Karaj home. Mohammad was beaten during the arrest and both were taken to Rajai Shahr prison for a short time. Nazli was released after twenty-four hours on a 20-million toman bail. William was transferred to the Pelak Sad prison of Shiraz and released after two months on 19 March 2010 on a 20-million toman bail.

21. Vahik Abrahamian was arrested on 20 February on charges of Christian activities among Muslims. He was detained for two months and released on bail on 24 April pending trial.

22. On 28 February Christian couple Hamid Shafiee and Reyhaneh Aghajary, who were house-church leaders in Isfahan, were arrested in their home by fifteen plain-clothed intelligence agents. They were held in Dastgerd prison for seventy-five days and released on 16 and 19 May on bail of $100,000 (USD) for each of them. For those seventy-five days, their two young sons were left without their parents.

23. Saeed Beyrami was arrested in Tabriz on 7 March. No formal charges were issued. He was released on bail with signs of physical torture. It is unknown whether a case was pursued against him.

24. A young member of Hamid and Reyhaneh's house church was arrested on 11 April. Daniel Shahri, the son of a blind Christian couple who attended St Luke's Episcopal Church in Isfahan, was nineteen at the time of his arrest. For the first four days following his arrest, his family had no idea where he was and searched everywhere for him. He was detained in Dastgerd prison for two weeks, and suffered beatings during interrogation. He was released on bail. He

was charged with web management of the home church, blasphemy and publishing lies, evangelism, and forming and participating in home church. He was told his case remained open and he could be summoned to court at any time. In December 2010, Daniel left Iran.

25. On 14 April Behnam Irani, the pastor of the Church of Iran house church in Karaj, was arrested at his home by intelligence agents, and endured beating during the arrest. A service was taking place at the time and the security officials interrogated those attending, as well as confiscating Bibles, Christian literature, and DVDs. Behnam was held for seventy-six days in solitary confinement at Rajai Shahr prison and then released on bail in June 2010. In January 2011 he was tried for, and convicted of, crimes against national security (4.6).

26. Ali Golchin, a Christian from Varamin (near Tehran), was arrested on 28 April; he was blindfolded and beaten during the arrest. Ali's father was summoned to the Ministry of Intelligence office in Varamin the day after the arrest, and warned not to speak out publicly about his son's situation. Ali Golchin was held for eighty-seven days in solitary confinement in Evin prison and during interrogations he was psychologically tortured, including being threatened with execution. He was released after about three months, in late July 2010 on a $200,000 (USD) bail. He was tried in court in April 2011 (4.10).

27. Amin Khaki, of the Karaj Church of Iran group was arrested on 10 May. The duration of this detention is unknown.

28. Fatemeh Passandideh, the wife of Church of Iran leader Youcef Nadarkhani, was arrested in June 2010 and faced apostasy charges. She was held for four months, before being released in October. Her release came ten days after the announcement of the death sentence for her husband.

29. Behruz Sadegh-Khanjani (a Church of Iran leader) was again taken into custody on 16 June 2010 upon arriving in Shiraz to attend a court hearing related to a previous charge. Behruz was held in solitary confinement until late November 2010 and was given access to his lawyer only once in this period. He was held in very unhygienic conditions and deliberate harm was inflicted on him. Behruz was charged with apostasy, blasphemy, and contact with the enemy. Behruz and five others from the Church of Iran group were tried in court in mid-February 2011 (4.7), after which Behruz was released on bail.

30. Six members of Behruz Sadegh-Khanjani's house church were arrested in Behruz's home on 18 June. The arrestees were Omid Khalidarnejad (released on bail on 14 July), Afshin Vafdarn (released on bail on 15 July), Mehdi Karbalaei-Ali (released on bail on approximately 19 July), Nahid Karoubian, Fatemeh Tork-Kajouri (wife of Behruz; released on bail on 22 July), and Alireza Seyyedian (released on bail on 25 July) and later brought to trial (4.13). Intelligence agents were equipped with electric shock batons during the house raid.

31. Ali Shahvari was arrested on 25 June in Zahedan. He spent at least three months in detention in solitary confinement. The date of his release is unknown, as is whether he later faced trial and was required to serve a judicial sentence.

32. Neshan Saeedi, a young husband and father, was arrested with his wife and six-year-old daughter at their Ahvaz home on 24 July. They were taken to a detention centre and subjected to hours of interrogation. The wife and daughter were released following questioning, but Neshan remained in solitary confinement, enduring regular interrogation and brutal treatment, until 3 October. He was released after posting $250,000 bail. During his incarceration, his

wife was allowed only very minimal contact with him, and the agents threatened her that she would never see her husband again if she tried to hire a lawyer or if she spoke out about the situation.

33. Eleven converts were arrested on a journey between Mashad and Bojnurd on 18 July. Eight of them were released after one week, but three remained in detention because they refused to sign declarations that they would refrain from any further Christian activity: Ehsan Behrooz (a student aged twenty-three at the time), and married couple Maria and Reza. For fifty days the security agents attempted to make them return to Islam, through solitary confinement and torture. On 29 August, court officials and security agents called in and pressured the three detainees' family members to persuade the three to recant their faith, or they would face apostasy charges. It is unknown when Reza and Maria were released. Ehsan was released on bail three months after the arrest, pending future trial.

34. On 28 July, the Tabriz home of Jamal Zarrin-Kamari and his wife, Solmaz Farzaneh Momtaz, was raided by intelligence officers while the couple were absent. The agents confiscated many Christian materials, and Jamal's parents were forced to call him to return home. On their arrival at home, Jamal and his wife were given a written order to report to the Ministry of Intelligence office on 1 August. It is believed that the couple fled Iran.

35. Hamed Pishkar, a Christian resident of Rasht, was arrested in his home on 15 August. He was released on bail from Lakan prison on 4 September.

36. On 3 September, eleven Christians from the "Church of Iran"[402] group of Bandar Anzali were arrested and charged with action against national security and consuming

402   See footnote 400.

wine, for their involvement in a house church and taking Communion. The eleven are: Abdolreza Ali Haghnejad (the leader of the group), his wife Anahita Khademi, Mahmoud Khosh-Hal and his wife, Hava Saadetmend, Fatemeh Modir-Nouri, Mehrdad Habibizadeh, Milad Radef, Behzad Taalipas, Amir Goldoust, his sister Mina Goldoust, and his grandmother Zainab Bahremend. The length of their detention is unknown. Their trial took place on 28 April 2011 (4.9) and they were acquitted on 14 May 2011.

37. On 4 September, ten Christian converts were arrested in the city of Hamedan. Six were released after signing documents stating they would not engage in further Christian activities. Four remained imprisoned: Vahik Abrahamian, his wife Sonia Keshish-Avanessian (who was reportedly pregnant at the time of the arrest), Arash Kermanjani, and his wife Arezo Teymouri. An incredibly high bail sum was demanded, which they could not afford. They were held without charge for a very long period, and were not given access to their families or the lawyer that their families hired for them. They were finally brought to trial in April 2011 (4.11). All were acquitted and Sonia, Arash, and Arezo were released following the trial, but Vahik continued to be detained until 29 August 2011.

38. On 14 September, Christian couple Mojtaba Keshavarz Ahmadi and Shahin Rostami Azar-Kord disappeared in Arak. For about a week their family members were terrified and were looking for them in hospitals and in morgues, until they were contacted by the Intelligence Ministry and were told that the two were in custody in Arak's central prison. Shahin suffered three heart attacks while in prison and was paralysed on one side of her body. Mojtaba suffered lung problems while in prison. Neither was granted the medical treatment they needed. Their lawyer was not allowed to see them for a month. In the Revolutionary Court, they were

acquitted of the charge of acting against national security, but were found guilty of "insulting the sacred principles of Islam" and were sentenced to three years in prison (4.5). The prosecution brought in someone who was a drug addict to be a witness, and he gave evidence that was later found to be falsified. Shahin and Mojtaba were eventually acquitted and released following an appeal in February 2011.

39. Mohsen Mahdian was arrested on 14 September in Arak, and detained in Arak prison until he was released on bail on 22 December 2010.

40. A new Christian called Alireza Najafzadeh was arrested on 26 September and tortured for three days in the Shahryar detention centre. He endured sensory disorientation, beatings, and whippings with a cable or water hose while being hung from the ceiling. He regularly passed out from the beatings. He was released on bail but was threatened not to share his experiences with anyone, or he would be killed. He fled Iran soon after this incident.

41. Ten converts were arrested at a house-church meeting in Pakdasht on 14 November. Two – the wife and young son of the homeowner – were released after a few hours, six others on bail after a few days. Ali Keshavarz and Mohammad Mohammadi were detained in Khorin prison until an unknown date. It is known that they remained in Khorin until at least 17 December.

42. Another church meeting was raided on 30 November, in the house of Reza T in Karaj. Fourteen converts were arrested, detained overnight, and subjected to severe interrogations. Reza T was detained for a month and released on bail on 29 December.

43. Another sixty-nine are reported to have been arrested in Bandar Abbas, Bandar Mahshahr, Ardabil, Tabriz, Khoramabad, and Elam between September and November

2010. They were released upon signing declarations that they would take no further part in Christian activities.

44. On 3 December, a house church in the care of Hossein Karimi was attacked by Karaj intelligence agents. Many items were confiscated and one member of the church was arrested. The duration of his/her detention is unknown.

45. In early December, Bahar Shokrollahi was arrested at the airport on her return from an overseas Christian conference. Her bags were searched and she was interrogated about what she had been doing overseas. She was not detained, but she and her husband later faced further questioning and her husband later endured a long pre-trial detention.

46. On 6 December 2010, Hashem Karimi was arrested and detained for thirteen days. Hashem is the father of Hossein Karimi, a Christian young man who was previously arrested in 2009 (2.3). Agents had intended to arrest Hossein, but finding him absent, arrested his father instead. Hashem suffered extreme ill-treatment in prison, and upon release was transferred immediately to an intensive care unit.

47. A house church in Dezful was raided on 24 December and the eleven attendees were arrested. Ten were held for several hours for questioning, and were then released with instructions to report to the Ministry of Intelligence in their hometowns. The leader of the group, Noorollah Qabitizadeh, was detained for nineteen months: he was subjected to intense interrogation and repeated pressure to renounce his Christian faith. He was brought to trial in shackles in September 2011, where he was threatened with the death penalty if he did not return to Islam. It is not known whether a sentence was issued following this trial. In February 2012 he was moved to Dastgerd prison due to his sharing his Christian faith with fellow inmates. He was later moved to Karoon prison (in Ahvaz), from which he

was released on 16 July 2012. It is unclear on what basis he was released.

48. On 26 December around seventy Christians from across Iran were arrested in a carefully coordinated wave of persecution. Many were detained and interrogated for just a day, and then released. But many were detained for over a month and endured regular interrogations, long periods of solitary confinement, harsh physical and psychological mistreatment, and threats of being charged with apostasy. Among those released in late January or early February 2011 pending trial were: Abbas Sadeghi, Leila and Sara Akhavan, Anahita Zare, Ladan Nouri, Nasrin Hosseini Nia, Mohammad Zardouz, Maryam Abdollahi, and Davoud Abdi. Released in March 2011 were: Matthew Zare and Rasoul Abdollahi. Released in April 2011: Mehdi Forootan. Most of these individuals then faced further harassment and some, during 2012, received court summons. Some have since left Iran. Rasoul Abdollahi began serving a three-year sentence in Evin prison in December 2013 (4.26). Some remain in Iran and could be re-arrested or summoned to court at any time.

49. Farshid Fathi, husband and father to two young children, was one of the seventy Christians arrested on 26 December in the mass crackdown. He spent over 100 days in solitary confinement during his first year of imprisonment. Over a year after his arrest, he finally faced trial in February 2012 (4.16). He was sentenced to six years for action against national security. His appeal later that year was unsuccessful. He has been in Evin prison since 26 December 2010, and remains there at the time of writing.

50. An elderly Christian couple were arrested on 27 December in Mashad: 65-year-old Hassan Razavi Derakhshan and 61-year-old wife Parya. Both had severe health issues. They

were held in Vakilabad prison until 31 January 2011, when they were released on bail. It is unknown whether the case against them was pursued.

51. Zohreh Taslim, a young single lady, was arrested on 27 December in Mashad and held for over a month. She was repeatedly pressured into recanting her Christian faith. She was later sentenced to six years in prison, but her lawyer sought an appeal. The outcome of the appeal is unknown.

52. Four were arrested on 29/30 December in Isfahan: Basir Amini, Yasaman Yar-Ahmadi, Hooman Tavakoli, and Rafi Nadipoor. They were detained in Evin prison and released on bail in late January 2011.

2011

53. Leonard Keshishian, the pastor of the Assemblies of God church in Isfahan, was summoned to the Intelligence Office in Isfahan. On arrival he was arrested in the early hours of 1 January. He was released on bail on 22 January.

54. On 8 January, Ebrahim Firouzi was arrested in his father's home in Robat Karim. He was released the same day after questioning. He was called in for further questioning on 9 January, and then arrested on 11 January. He had a court hearing on 29 January where he was charged with evangelizing, apostasy, and association with foreign organizations. A further hearing occurred in April – it is not believed that he was sentenced – and he was released on 6 August 2011.

55. Up to twenty Christians in Khorasan province were reported to have been taken in for questioning during January 2011.

56. In January, two young Christian women, Nazak Jalilpoor and her friend Samaneh from Urmia, were arrested upon returning to Iran from an overseas conference. Samaneh

was held for three days and Nazak for an unknown length of time.

57. In early January, church leaders Mostafa Shokrollahi and Khalil Yar-Ali were called in on various days for questioning by the Ministry of Intelligence. Their wives Bahar and Mahnaz were also called in. On 25 January, they were both detained. Both their homes were searched for evidence of their Christian ministry. During detention they endured long periods of solitary confinement and were psychologically and physically tortured during regular interrogation sessions. Mostafa was threatened with rape if he did not comply with questioning, and both were pressured to return to Islam and threatened with execution. After the cycle of interrogations, they were held in extremely poor, over-crowded conditions in Karoon prison. They were released on a high bail in late March. Khalil went to the Revolutionary Court in May 2011, on charges of acting against the security of the state, through evangelism. The judge informed Khalil that the intelligence agents had ordered him to issue a sentence of three years, but the judge bravely acquitted Khalil instead, stating that Christians are free to practise their faith under Iran's constitution. The prosecution appealed but Khalil was again acquitted in September 2011. After his release, Khalil was harassed so intensely that he left the country. Mostafa also left Iran.

58. On 10 February, Arash and Azadeh Attarzadeh were arrested in east Tehran. They are believed to have been detained for a short period. A further four Christians in east Tehran, probably linked to Arash and Azadeh, were arrested on 11 February.

59. On 13 February an estimated forty-five Christians were arrested in various cities: Tehran, Ahvaz, Dezful, Karaj,

Robat Karim, and Mashad. Most were detained overnight for questioning. One man and his pregnant wife were informed that they would be called for questioning once their child was born.

60. In mid-March married Christian couple Hamid Najafi and Mahzar Najafi were arrested while attempting to cross the border to Turkey. Their home had been among those raided by intelligence agents on 26 December 2010, and they had twice subsequently been called into the local Intelligence Office for questioning. During the second round of questioning the interrogators made implicit threats against their young daughter, which persuaded the family to try to leave Iran. Upon their arrest, they were held for fifteen days, and Hamid was beaten during his detention in Salmas prison. They were later fined and the case was closed.

61. On 17 March, ten believers were arrested at a house-church meeting in Kermanshah. All were subjected to interrogation overnight, and seven of the group were released the following day. Two of the group, Nahid Shirazi and Meghdad Babakarimi, were released on bail in early April. The final member of the group, Masoud Delijani (husband of Nahid Shirazi), was held for a long period in solitary confinement and was finally released after 114 days on 9 July 2011, on bail of $100,000 (USD). He would go on to be re-arrested (point 65 below).

62. Shahla Rahmati, a member of the registered Assemblies of God church in Tehran, was arrested on 26 April and sent to Evin prison on 28 April. She was held in solitary confinement for five months and endured regular interrogation. Subsequently she was transferred to the women's ward where her blood pressure dropped very low and she was not given adequate treatment. Although

an Iranian lawyer agreed to take up Shahla's case, she was not allowed to see him until a few days before her court hearing, which was held in the midst of her incarceration, on 18 September (4.12). The hearing was held at Branch 28 of the Revolutionary High Court in Tehran. Her lawyer was called to the court on 17 November 2011: Shahla had been sentenced to three years' imprisonment. On 20 December 2011, she was released, having been cleared of all charges.

63. In early summer 2011, Mitra Zahmati and Maryam Jalili were taken into custody once more, following their release on bail in March 2010. They were sentenced to two and a half years' imprisonment on 4 December 2011 (4.14). They were released early from prison on 17 September 2013, as part of a group of about eighty political prisoners who were released just prior to President Rouhani's visit to the United Nations General Assembly (UNGA) in New York.

64. Vahid/Natan Roufegarbashi and Reza Khanamoei, two young Azeri Christians, were arrested in mid-July near the city of Kalibar. They were found distributing Scriptures in a village, and the pair was chased by police as they fled on their motorbike. The motorbike was driven off-road and crashed, causing Reza to break his leg and Vahid to injure his head. The police caught them and began beating them. They were detained for over a month, much of which was spent in solitary confinement, and they received no treatment for their injuries. Following their release on bail on 21 August, they were harassed by intelligence agents, and so both fled the country before being summoned to court.

65. In July, two weeks after being released on bail, Masoud Delijani was re-arrested. He was tried in the Revolutionary Court of Kermanshah, with no access to a lawyer, and sentenced in February 2012 to three years in prison (4.15).

He was incarcerated in Diesal-Abad prison of Kermanshah. It is unknown whether he served out his full sentence.

66. Leila Mohammadi was detained on 30 July when her east Tehran home was raided. She was taken to an unknown place and later transferred to Evin prison, where she was held for five months. She was released on bail on 28 December. She was later tried on 18 January 2012 (4.17).

67. Fatemeh Nouri, an art student and Christian convert, was arrested in September in her home in east Tehran. The Revolutionary Court convicted her of attending a house, insulting sacred figures, and action against national security. The court ruled that she be deprived of education for one year. She was released on 30 November after nearly three months in prison.

68. Abdolreza (Matthias) Ali Haghnejad, the pastor of the Church of Iran group of Bandar Anzali, was arrested in Rasht on 17 August. He was released ten days later on bail: a family member posted their property deeds as bail.

69. On 17 October Fariborz Arazm, a 44-year-old married Christian convert from Robat-Karim, was arrested in his own residence. Fariborz was initially held in Rajai Shahr prison of Karaj, spending twenty-one days in solitary confinement. He was then transferred to Ward 350 of Evin prison in Tehran for further interrogation. It was while on this ward that he made friends with Farshid Fathi until his temporary release on 11 April 2012, following nearly six months of imprisonment. Reportedly a court announced he would be charged with being in contact with missionaries and also of promoting the Christian faith among Iranian Muslims. It is unknown if this trial went ahead.

70. On 24 October, a Christian student activist called Sahar Mousavi was summoned and arrested. It is assumed that she remains detained at the time of writing.

71. In November 2011, Ehsan Behruz, who was then a 24-year-old student at the university of Mashad, was re-arrested. He spent 105 days in solitary confinement, and the authorities continued to threaten him with apostasy and to pressure him to recant his Christian faith. He was finally released on 16 June 2012.

72. On 23 December 2011, at least fifty-five Christians were arrested when the sanctioned Assemblies of God church in the city of Ahvaz was raided during a Christmas service. All those in the building, including about fifteen children attending Sunday school, were detained, interrogated, and threatened, and most were eventually released. However, the church's senior pastor, Pastor Farhad Sabokroh, his wife Shahnaz Jayzan, and two elders of the church, Naser Zamen-Dezfuli and Davoud Alijani, were held for much longer. Shahnaz was released on bail on 1 January, Farhad and Naser were released on 21 February, and Davoud on 8 March. Davoud recalled that he spent eighty days in solitary confinement during his detention. They would later be sentenced and required to serve more time in prison (4.18).

2012

73. On 8 February 2012, intelligence agents raided a house-church gathering in Shiraz, confiscating religious materials and arresting eight Christian converts: Mojtaba Hosseini, a couple – Fariba Nazemian-Pour and Homayoun Shokoohi – and their 17-year-old son Nima, Vahid Hakkani, Sharifeh Dookh, Mohammad-Reza Partoei (Kourosh), and Masoud Golrooyan. Masoud, Sharifeh, and Nima were released on 14 March 2012 after the Revolutionary Court demanded the payment of a large bail from each. Fariba was released on bail in October 2012. Three of the group have remained imprisoned since their February 2012 arrest and are

serving sentences (4.22) in Adelabad prison at the time of writing, including Vahid Hakkani who went on hunger strike multiple times in early 2014.

74. An evening church meeting in Kermanshah was raided on 21 February 2012, and thirteen Christians were arrested and transferred to an unknown location. Nine of these detainees were released the following day after their photos were taken, their details and fingerprints recorded, and after they signed a disclaimer stating they would not attend any further Christian gatherings. A further detainee, Azadeh Sharifi, was released after eight days of detention; one, Shirin Ghanbari, was released some weeks later. But two, Mojtaba Baba-Karimi and Mehdi Chaghakaboudi, were never reported as released, and may remain detained at the time of writing.

75. A broad wave of arrests occurred in Isfahan on 22 Feburary 2012: Hekmat Salimi, pastor of the official Episcopal Church of St Paul was arrested, and his home raided at 7 a.m. on 22 February. The authorities did not provide any explanation and transferred him to an unknown location. Hekmat was reportedly released on 3 May following seventy-three days in prison. He reportedly was forced to submit as bail a title deed valued at the equivalent of $40,000 (USD).

76. Shahram Ghaedi, a member of St Paul's Episcopal Church, and an actor, was also arrested that morning. He was reportedly released on bail in late April 2012.

77. Maryam Del-aram was arrested on 22 February. Plain-clothes agents raided her house early in the morning, and seized Bibles and Christian materials. They transferred her to an unknown location. She was temporarily released on bail in early May.

78. Giti Hakimpour, a 78-year-old Christian lady, had her house raided on 22 February at 6 a.m. by agents. She

endured three days of custody in the Intelligence Office of Isfahan and was released on 25 February. Ms Hakimpour is a member and minister at St Luke's Episcopal Church in Isfahan.

79. Shahnaz Zarifi is a Christian mother of two who had her home raided on the morning of 22 February. The agents searched her apartment, threatened her, and then arrested her. Unconfirmed reports indicate that she has been transferred to the Dastgerd prison in Isfahan. She was temporarily released on bail in early May.

80. Further Christians who were reported to have been arrested in Isfahan around this time are: Majid Enayat, Enayat Jafari, Fariborz Parsi-Nejad, Keyhan Amirian, Khodadad Nasiri, and Misem Hojatti. It is unknown whether any of the above Isfahan detainees were subsequently tried in court and issued judicial sentences.

81. In March 2011 Alireza Seyyedian was arrested while attempting to flee the country. He was then sentenced to six years' imprisonment in November 2011. At the time of writing, he remains incarcerated in Ward 350 of Evin prison.

82. On 14 April in Tehran, intelligence agents simultaneously arrested two Christian converts by the names of Ladan and Hooman. The authorities entered the two homes without showing any warrant and arrested the two Christians without providing any explanation. Both Christians were then transferred to an unknown location immediately following their arrest. They were detained for fifty-eight days before being released on 10 June, after posting bail worth $325,000 (USD). They were charged with forming a house church and evangelism. It is unknown whether the pair later faced trial and if they were required to serve a judicial sentence.

83. In early May a Christian called Nazak presented herself to the Ministry of Intelligence Office in Urmia, following weeks of harassment by the intelligence agents via telephone calls. She was detained and interrogated for an unknown period.

84. On 30 May, Iran's cyber police raided the home of Alireza Ibrahimi, who ran a Christian website. He was not home, but his personal belongings, which included his laptop, articles, notes, and Christian literature were confiscated. Prior to this raid the plain-clothed authorities had attempted to arrest him on May 27, but he was not at home on this occasion either. The cyber police also raided the home of two of Alireza's Christian friends, Saeed Mirzaei and Sadegh Mirzaei, and arrested them. They were charged with propagating against Islam and actions against national security. It is unknown whether the pair later faced trial and if they were required to serve a judicial sentence.

85. On 25 and 26 May, two house churches in Khorasan province were raided, and some members arrested. On 25 May, a house church in the city of Neyshabur was raided and two men, Hadi and Alireza, were taken into custody. The length and conditions of their detention is unknown. On 26 May, a house church in Mashad was raided and Vahid Zardi and his wife were arrested. Vahid's wife was held for questioning for one day only, but Vahid remained in prison for 136 days until he was released on bail on 14 October. A case against the Khorasan Christians is understood to be pending.

86. On 24 May, Mehrdad Sajadi and his wife Forogh Dashtianpoor were arrested in Tehran. They were elders of the registered Emmanuel Presbyterian church in Tehran. Forogh was released on bail on 7 June, but Mehrdad was held for over a year without formal charge, until his release on bail in July 2013. It is unknown whether the couple

later faced trial and if they were required to serve a judicial sentence.

87. Saeed Abedini, an Iranian-American Christian convert, was arrested in July, held under house arrest initially and then transferred to Evin prison on 26 September, where he endured prolonged interrogations. At the time of his arrest he was visiting Iran from his home in the USA, in order to establish an orphanage in Iran. Prior to this he had been arrested on a couple of occasions. He was sentenced to eight years' imprisonment in January 2013 (4.19) and his appeal was unsuccessful. He has endured much physical mistreatment during his imprisonment. He remains imprisoned at the time of writing.

88. A Church of Iran prayer meeting in Shiraz was raided on 12 October and seven church members arrested: Mohammad Roghangir, Suroush Saraie, Roxana Forughi, Eskandar Rezaie, Bijan Farokhpour Haghighi, Mehdi Ameruni, and Shahin Lahooti. Two further members of the group were arrested on 18 October: Afsar Bahmani and Masoud Rezaie. Asfar was released unconditionally the following day and was not later called to court. Three of the others were released on bail within a month of the arrest: Mohammad, Suroush, and Esakandar were released on bail in March 2013; Shahin, a Christian musician, was detained until December 2013. The group were sentenced on 16 July 2013 (4.24) and their appeal in March 2014 was unsuccessful. Three of them are in custody at the time of writing.

89. In late 2012 (date unknown), Maryam Naghash Zargaran (called "Nasim") was arrested in Tehran. On the day of her arrest, agents searched her home and took all her Christian books and materials and her computer. She spent three days initially in Vozara (a detention centre in Tehran run by the Ministry of Intelligence) before being sent to Evin

prison, where she endured interrogations. She remained there for nineteen days, until a 70-million toman bail was demanded and the title deed of a family home was posted. She faced trial in January 2013 (4.20) and was sentenced to four years' imprisonment, which she began serving in Evin prison on 15 July 2013.

90. On 27 December, Revd Vruir Avanessian and about fifty other Christians were arrested while celebrating Christmas together. Revd Avanessian had been an ordained pastor of the Armenian and Persian-language congregations of the central Assemblies of God church in Tehran for more than seventeen years. Most of the fifty gathered Christians were questioned and released later that day, but Revd Avanessian was held longer, despite being very ill and requiring regular treatment. He was released on 10 January 2013 after property title deeds were submitted as bail payment. He was informed in December 2013 that he had been sentenced to three and a half years in prison (4.25).

91. Mostafa Bordbar (age twenty-six at the time) was among those arrested on 27 December with Revd Avanessian. He was detained in Ward 350 of Evin prison from the time of his arrest and throughout the court proceedings against him. He was sentenced to ten years' imprisonment (4.21), but was later acquitted at appeal and released on 3 November 2013, nearly a year after his arrest.

92. On 25 December, Youcef Nadarkhani was re-arrested, following his being acquitted of apostasy and released in September. He was held for two weeks and released on 7 January 2013.

93. On 31 December, four members of the Church of Iran network were arrested. They were later sentenced to eighty lashes for drinking wine during Communion (see Section 3: Corporal punishment).

2013

94. On 9 January 2013, Shahrzad (aged twenty-five) and Sam (aged twenty-seven) were arrested in a home in Tehran. They were missing for two months before their family learned they were detained in prison. They were accused of establishing a house church. It is unknown whether they were subsequently released or if they remain detained.

95. In February, there were unconfirmed reports that a Christian in Rasht had been detained and interrogated, and subsequently informed that she would be whipped for drinking alcohol during Communion, and her daughter would be expelled from school.

96. On 7 March, Ebrahim Firouzi was at his workplace when he was taken into custody once more. He was held for fifty-three days before being released on bail, in the form of a property deed. He was later brought to trial, sentenced, and imprisoned to serve his sentence in August 2013 (4.23).

97. Somayeh Bakhtiari and Ronak Samavat were arrested on 24 and 25 April respectively, for their involvement in a house church. It is possible they remain detained at time of writing.

98. Revd Robert Asserian, an Armenian pastor of the central Assemblies of God church in Tehran, was arrested on the morning of 21 May, when he arrived at the church to lead a prayer meeting. He spent forty-three days in custody in Evin prison before being released on bail on 2 July. Revd Asserian had been a well-loved and respected leader at the church for over twenty-five years. His arrest was the peak of a sustained campaign of pressure inflicted on the central church by the authorities. Following his arrest, the church was closed and, at the time of writing, has not been re-opened.

99. Three young men who ran a Christian website were arrested on 29 May in Isfahan. Mohammad Reza Farid,

Saeed Safi, and Hamid Reza Ghadiri were arrested at Hamid's home during a worship meeting; agents entered the property, acted violently towards the gathered group, and confiscated their ID cards. Prior to the arrest, various members of their house church had been contacted by intelligence agents and asked questions about the three men. No further information is obtainable about the situation: it is possible that the three men remain detained at the time of writing.

100. Farshid Modares-Aval, Samad Kazemi, and Hamid Reza were arrested on 10 July 2013 following raids on their homes in Tabriz. Fellow believer Yashar Farzin No was arrested the following day while Mohammad Reza Piri was arrested on 17 July. There were reportedly other Christians subsequently arrested in Tabriz whose identities are unknown. Mohammad Reza Piri sustained serious injuries after being tortured and severely beaten during interrogations and had to spend four days in the hospital of the central prison of Tabriz. Prior to the arrests, Yashar Farzin No and his wife had been repeatedly put under pressures to recant their new Christian faith and return to Islam. Samad Kazemi was released on bail a few days after his arrest and the rest of the group were also later released on bail. They will continue to be monitored and may be summoned to court.

101. On 12 July, Nasim Zanjani was arrested at her parents' home in Tehran. Her house was searched, and her computer, Christian books, and CDs were confiscated. No further information on her situation is available. It is possible that she remains detained at the time of writing.

102. Hossein Saketi Aramsari (Stephen) was arrested on 23 July 2013 in Golestan province. For the majority of his detention he has been held in Rajai-Shahr prison in Karaj. He was subsequently transferred to the Ghezel Hesar

prison Karaj in late October 2013. During November 2013 he was charged with evangelism. In January 2014 he was sentenced to one year in prison (4.27).

103. Plain-clothed agents raided a house church meeting in Isfahan on 1 August. Three were arrested: Sedigheh Amirkhani, Mahnaz Rafiee, and Mohammad Reza Peymani. It is unknown for how long the three remained detained or if they subsequently faced trial. It is possible that they remain detained at the time of writing.

104. Five Christian converts were arrested on 9 August during a raid on a house-church meeting in western Tehran. There were fifteen participants of the meeting and the raid was reportedly violent. The five arrestees, Parham Farazmand, Sara Sardsirian, Sedigheh Kiani, Mona Fazli, and one unnamed other, were taken to an unknown location.

105. On 21 August, Ebrahim Firouzi, Masoud Mirzaei, and Sevada Aghasar were arrested in Karaj. Ebrahim was taken to serve his sentence. Masoud was released after a short detention. Sevada (of Armenian ethnicity) was detained for over six months until he was released on bail on 2 March 2014. It is likely that he will be summoned to court during 2014 or 2015.

106. Three Tehran-based Christians named Sahar Barzegar and Kaymar Barzegar (a married couple with a young daughter) and their pastor Amir Ebrahimi were reported as going missing on 29 August. Each of the three was sentenced to six months' imprisonment and forty lashes because of their house church activities.

107. The homes of four Christians in Karaj were raided on 15 December. Among the four was Kristina Irani, the wife of imprisoned Church of Iran leader, Behnam Irani. The other three homes belonged to Silas Rabbani, Amin Khaki, and an unnamed Christian. Many Christian materials were

confiscated during the raids. The three men were told to expect a summons for a court hearing.

108. On 24 December 2013, a house in eastern Tehran was raided: five Christians who were celebrating Christmas were arrested and taken to an unknown location. The neighbouring house was also searched; the neighbour, who had observed the raid of the Christmas meeting, was beaten and insulted and warned not to speak out about what he had witnessed. The five arrested Christians were Mr Hosseini (the homeowner), Ahmad Bazyar, Faegheh Nasrollahi, Mastaneh Rastegari, and Amir-Hossein Ne'matollahi. A family member of Ahmad's later learned that they were arrested by the Iranian Revolutionary Guard Corps (IRGC) and that the group was being held in Ward 2A of Evin prison (which is run by the IRGC). No further news is available; it is possible that they remain detained at the time of writing.

109. Sara Rahimi-Nejad, Mostafa Nadri, Majid Sheidaei, and George Isaian were arrested in Mr Isaian's home in Karaj on 31 December 2013. They were taken to an unknown location. It is possible that they remain detained at the time of writing.

2014

110. Two unnamed Christian men, a young man and his uncle, were arrested at Tehran airport on 10 February 2014 upon returning from an overseas trip. A week after their arrest, the Ministry of Intelligence contacted their families and said they had been charged with making contact with Christian networks abroad, apostasy, and for promoting Christianity inside the country. It is possible that they remain detained at the time of writing.

111. Amin Khaki, Hossein Barunzadeh, and Rahman Bahman, members of Behnam Irani's Church of Iran fellowship in Karaj, were arrested by intelligence agents during a picnic on 5 March 2014. Eight Iranian Christians in total were arrested during the incident, and taken for interrogation; the five others[403] were released after questioning. It is possible the three men remain detained at the time of writing. Amin Khaki was transferred to the Interim Ward of Ahvaz Prison on 7 May, while Hossein Baraunzadeh and Rahman Bahma were transferred from Ahvaz Prison to a prison in the city of Dezful. Amin Khaki was reportedly beaten violently in Ahvaz prison.

112. Mohammad Bahrami, a new convert to Christianity, was arrested on 7 April 2014 after being summoned to the Intelligence Office in Ahvaz. He was taken to an undisclosed location and it is possible that he remains detained at the time of writing.

113. Six Christians: Ehsan Sadeghi, Nazi and Maryam Azadi, Ali Arfa'e, Vahid Safi, and Amin Mazloomi were arrested during an Easter service on 18 April 2014 in south Tehran. They were taken to an unknown location. It is possible that they remain detained at the time of writing.

114. In April 2014, Shahin Lahooti (4.28) was taken back into custody after his two-and-a-half-year sentence was upheld at appeal in March 2014. It is believed he is now serving his sentence.

115. Silas Rabbani, a deacon within the Church of Iran fellowship of Karaj was arrested on 5 May 2014 and transferred to section 8 of Gohardasht prison.

116. On 5 July Church of Iran leader Abdolreza (Matthias) Ali Haghnejad and members Suroush Saraie and Mohammad

---

403 Mohammad Bahrami, Fatemeh Bagheri, Amineh Moalla, Saiede Rahimi, and Hossein Etemadifar.

Roghangir were arrested in an early morning raid on Abdolreza's home in Bandar Anzali. It is assumed Suroush and Mohammad have begun to serve their prison sentences (4.28), which they were issued on 16 July 2013 as part of a larger group of defendants. Abdolreza has been targeted regularly by the Iranian regime and has been imprisoned on three former occasions.

3. Corporal punishment and prison assaults

On 30 October 2013, two Christians were flogged with eighty lashes each, served as punishment for taking wine during a Communion (Eucharist) service. It not clear whether two others who received the same sentence were also subsequently flogged. The verdict was against four Christians – Behzad Taalipasand, Mehdi Reza Omidi (Youhan), Mehdi Dadkhah (Danial), and Amir Hatemi (Youhanna) – and had been received on 20 October. The verdict from a Rasht court dated 6 October 2013 sentenced each of them to eighty lashes for the consumption of wine during a Communion, and for the possession of satellite equipment.

It is highly likely that other Christians in Iran have suffered judicially mandated corporal punishment since 2009, but this is the only case that has been reported publicly. Many Christians endure physical torture during interrogations and some have faced physical assault while in prison. For example, the following three incidents occurred during the first half of 2014:

1. On Thursday 17 April, a brutal incident occurred in Evin prison (Tehran), resulting in the injury of over thirty inmates, including Farshid Fathi, who is the longest-serving Christian prisoner in Iran at time of writing. The attack, which occured in ward 350 of Evin among prisoners of conscience, was perpetrated by armed, armoured guards who were supposedly there to conduct a routine inspection. However, for over five hours, the inmates were beaten and

brutalized by the guards. During the incident, Farshid went to help one of the injured inmates, but was stopped by one of the guards who stamped on Farshid's bare foot with his heavy boot. Farshid sustained a broken foot. Though he was in great agony, the guards did not allow him any medical treatment for three days until Sunday morning (Easter Sunday). He was taken to hospital in chains; there he was treated and his foot bandaged. Many other victims were also denied the treatment they needed and many were put in solitary confinement.

2. In March, imprisoned Christian leader Saeed Abedini was transferred from Rajai Shahr prison to hospital so that he could be treated for numerous serious injuries he had sustained during beatings in prison. On 20 May, he was beaten again in hospital. Without advance notice he was dragged from his hospital bed, beaten, and taken back to prison. His medical condition is worsening because he is not receiving proper treatment. He has been in custody since September 2012.

3. On 7 June, Behnam Irani (a Christian prisoner who has been incarcerated in Ghezel Hesar prison since May 2011) was beaten violently in his cell and then taken to an unknown location. Behnam was summoned by Judge Mohammad Yari, Chief of the Sixth Chamber of the Revolutionary Tribunal, but as the summons appeared irregular and contrary to judicial process, Behnam rejected it and wrote a letter of protest. However, at 9 a.m. intelligence agents entered his prison cell and proceeded to beat him before he was taken to see Mohammad Yari. He was subsequently taken to a detention centre where he was interrogated and subjected to solitary confinement. He was returned to Ghezel Hesar later in June. Two weeks prior to the assault, the authorities confiscated Behnam's Bible and other Christian literature.

4. Custodial sentences issued to Christians

1. Hossein Karimi (2.3) from Karaj was given a two-year suspended prison sentence on 15 March 2009 for his Christian ministry work and evangelism.

2. Youcef Nadarkhani (2.10) was informed orally in late September 2010 that the Court in Gilan province had sentenced him to death for apostasy. The ruling of an appeal court in June 2011 called for the Gilan court to re-examine the case; this re-examination occurred on 25–28 September 2011. During this hearing, he was given three opportunities to recant his faith and he refused each time. Finally another hearing occurred in September 2012, where he was acquitted of apostasy, and sentenced instead to three years for "evangelizing Muslims". He had already served three years in prison, and so was released.

3. On 30 December, Hamideh Najafi (2.11) was sentenced by the Mashad Revolutionary Court to three months of house arrest. Her daughter suffered from a serious kidney condition and the court ordered her to be placed in foster care. However, the court relented on this point on the condition that Hamideh cease believing in Christ and stop speaking of her faith.

2010

4. In August 2010, Davoud Nejat-Sabet (2.18) and Shahin Taghizadeh were given a suspended sentence of one year. Both were members of a church in Rasht.

5. In late 2010, a Christian couple from Arak (Mojtaba Keshavarz Ahmadi and Shahin Rostami (2.38)) were sentenced to three years for insulting Islamic sanctities. The sentence was overturned at appeal in February 2011.

2011

6. In January 2011, Behnam Irani (a leader of a Church of Iran fellowship in Karaj – 3.25) was tried, convicted of crimes against national security and given a one-year sentence. On 31 May a warrant was issued for his arrest so he turned himself into Ghezel Hesar prison and began serving his sentence. Shortly before the time he was to be released (18 October 2011) he was informed by letter that he was now required to serve a five-year prison sentence that he had received in 2008, but which had been suspended. He is expected to remain in prison until October 2016. He has been seriously ill while in prison and has been regularly denied adequate medical treatment.

7. On 15 February six members of the Church of Iran group (2.29) faced trial in the Shiraz Revolutionary Court. Behruz Sadegh-Khanjani, Mohammad (William) Beliad, Nazli Makarian, Parviz Khalaj, Amin Farzad-Manesh, and Mehdi Forutan were tried on national security charges. Following the trial Behruz was released on a bail of $150,000 (USD). It was later announced that the court had sentenced the group to one year in prison on account of "propaganda against the order of the Islamic Republic of Iran" (article 500 of the penal code). The case went to appeal, but was unsuccessful. One member of the group, Mehdi Forutan, began serving this one-year sentence in Adel Abad prison in October 2011; the others are believed to have absconded.

8. On 5 April the Church of Iran Shiraz group (4.7) also had a scheduled hearing in the ordinary criminal court on charges of apostasy and blasphemy, but the court postponed the hearing until 12 April, and then postponed again due to lack of evidence. Whether this second trial occurred is not known.

9. The trial of eleven Church of Iran believers from Bandar Anzali (2.36) took place on 28 April 2011 in the Revolutionary Court of Bandar Anzali. They were charged with action against national security and consuming wine during a Communion service. They were acquitted on 14 May 2011. They were legally represented by Mohammad Ali Dadkhah (a well-known human rights defender who is now imprisoned himself for his work).

10. Ali Golchin, a Christian from Varamin (2.26), was sentenced to one year in prison by Branch 28 of the Tehran Revolutionary Court on 19 April 2011. His lawyer was reportedly not allowed to speak during the court session. Ali was acquitted at appeal six months later but he received no documentation to prove the acquittal. He continued to face intense harassment following his acquittal and so later left Iran.

11. Four Christians from Hamedan (2.37) were tried in late April. They were acquitted and three were released but one, Vahik, remained in detention until August 2011.

12. On 17 November, a three-year sentence was handed down to Shahla Rahmati (2.62) via her lawyer, following a court hearing on 18 September 2011 at Branch 28 of the Revolutionary High Court in Tehran. The name of the judge was Mr Moghaysi, who normally presides over the trials of Muhajideen prisoners (who usually receive the sentence of execution). Shahla was convicted of being a vehicle to give funds to church house group leaders in Iran. The prosecutor argued that this constituted "action against the national security of the country". Shahla's lawyer appealed, and she was released on 20 December 2011.

13. In December Alireza Seyyedian (2.30) was sentenced to six years in prison by Branch 26 of Iran's Revolutionary Court for crimes against national security and propaganda

against the regime (the latter for his baptism in Turkey). He was also accused of holding regular meetings with converts. He began serving this sentence in March 2012, when he was arrested while attempting to flee the country. At the time of writing, he remains incarcerated in ward 350 of Evin prison.

14. On 4 December 2011, two Christian ladies, Mitra Zahmati and Maryam Jalili (2.63), were sentenced to two and a half years' imprisonment for their membership of an illegal group: a house church.

2012

15. In February 2012, Masoud Delijani (2.65) was sentenced to three years' imprisonment by the Revolutionary Court of Kermanshah. He was convicted of holding illegal house-church gatherings, evangelizing to Muslims, and action against national security.

16. On 5 February Farshid Fathi (2.49) was tried at Branch 15 of Revolutionary Court in Tehran, fourteen months after his arrest. He was convicted of action against national security, cooperating with foreign organizations, and evangelism, and sentenced to a total of six years' imprisonment. The name of the judge was Mr Salavati. The unsuccessful appeal hearing took place on 23 May 2012.

17. Leila Mohammadi (2.66) was tried on 18 January and sentenced to two years in prison for forming a house church, insulting sacred figures, and action against national security. The case was sent to the high court of Tehran province. It is not known whether she was acquitted or whether she was required to serve the sentence.

18. Four leaders of the Assemblies of God church of Ahvaz (2.72) were taken to Branch 2 of the Revolutionary Court of Ahvaz on 21 October 2012. On 29 October 2012, Judge

Seyed Mohammad Bagher Mousavi handed down his verdict: they were all found guilty, convicted under article 500 of the penal code, of gathering in an illegal group and working against the national and international security of the nation, of preaching against the Islamic regime, and of evangelizing. Under Article 10 of the penal code, the church's resources and belongings were permanently confiscated. The appeal in April 2013 was unsuccessful and the four were called to serve their sentences on 1 May 2013. Farhad Sabokroh and Naser Zamen Dezfuli were released from Sepidar prison on 4 December after serving 236 days. Davoud Alijani was released from Karoun prison on 13 January 2014. Shahnaz Jayzan was released from Sepidar on 28 January 2014. They now are unable to continue their Christian ministry.

2013

19. In January, Saeed Abedini (2.87) was tried on the charge of action against national security. He was sentenced by Judge Pir-Abassi to eight years' imprisonment, which was upheld following an appeal hearing on 25 August 2013. In November he was transferred to the notorious Rajai Shahr prison in Karaj. He has suffered beatings inside that prison, and was sent to hospital in March 2014 because of the injuries he sustained, but during May of that year he was beaten in hospital and hauled back to prison.

20. On 9 March 2013, the Revolutionary Court of Tehran handed down its judgment against Christian lady, Maryam Naghash Zargaran (2.89). She was sentenced to four years' imprisonment. Judge Mohammad Moghiseh had determined that she had set up and formed house churches with the aim of drawing youth to Christianity and herself had propagated Christianity, among other Christian activities. The court regarded these activities as "being in

line with the hostile aims of the UK and Israelis to spread house churches inside Iran and corrupt Islamic society". The case went to appeal but it was unsuccessful. She was summoned on 15 July to begin serving her sentence.

21. On 9 June, Mostafa Bordbar (who had been arrested in late December 2012 – 3.91) was tried and charged with illegal gathering and participation in a house church. The verdict was handed down in July: he had been sentenced to ten years in prison, which combined five years for membership of an anti-security organization and five years for action against national security. This was the longest prison sentence that had been issued to a Christian in recent years. The case went to appeal, and on 30 October 2013, Branch 43 of the Appeal Court overturned the sentence and acquitted him of all charges. Mostafa was released in early November.

22. On 18 June, six members of a Shiraz house church (2.73) were tried and convicted of attending a house church, spreading Christianity, having contact with foreign ministries, propaganda against the regime, and disrupting national security. The six were: Mojtaba Hosseini, Mohammad Reza-Partoei, Vahid Hakkani, Homayoun Shokouhi, his wife Fariba Nazemian-Poor, and their son Nima. Fariba and Nima were given two-year suspended sentences. The four men were sentenced to forty-four months each. The four men had already been incarcerated for fifteen months by the time they were brought to trial. The sentences were upheld on appeal in October 2013. Homayoun, Mojtaba, and Vahid continue to be incarcerated at time of writing. Mohammad Reza-Partoei was reportedly released on parole in May 2014.

23. Ebrahim Firouzi (2.96) was tried at the Robat Karim Revolutionary Court on 6 July and on 14 July received the court ruling: he was sentenced to one year imprisonment

and two years' exile to Sarbaz (a remote border town), for propaganda against the system, establishing and managing a deviant evangelical Christian organization, relationships with anti-revolutionary groups outside the country, acquisition and distribution of Christian literature, including the Bible, and participation in house churches. He was taken into custody to begin serving his sentence in August 2013.

24. Eight members of a Church of Iran group from Shiraz were sentenced on 16 July. They had been arrested on 12 October 2012 (2.88). Mohammad Roghangir was sentenced to six years, Massoud Rezaie to five years, Mehdi Ameruni and Bijan Farokhpour Haghighi to three years each, Shahin Lahooti and Suroush Saraie to two and a half years each, and Eskandar Rezaie and Roxana Forughi to one year in prison. The case went to appeal in March 2014.

25. Revd Vruir Avanessian (2.90) was tried on 7 September at Branch 26 of the Revolutionary Court in Tehran on charges of action against national security and of evangelizing. In December he was informed that he had been sentenced to three and a half years' imprisonment. He is an elderly man who suffers with severe medical conditions and requires regular medical treatment, which probably explains why, at the time of writing, he has not been called to serve his sentence in prison. He is believed to be under house arrest.

26. Rasoul Abdollahi (who was originally arrested in a mass crackdown on Christians at Christmas 2010 – 3.48) was sentenced to three years' imprisonment in 2013 and began serving his sentence in Evin prison on 2 December 2013.

2014

27. In January 2014 Hossein Saketi Aramsari (Stephen) (2.102) was sentenced to one year in prison for evangelizing. Judge

Asef Hosseini convicted him in Branch 1 of Revolutionary Court in Karaj.

28. The case of eight Church of Iran Christians (2.88) went to appeal in March 2014. The sentences of seven of the group were upheld. Roxana Foroughi was acquitted. Shahin Lahooti was taken into custody again in April 2014, and is presumed to have begun serving his sentence. Two other members of the group were taken into custody on 5 July, and are presumed to have also begun serving their sentences. The remaining four members of the group could be summoned at any time to serve their sentences.

It is highly likely that considerably more Christians have been tried and sentenced than section 4 catalogues, but often information about court cases is not disseminated for security reasons.

However, it seems that the Iranian regime's preferred method of crushing the church is to intimidate Christians into leaving the country as refugees. Christians who are dedicated to evangelizing and discipling other believers are so closely monitored, and so frequently harassed, arrested, and threatened, that many leave Iran because they are not able to continue in their ministry inside Iran. Christians who leave Iran as refugees save the Iranian government the high costs of court cases, the costs of housing Christians in prisons for many years and, crucially, it saves Iran from further international outcry. It seems that Iran's chief aim is to persuade the Christian community to remove itself from the country, rather than to imprison all Iran's Christians, for, as the title of this book suggests, there are simply "too many to jail".

THE FINAL TESTAMENT OF MEHDI DIBAJ

Mehdi Dibaj's courageous suffering and witness to Jesus Christ is an inspiration to Iran's churches, old and new, and to Christians everywhere.

In particular Christians around the world have been deeply moved by the defence Mehdi Dibaj gave in 1993 before an Islamic court which sentenced him to death for apostasy.

This is the background to how this document came to the international church.

Back in 1986 Mehdi Dibaj had been sentenced to death for apostasy by the court of the Islamic Republic in the city of Sari in the north of Iran.

However, Mehdi Dibaj had appealed against his sentence on the grounds that the Koran does not demand the death sentence for apostates from Islam. After making his appeal, Mehdi Dibaj remained in prison, not knowing whether or not he would be acquitted or executed.

Eventually in December 1993 the court convened to consider Mehdi Dibaj's case. During the hearing Mehdi Dibaj gave his final testimony, printed here.

This extraordinary statement was smuggled out of the prison and eventually found its way to Revd Haik Hovsepian Mehr, the Chairman of the Council of Protestant Ministers in Iran.

Haik Hovsepian Mehr faxed the statement to his close friend Sam Yeghnazar in the UK. Sam Yeghnazar was meant to be on holiday with his family, but he had sensed he might be needed to play a part in the campaign to help Mehdi Dibaj. So the holiday plans had been cancelled and he had stayed at his desk.

The fax arrived in Sam Yeghnazar's office on 12 January 1994. Sam immediately translated Mehdi Dibaj's final testament into English and sent it to church leaders and the press.

The next day the whole world knew about Mehdi Dibaj, not least because Bernard Levin, the famous journalist for the *The Times* newspaper dedicated his entire column to the testimony.

As detailed in Chapter 8, the Iranian authorities released Mehdi Dibaj from prison on 16 January 1994 after an international campaign for his freedom. The man in Iran who had made the campaign happen, Haik Hovsepian Mehr, paid with his life. He went missing on 19 January. Ten days later his son identified his murdered corpse.

Mehdi Dibaj only enjoyed a few months of life outside prison. On 24 June he also went missing; on 5 July his murdered body was identified.

He left behind an example to follow – and this is his final testament.

"In the Holy Name of God who is our life and existence"

With all humility I express my gratitude to the Judge of all heaven and earth for this precious opportunity, and with brokenness I wait upon the Lord to deliver me from this court trial according to His promises. I also beg the honored members of the court who are present to listen with patience to my defense and with respect for the Name of the Lord.

I am a Christian. As a sinner I believe Jesus has died for my sins on the cross and by His resurrection and victory over death, has made me righteous in the presence of the Holy God. The true God speaks about this fact in His Holy Word, the Gospel (Injil). Jesus means Savior "because He will save His people from their sins." Jesus paid the penalty of our sins by His own blood and gave us a new life so that we can live for the glory of God by the help of the Holy Spirit and be like a dam against corruption, be a channel of blessing and healing, and be protected by the love of God.

In response to this kindness, He has asked me to deny myself and be His fully surrendered follower, and not to fear people even if they kill my body, but rather rely on the creator of life who has crowned me with the crown of mercy and compassion. He is the great protector of His beloved ones as well as their great reward.

I have been charged with "apostasy!" The invisible God who knows our hearts has given assurance to us, as Christians, that we are not among the apostates who will perish but among the believers who will have eternal life. In Islamic Law (Sharia'), an apostate is one who does not believe in God, the prophets or the resurrection of the dead, We Christians believe in all three!

They say "You were a Muslim and you have become a Christian." This is not so. For many years I had no religion. After searching and studying I accepted God's call and believed in the Lord Jesus Christ in order to receive eternal life. People choose their religion but a Christian is chosen by Christ. He says, "You have not chosen me but I have chosen you." Since when did He choose me? He chose me before the foundation of the world. People say, "You were a Muslim from your birth." God says, "You were a Christian from the beginning." He states that He chose us thousands of years ago, even before the creation of the universe, so that through the sacrifice of Jesus Christ we may be His. A Christian means one who belongs to Jesus Christ.

The eternal God who sees the end from the beginning and who has chosen me to belong to Him, knew from the beginning those whose heart would be drawn to Him and also those who would be willing to sell their faith and eternity for a pot of porridge. I would rather have the whole world against me, but know that the Almighty God is with me. I would rather be called an apostate, but know that I have the approval of the God of glory, because man looks at the outward appearance but God looks at the heart. For Him who is God for all eternity nothing is impossible. All power in heaven and on earth is in His hands.

The Almighty God will raise up anyone He chooses and bring down others, accept some and reject others, send some to heaven and other to hell. Now because God does whatever He desires, who can separate us from the love of God? Or who can destroy the relationship between the creator and the creature or defeat a life that is faithful to his Lord? The faithful will be safe and secure under the shadow of the Almighty! Our refuge is the mercy seat of God who is exalted from the beginning. I know in whom I have believed, and He is able to guard what I have entrusted to Him to the end until I reach the Kingdom of God, the place where the righteous shine like the sun, but where the evil doers will receive their punishment in the fire of hell.

They tell me, "Return!" But to whom can I return from the arms of my God? Is it right to accept what people are saying instead of obeying the Word of God? It is now 45 years that I am walking with the God of miracles, and His kindness upon me is like a shadow and I owe Him much for His fatherly love and concern.

The love of Jesus has filled all my being and I feel the warmth of His love in every part of my body. God, who is my glory and honor and protector, has put his seal of approval upon me through His unsparing blessings and miracles.

This test of faith is a clear example. The good and kind God reproves and punishes all those whom He loves. He tests them in preparation for heaven. The God of Daniel, who protected his friends in the fiery furnace, has protected me for nine years in prison. And all the bad happenings have turned out for our good and gain, so much so that I am filled to overflowing with joy and thankfulness.

The God of Job has tested my faith and commitment in order to increase my patience and faithfulness. During these nine years he has freed me from all my responsibilities so that under the protection of His blessed Name, I would spend my time in prayer and study of His Word, with a searching heart and with brokenness, and grow in the knowledge of my Lord. I praise the Lord for this unique opportunity. God gave me space in my confinement, brought healing in my difficult hardships and His kindness revived me. Oh what great blessings God has in store for those who fear Him!

They object to my evangelizing. But if one finds a blind person who is about to fall in a well and keeps silent then one has sinned. It is our religious duty, as long as the door of God's mercy is open, to convince evil doers to turn from their sinful ways and find refuge in Him in order to be saved from the wrath of the Righteous God and from the coming dreadful punishment.

Jesus Christ says "I am the door. Whoever enters through me will be saved." "I am the way, the truth and the life. No-one comes to the father except through me." "Salvation is found in no-one else, for there is no other name under heaven given to men by which we must be saved." Among the prophets of God, only Jesus Christ rose from the dead, and He is our living intercessor for ever.

He is our Savior and He is the (spiritual) Son of God. To know Him means to know eternal life. I, a useless sinner, have believed in this beloved person and all His words and miracles recorded in the Gospel, and I have committed my life into His hands. Life for me is an opportunity to serve Him, and death is a better opportunity to be with Christ. Therefore I am not only satisfied to be in prison for the honor of His Holy Name, but am ready to give my life for the sake of Jesus, my Lord, and enter His kingdom sooner, the place where the elect of

God enter everlasting life. But the wicked enter into eternal damnation.

May the shadow of God's kindness and His hand of blessing and healing be and remain upon you for ever. Amen. With Respect,

Your Christian prisoner,
Mehdi Dibaj

Written by Mehdi Dibaj, translated into English by Sam Yeghnazar.

FINAL NOTE

If you want to get involved in the story of Iran's new Christians by prayer, the author would recommend you use the excellent guide, *Iran 30*. This widely used free booklet is available from www.elam.com; and there are regular updates posted at www.iran30.org.

SELECT BIBLIOGRAPHY

Ahmadi, N., and F. *Iranian Islam: The Concept of the Individual*, Macmillan, 1998

Alavi, N. *We Are Iran*, Portobello Books, London, 2005

Alizadeh, P. (ed.). *The Economy of Iran: Dilemmas of an Islamic State*, I.B. Tauris, 2000

Ansari, A. *Iran, Islam and Democracy: The Politics of Managing Change*, Chatham House, 2000

Arberry, A. *Sufism: An Account of the Mystics of Islam*, Dover Publications, New York, 1950

Axworthy, M. *Iran, Empire of the Mind: A History of Iran*, Penguin Books, 2007

Axworthy, M. *Revolutionary Iran: A History of the Islamic Republic*, Allen Lane, 2013

Bahari, M. *Then They Came for Me: A Story of Injustice and Survival In Iran's Most Notorious Prison*, Oneworld, 2011

Banisadr, M. *Masoud: Memoirs of an Iranian Rebel*, Saqi, 2004

Behrooz, M. *Rebels With a Cause: The Failure of the Left in Iran*, I.B. Tauris, 2000

Bill, J. A. and Williams, J. A. *Roman Catholics and Shi'i Muslims: Prayer, Passion and Politics*, The University of North Carolina Press, 2002

Blunt, W. *Pietro's Pilgrimage*, James Barrie, 1953

Blunt, W. *Persian Spring*, James Barrie, 1957

Boroujerdi, M. *Iranian Intellectuals and the West: The Tormented Triumph of Nativism*, Syracuse University Press, 1996

Bosch, D. *Transforming Mission: Paradigm Shifts in Theology of Mission*, Orbis Books, 1991

Bradley, M. *Iran: Open Hearts in a Closed Land*, Authentic, 2007

Bradley, M. *Iran and Christianity: Historical Identity and Present Relevance*, Continuum, 2008

Corbin, H. *Spiritual Earth and Celestial Earth: From Mazdean Iran to Shi'ite Iran*, I.B. Tauris, 1990

Dabashi, H. *Close-Up: Iranian Cinema*, Verso, 2001

Dehqani-Tafti, H. *The Hard Awakening*, Triangle, 1981

Dehqani-Tafti, H. *Christ and Christianity in Persian Poetry*, Sohrab Books, 1986

Donaldson, D. *The Shi'ite Religion*, Luzac, 1933

Edabi, S. *Iran Awakening: A Memoir of Revolution and Hope*, Rider, 2006

Fisk, R. *The Great War for Civilisation: The Conquest of the Middle East*, Harper Perennial, 2006

Foltz, R. *Spirituality in the Land of the Noble: How Iran Shaped the World's Religions*, Oneworld Publications, 2004

Foltz, R. *Religions of Iran: From Prehistory to the Present*, Oneworld, 2013

Francis-Dehqani, G. *Religious Feminism in an Age of Empire*, Bristol University, 2000

Frye, R. N. *The Golden Age of Persia*, Phoenix, 1975

Hiro, D. *The Longest War: The Iran–Iraq Military Conflict*, Paladin, 1990

Hiro, D. *Iran Today*, Politicos, 2005

Humphreys, E. *The Royal Road: A Popular History of Iran*, Scorpion Publishing, 1992

Hunt, P. *Inside Iran*, Lion Publishing, 1981

Issa, R., and Whitaker, S. (eds) *Life and Art: New Iranian Cinema*, British Film Institute, National Film Theatre Publishing, 1999

Karsh, E. *The Iran–Iraq War, 1980–1988*, Osprey Publishing, 2002

Keddie, N. R. *Modern Iran: Roots and Results of Revolution*, Yale University Press, 2003

Khalidi, T. *The Muslim Jesus: Sayings and Stories in Islamic Literature*, Harvard University Press, 2011

Lewis, B. *What Went Wrong? Western Impact and Middle Eastern Response*, Harper Perennial, 2002

Mackay, S. *The Iranians*, Penguin,1996

Malm, A., and Esmailian, S. *Iran on the Brink: Rising Workers and Threats of War*, Pluto Press, 2007

Milani, A. *Lost Wisdom: Rethinking Modernity in Iran*, Mage Publishers, 2004

Miller, W. *My Persian Pilgrimage: An Autobiography*, William Carey Library, 1989

Moffett, S. *History of Christianity in Asia*, Vol. 1, Orbis Books, 1998

Moffett, S. *History of Christianity in Asia*, Vol. 2, Orbis Books, 2005

Moin, B. *Khomeini: Life of the Ayatollah*, St Martin's Press, 1999

Mottahedeh, R. *The Mantle of the Prophet: Religion and Politics in Iran*, Oneworld Publications, 1985

Nafisi, A. *Reading Lolita in Tehran: A Memoir in Books*, Fourth Estate, 2004

Naji, K. *Ahmadinejad: The Secret History of Iran's Radical Leader*, I.B. Tauris, 2008

Nasr, V. *The Shia Revival*, W. W. Norton, 2006

Nazir-Ali, M. *Islam: A Christian Perspective*, Paternoster Press, 1983

Nima, R. *The Wrath of Allah*, Pluto Press, 1983

Peterson, S. *Let the Swords Encircle Me: Iran – A Journey Behind the Headlines*, Simon & Schuster, 2010

Pollack, K. *The Persian Puzzle: The Conflict Between Iran and America*, Random House, 2004

Rasooli, J., and Allen, C. *Dr Sa'eed of Iran*, Good News Publishers, 1964

Rostampour, M and Amirizadeh, M. with Perry, J. *Captive In Iran: A Remarkable True Story of Hope and Triumph Amid the Horror of Tehran's Brutal Evin Prison*, Tyndale, 2013

Sciolino, E. *Persian Mirrors: The Elusive Face of Iran*, Free Press, 1997

Selby, P. *Persian Springs*, Highland Books, 2001

Shah, I. *The Sufis*, Doubleday and Company, Garden City, 1964

Shortt, R, *Christianophobia: A Faith Under Attack*, Random House, 2012

Takeyh, R. *Hidden Iran: Paradox and Power in the Islamic Republic*, Henry Holt and Company, 2006

Takeyh, R. *Guardians of the Revolution: Iran and the World in the Age of the Ayatollahs*, Oxford University Press, 2009

Waterfield, R. *Christians in Persia: Assyrians, Armenians, Roman Catholics and Protestants*, George Allen and Unwin, London, 1973

Wright, D. *The English amongst the Persians during the Qatar Period, 1787–1921*, Heinemann, 1977

Wright, R. *In the Name of God*, Bloomsbury, London, 1990

Wright, R. *The Last Great Revolution: Turmoil and Transformation in Iran*, Alfred A. Knopf, 2000

Yaghmaian, B. *Social Change in Iran: An Eyewitness Account of Dissent, Defiance, and New Movements for Rights*, State University of New York Press, 2002

Ye'or, B. *The Decline of Eastern Christianity Under Islam: From Jihad to Dhimmitude*, Associated University Press, 1996

INDEX